EARLY BILITERACY DEVELOPMENT

"This detailed, empirical look at biliteracy development in young children is very welcome. Across a range of languages and instructional contexts in the United States, the authors paint a portrait of bilingual children's rich repertoires of complex metalinguistic strategies and interpretations as they go about reading, writing, and constructing literacy across two languages. The book points unmistakably to the promise and potential of purposefully biliterate classrooms and teaching practices in our schools."

Nancy Hornberger, Goldie Anna Professor of Education, University of Pennsylvania Graduate School of Education

"The editors have brought together an eminent group of scholars who present fascinating studies of children learning a variety of languages and, who are, at the same time, becoming biliterate. This volume will appeal to anyone interested in the early reading and writing development of young children who are learning more than one language."

Robert T. Jiménez, Professor of Education, Vanderbilt University

Focused exclusively on biliteracy development in early childhood across a variety of languages, this book provides both findings from empirical research with young bilinguals in home and school contexts, and practical applications of these findings.

Eurydice Bouchereau Bauer is Associate Professor at the University of Illinois, Urbana-Champaign.

Mileidis Gort is Assistant Professor of Language and Literacy at the University of Miami, School of Education.

EARLY BILITERACY DEVELOPMENT

Exploring Young Learners' Use of Their Linguistic Resources

Edited by Eurydice Bouchereau Bauer and Mileidis Gort

Routledge
Taylor & Francis Group

LONDON AND NEW YORK

First published 2012
by Routledge
711 Third Avenue, New York, NY 10017

Simultaneously published in the UK
by Routledge
2 Park Square, Milton Park, Abingdon, Oxon OX14 4RN

Routledge is an imprint of the Taylor & Francis Group, an informa business

© 2012 Taylor & Francis

Library of Congress Cataloging in Publication Data
Early biliteracy development : exploring young learners' use of their linguistic resources / edited by Eurydice Bouchereau Bauer & Mileidis Gort.
    p. cm.
    1. Spanish language–Study and teaching (Elementary)–United States.
    2. English language–Study and teaching (Elementary)–United States.
    3. Bilingual education–United States. 4. Multilingualism. I. Bauer, Eurydice B. (Eurydice Bouchereau) II. Gort, Mileidis.
    LC3731.E25 2011
    370.117'50973–dc22   2011004181

ISBN: 978-0-415-88017-6 (hbk)
ISBN: 978-0-415-88018-3 (pbk)
ISBN: 978-0-203-85040-4 (ebk)

Typeset in Bembo
by Wearset Ltd, Boldon, Tyne and Wear

Printed and bound in the United States of America
by IBT Global.

CONTENTS

PREFACE

We invited literacy researchers and teacher educators to contribute to this book based on their understanding of and engagement with research in the area of early childhood bilingualism, their reflective pedagogical practices, and their careful attention to emergent bilingual learners' interests and instructional needs. The chapters are organized around two general age/grade bands representing the early childhood education years: preschool and early elementary grades. Together, the chapters shed light on the various factors and skills that impact young bilinguals' literacy development across different languages with attention to both reading and writing as constituted and manifested in concrete social contexts, including homes and classrooms. Each chapter is structured in a similar format to offer parallel descriptions of the research, including a brief review of related empirical studies, an overview of the methods for data collection and analysis, a description of the main findings, and specific pedagogical implications to support educators' efforts in constructing meaningful, challenging, and dynamic literacy and language learning communities where one or more languages are used for communicating and learning.

Part I, *Emergence of Biliteracy: The Preschool Years*, opens with a vignette that introduces key issues and questions on early biliteracy development in preschoolers. The three chapters that follow challenge readers to view differences as opportunities for learning and building on the diversity among our youngest students. In Chapter 2, *Supporting the Early Development of Biliteracy: The Role of Parents and Caregivers*, Eurydice Bouchereau Bauer and Dumisile Mkhize examine the role of caregivers in shaping young bilinguals' literacy development in two languages. The authors describe how members of one family scaffolded their literacy interactions with a German/English emergent bilingual child and analyze the impact of those scaffolded interactions on the child's early biliteracy development. The analysis of Elena's case reveals how a supportive and nurturing literacy-rich home context was one of the main contributing factors to her early biliteracy development. The integration of different modes of literacy – reading, acting out, and talking about text – also appeared to nurture Elena's exploration of literacy across two languages.

The next two chapters in this part take somewhat different approaches – with respect to learning contexts and issues explored – on the topic of development and application of early literacy concepts. In Chapter 3, *Literacy Practices and Language Use among Latino Emergent Bilingual Children in Preschool Contexts*, Lucinda Soltero-González and Iliana Reyes apply a sociocultural lens to examine the ways in which Spanish–English emergent bilingual children experienced learning to read and write in an English immersion context under the restrictive conditions of Arizona's Proposition 203. Their analysis focuses on the role of the children's native language in their explorations and use of English literacy in the classroom. Their analyses reveal how, despite a restrictive political climate that dismisses native-language instruction, young emergent bilinguals relied on their own cultural and linguistic resources in Spanish and English to make school literacy relevant to their lives.

We end the preschool section of this text with David Yaden, Jr. and Tina Tsai's chapter on the developmental pathways of the early English/Chinese biliterate writing of 11 young children ranging in age from four to six years (Chapter 4: *Learning How to Write in English and Chinese: Young Bilingual Kindergarten and First Grade Children Explore the Similarities and Differences between Writing Systems*). Their work presents a detailed examination of the ways in which children conceptualize both the symbols and processes they use to represent what they want to mean as they learn to write in two typologically diverse languages. Yaden and Tsai specifically focus on the conceptual differences and crossovers between Chinese and English writing and draw on the clinical methodology developed by Vygotsky and colleagues (Luria, 1998; Vygotsky, 1997) in the 1920s and more recently by Ferreiro and Teberosky (1982) to elicit children's thinking during the act of writing.

We introduce Part II, *Biliteracy Development in Early Elementary School*, with a vignette that addresses issues and questions on biliteracy development in early primary grades. This part consists of four chapters, each of which looks at literacy learning and teaching within a variety of instructional contexts. Mileidis Gort's chapter, *Evaluation and Revision Processes of Young Bilinguals in a Dual Language Program* (Chapter 5), presents selected examples from case studies of the evaluation and revising processes of six emergent bilingual/biliterate first graders from English- and Spanish-language backgrounds learning both languages in a Two-Way Immersion program. Through a year-long ethnographic study, Gort documents and highlights children's numerous strategies for revising their written work, including rereading, using available print resources, asking for help, thinking aloud, self-correcting, and code-switching. Findings expand our understanding of the processes and strategies young bilingual writers engage in when making decisions about their writing and have important implications for the design and implementation of effective language and literacy environments for emergent bilinguals from minority- and majority-language backgrounds.

In Chapter 6, *Zehra's Story: Becoming Biliterate in Turkish and English*, Zeynep Çamlibel and Georgia Garcia describe what they learned from Zehra, a young Turkish-speaking first grader who was in the process of acquiring English as a second language and receiving initial formal literacy instruction in both of her languages at the same time. Through sociolinguistic, sociocultural, and cognitive perspectives, the authors explore Zehra's language learning processes and experiences over the course of her first year in a U.S. school in three different classroom contexts: mainstream (general education), English-as-a-Second-Language, and native language, while considering contextual, cultural, and social factors affecting her language and literacy development in and out of school. Findings reveal how prior experience with metalinguistic tasks in Turkish appeared to support Zehra's acquisition of literacy in both languages and facilitated transfer.

In Chapter 7, *Traveling the Biliteracy Highway: Framing Biliteracy from Students' Writings*, María Fránquiz discusses the potential for biliteracy in K-2 classrooms in a rural school where there is no official bilingual education program. A metaphor of children taking a successful trip on a biliteracy highway is used to show how students in a rural community in the U.S./Mexico borderlands took up opportunities to "unleash" their biliteracy potential (Reyes, 2001) during their journey in a planned unit of study on quilting. One of the critical strategies that assisted the young children in demonstrating their biliteracy potential was code switching, or moving easily between one linguistic code and another within a sentence or an utterance. This strategy became available through collaborative efforts between guest artists and the school personnel and through effective use of culturally relevant literature.

The last chapter in Part II, *The Evolution of Biliterate Writing Development through Simultaneous Bilingual Literacy Instruction* (Chapter 8, by Wendy Sparrow, Sandra Butvilofsky and Kathy Escamilla), explores the longitudinal writing development of 25 emerging Spanish/English bilingual children from first through third grade through T-unit and qualitative analyses. By examining children's writing samples in both Spanish and English throughout the three years, the authors provide evidence of growth in linguistic complexity in both languages as students advanced in grade level. Findings demonstrate students' potential to develop writing skills simultaneously in two languages and illustrate the importance of viewing bilingual students' literacy development through a bilingual lens.

In the closing chapter, editors Eurydice Bouchereau Bauer and Mileidis Gort offer a summary that highlights the various perspectives provided on emergent biliteracy by each of the chapters, shows how the findings in the book extend earlier research on children's biliteracy as well as collectively address current issues in the field of biliteracy, and delineate areas of research that still need to be investigated if we are to better understand the biliteracy development and instruction of young bilingual children. As a support for all readers, a glossary of key terms is provided at the end of the book.

References

Ferreiro, E., & Teberosky, A. (1982). *Literacy before schooling*. Portsmouth, NH: Heinemann.

Luria, A. R. (1998). The development of writing in the child. In M. K. de Oliveira & J. Valsiner (Eds.), *Literacy in human development* (pp. 1–56). Stamford, CT: Ablex.

Vygotsky, L. S. (1997). *The collected works of L. S. Vygotsky. Vol. 4. The history of the development of higher mental functions* (R. W. Rieber, Ed.; M. J. Hall, Trans.). New York: Plenum Press.

Acknowledgments

Our sincere appreciation goes to the contributors who have written so provocatively on the issues of early biliteracy. The idea for this book emerged several years ago from a panel presentation at AERA, which was organized by the first editor. Since that presentation, we have added a few more contributors to complement our discussion on young children's biliteracy development at different developmental points and across a variety of languages. Without the collective efforts of all these authors, this book would not have come to fruition.

We also would like to thank our true inspirations for this book, the many children who defiantly embrace their bilingualism despite efforts to keep them monolingual in the United States. To our own bilingual children at home, we say thank you for being our teachers and giving us a glimpse into what it means to own one's linguistic heritage.

Finally, we would like to thank our graduate students who have helped us at different stages of writing this book. Your hard work is much appreciated – Dimisile Mkhize, Language and Literacy at University of Illinois, Kirsten Letofsky, Language and Literacy at University of Illinois, and Ryan Pontier, Language and Literacy in Multilingual Settings at University of Miami.

1

INTRODUCTION

Holistic Approaches to Bilingual/Biliteracy Development, Instruction, and Research

Mileidis Gort and Eurydice Bouchereau Bauer

In the United States, a large and growing number of students from culturally and linguistically diverse backgrounds have the potential to develop bilingualism and biliteracy if supported in their immediate environment. Throughout this book, we adopt the term *emergent bilingual* to more accurately describe the realities of young children who have been in the process of developing two (or more!) languages from a young age or who speak a language other than English and are in the process of acquiring English as an additional language (Garcia et al., 2008). We see so much promise in children who grow up with two languages and cultures and become biliterate – sometimes supported by, but often in spite of, an educational system that has little understanding of the linguistic and cultural resources they possess (Reyes & Halcon, 2001) – and contend that they are intellectually capable and serve as true models of the potential for all children to become active, engaged, and successful bilinguals and biliterates.

A great deal is known about the early literacy development of monolingual children (e.g., Teale & Sulzby, 1989; Dyson, 1984; Clay, 1991; Adams, 1990; Venezky, 1999); however, in spite of the ubiquity of bi/multilingualism in the world, research on the early literacy development of young bilinguals remains disproportionately scant (Dworin & Moll, 2006; Garcia, 2000; Jiménez et al., 1999; Vernon-Feagans et al., 2001). This gap in scientific knowledge presents a practical problem for the growing number of educational professionals working with children who live with two or more languages in their home, community, and school environments, but who lack adequate information about the developmental pathways to bilingualism and biliteracy and research-based educational practices that best serve emergent bilinguals.

This book shares with prospective and in-service teachers, literacy teacher educators, graduate students, and researchers whose work involves bilingual learners, original research examining issues related to early biliteracy development across different languages (e.g., Spanish/English, German/English, Turkish/English, and Chinese/English), and offers practical applications of those research findings. We focus specifically on the literacy and language development of emergent bilinguals during the early childhood years, from preschool to grade 3, across various learning contexts where literacy and language take shape. Chapters based on original empirical research address relevant questions concerning the nature of bilingual children's literacy learning experiences in bilingual and monolingual environments, as well as the course and processes of language and literacy development in two languages. The chapters are situated within the broader political/educational context, approach literacy learning from multiple perspectives, including cognitive, sociolinguistic, and sociocultural orientations, and adopt both bilingual and developmental lenses in the analysis of children's dual language and literacy competencies. Our primary goals are to continue to push the field forward, to support educators, preservice teachers, and researchers in their ongoing efforts to understand and nurture the development of emergent bilinguals, as well as to explore the capabilities and experiences of young bilingual children as competent and dynamic language users and learners.

Current Issues in Early Biliteracy Development

Biliteracy is a complex phenomenon with cognitive, sociocultural, and sociological dimensions. Through participation in multilingual and multicultural social networks that are not accessible to monolinguals, bilinguals can experience a range and variety of literacy practices and transact with two literate worlds to create knowledge and transform it for meaningful purposes. As such, biliteracy must be understood as a special form of literacy that is distinct from the literacy experiences and processes of monolinguals.

A growing research base in early biliteracy development suggests that bilingual children have the potential to develop literacy in two languages, either simultaneously or in succession, in supportive contexts. We refer to the ongoing process of early biliteracy development as emergent biliteracy, following others in the field (Edelsky, 1986; Moll et al., 2001), but adding a specific meaning to "emergent" since young children may not yet have developed conventional (i.e., adult-like) writing and reading competencies. Throughout this volume, thus, we use "emergent biliteracy" to refer to the ongoing, dynamic development of concepts and expertise for thinking, listening, speaking, reading, and writing in two languages (Reyes, 2006).

Research evidence suggests that there are multiple paths to children's biliteracy development and that these multiple paths are normal aspects of bilingual development. Further, when biliteracy is encouraged, nurtured, and promoted, literacy skills and strategies learned in either language influence, or transfer to, the other language through what appears to be a bidirectional process. Finally, the contexts in which children develop biliteracy and a number of personal variables affect the processes of biliteracy development and degree of biliteracy achieved.

Emergent bilinguals have the potential to develop literacy in two languages in supportive contexts that include the classroom, home, and community. Research shows that biliteracy can be attained with deliberate support in a variety of classroom (e.g., Dworin, 1998; Gort, 2006; Perez & Torres-Guzmán, 2002; Whitmore & Crowell, 1994) and home settings (Bauer, 2000, 2003). Some emergent bilingual children learn to read and write in both languages at the same time; this is referred to as simultaneous development of biliteracy. Many Two-Way Immersion or Dual Language programs in the United States follow this approach to bilingual and biliteracy acquisition, which often yields high degrees of biliteracy proficiency. Other young bilinguals are introduced to reading and writing in their home/native language first and later in their second language in a sequential fashion. For children from non-English speaking homes in the United States, this means learning to read and write in the non-English language first, and then introducing literacy in English. This can be a successful route to biliteracy only if the non-English language continues to be promoted and developed to high degrees, and not abandoned before it is fully developed, once English is introduced.

Homes and communities also can be supportive contexts for biliteracy development in young children. For example, the work of Gillanders and Jiménez (2004), Reyes and Azuara (2008) and Volk and DeAcosta (2001) highlights the ways in which Latino parents, siblings, and other family members actively support children's emergent biliteracy by engaging them in numerous formal and informal literacy-related activities. Families demonstrate a wide variety of communicative practices and ways in which they use written materials in the two languages, including writing and reading general notes, cards, letters, and religious texts, in support of children's biliteracy development.

The diversity that students display as they become biliterate suggests that context as well as personal characteristics play an important role in that process. Emergent bilinguals may engage with literacy tasks and activities in a language they do not yet speak fluently (Moll et al., 2001), suggesting that emergent bilinguals' literate ability may at times exceed their oral fluency in that language. This developmental pathway questions a common assumption that literacy is dependent on proficiency in the spoken language. Also, emergent bilinguals may be stronger writers than readers in either of their languages, a pattern also found in young monolinguals. Further, for some children, emergent biliteracy can develop without formal instruction. Reyes (2001) documented this phenomenon of "spontaneous biliteracy" in her study of four Spanish–English emergent bilinguals who "appeared to move rather successfully along the path of biliteracy without formal literacy instruction in *both* languages" (p. 97). Other emergent bilinguals evidence higher oral language skills in one language, but more advanced reading abilities in the other language. In these cases, formal literacy instruction in each language, or lack thereof, plays an important role in children's development toward biliteracy. These findings illuminate how emergent biliteracy is not unilinear. In other words, there is tremendous diversity in the ways in which young children progress and develop in their biliterate abilities.

A growing body of research suggests that relationships between bilingual children's languages and uses of each language in and out of school are fluid and reciprocal. Similarly, biliteracy development is a dynamic, flexible process in which children's transactions with two written languages mediate their language and literacy learning in both languages. Emergent bilingual children apply a number of reading and writing strategies across their languages (Dworin, 2003; Gort, 2006; Moll et al., 2001). Further, bilingual children tend to integrate and synthesize their multilingual/multicultural resources and demonstrate an awareness of the characteristics that differentiate two writing systems, an ability to highlight boundaries between writing in each of their languages, as well as an awareness of instances where written marks/symbols could cross boundaries and be interpreted differently in another system (Kenner, 2004). The bidirectional nature of biliteracy seems to play an especially important role at both oral and emergent literacy levels (Reyes, 2006) as young bilingual readers and writers apply what they learn in one language to their other language in ways that suggest that development in each language supports advances in the other.

The contexts in which children develop biliteracy and a number of other variables (e.g., contextual, linguistic, personal) affect the processes of biliteracy development and degree of biliteracy achieved (Brisk & Harrington, 2000). For example, the structural differences between, or similarities of, the languages involved influence in part the degree to which the learning to read and write process will be facilitated through cross-language transfer. The learning context and relevant formal instructional opportunities are other factors adding complexity to the biliteracy developmental process. For this reason, emergent bilinguals develop language and literacy skills at different rates.

We have evidence from classroom- and community-based research that suggests biliteracy can be attained with deliberate support, continued encouragement, opportunity, and quality instruction in two languages in classroom settings and beyond. Teachers who bring a dynamic, holistic, and bilingual philosophy and practice to their classroom facilitate biliteracy for their students (Dworin, 1998). However, in subtractive environments which threaten the status and maintenance of either of the languages (usually a minority language such as Spanish or Chinese in U.S. contexts), the development of bilingualism and biliteracy is limited and often only serves as a temporary bridge to English development.

Conceptual Framework

In this volume, the authors assume a view of literacy development that can be characterized as constructivist within a sociocultural context. A constructivist perspective views the learner as an active participant in purposeful and authentic meaning making (Bruner, 1996). A sociocultural framework foregrounds how children learn as they interact with and interpret their world within their culture and in their social group (Vygotsky, 1978; Wertsch, 1998). The children's environment and purpose provide the sociocultural context within which they construct or make meaning. From a sociocultural perspective, thus, emergent biliteracy encompasses the children's use of their cultural and linguistic experiences to co-construct meaning with parents, teachers, siblings, and peers in their environment (Whitmore et al., 2004). Emergent bilingual children's understanding of how to approach and represent ideas in writing is socially constructed and supported by the adults and expert readers and writers around them (Vygotsky, 1978).

Because a monolingual perspective does not suffice for understanding bilinguals, bilingualism, and biliteracy (Moll & Dworin, 1996; Valdés, 1992; Walsh, 1991), we apply a multilingual perspective in order to understand the emergent literacy development of young bilinguals. A multilingual perspective is based on a holistic view of the bilingual learner, including validation of students' cultural and linguistic backgrounds as resources for learning, an understanding of the role of primary language (including literacy) in the acquisition of a new language, and a consideration of sociolinguistic, socio-historical, and sociocultural factors that contribute to the child's development and experiences. This perspective acknowledges and encompasses students' linguistic, literacy, and cultural repertoires including languages, dialects, functions, and uses of language and literacy in different contexts (Gort, 2006). Across the chapters presented in this volume, we adopt both bilingual and developmental lenses when analyzing children's language and literacy competencies. Only in this way can we hope to understand how children's knowledge is intertwined within their two developing linguistic systems (Reyes, 2001) while exploring and recognizing how their abilities progress with time.

References

Adams, M. J. (1990). *Learning to read: Thinking and learning about print*. Cambridge, MA: MIT Press.

Bauer, E. B. (2000). Code-switching during shared and independent reading: Lessons learned from a preschooler. *Research in the Teaching of English, 35*(1), 101–130.

Bauer, E. B. (2003). Finding Esmerelda's shoes: A case study of a young bilingual child's response to literature. In A. Willis, G. E. Garcia, V. Harris, & R. Barrera (Eds.), *Multicultural issues in literacy and practice* (pp. 11–28). Mahwah, NJ: Lawrence Erlbaum.

Brisk, M. E., & Harrington, M. M. (2000). *Literacy and bilingualism: A handbook for all teachers*. Mahwah, NJ: Lawrence Erlbaum.

Bruner, J. (1996). *The culture of education.* Cambridge, MA: Harvard University.

Clay, M. M. (1991). *Becoming literate: The construction of inner control.* Auckland: Heinemann.

Dworin, J. E. (1998, April). Biliteracy development: Perspectives from research in children's reading and writing. Paper presented at the Annual Meeting of the American Educational Research Association, San Diego, CA (ERIC Document 420-845).

Dworin, J. E. (2003). Examining children's biliteracy in the classroom. In A. Willis, G. Garcia, R., Barrera, & V. Harris (Eds.), *Multicultural issues in literacy research and practice* (pp. 29–48). Mahwah, NJ: Lawrence Erlbaum.

Dworin, J. E., & Moll, L.C. (2006). Guest editors' introduction. *Journal of Early Childhood Literacy, 6*(3), 234–240.

Dyson, A. (1984). Learning to write/learning to do school. *Research in the Teaching of English, 18*(3), 233–264.

Edelsky, C. (1986). *Writing in a bilingual program: Había una vez.* Norwood, NJ: Ablex.

Ferreiro, E., & Teberosky, A. (1982). *Literacy before schooling* (K. Goodman, Trans.). Exeter, NH: Heinemann.

Garcia, G. E. (2000). Bilingual children's reading. In M. L. Kamil, P. B. Mosenthal, P. D. Pearson, & R. Barr (Eds.), *Handbook of reading research* (Vol. 3, pp. 813–834). Mahwah, NJ: Lawrence Erlbaum.

Garcia, O., Kleifgen, J. A., & Falchi, L. (2008). *From English language learners to emergent bilinguals. Equity matters: Research review no. 1.* New York: Teachers College, Columbia University.

Gillanders, C., & Jiménez, R. (2004). Reaching for success: A close-up of Mexican immigrant parents in the USA who foster literacy success for their kindergarten children. *Journal of Early Childhood Literacy, 4*(3), 243–269.

Gort, M. (2006). Strategic codeswitching, interliteracy, and other phenomena of bilingual writing: Lessons from first grade dual language classrooms. *Journal of Early Childhood Literacy, 6*(3), 323–354.

Jiménez, R. T., Moll, L. C., Rodriguez-Brown, F. V., & Barrera, R. B. (1999). Latina and Latino researchers interact on issues related to literacy learning. *Reading Research Quarterly, 34*(2), 217–230.

Kenner, C. (2004). *Becoming biliterate: Young children learning different writing systems.* Stoke on Trent: Trentham.

Luria, A. R. (1998). The development of writing in the child. In M. K. de Oliveira & J. Valsiner (Eds.), *Literacy in human development* (pp. 1–56). Stamford, CT: Ablex.

Moll, L. C., & Dworin, J. E. (1996). Biliteracy development in classrooms: Social dynamics and cultural possibilities. In D. Hicks (Ed.), *Child discourse and social learning: An interdisciplinary perspective* (pp. 221–246). Cambridge: Cambridge University Press.

Moll, L. C., Saez, R., & Dworin, J. E. (2001). Exploring biliteracy: Two student case examples of writing as a social practice. *Elementary School Journal, 101*(4), 435–450.

Perez, B., & Torres-Guzmán, M. E. (2002). *Learning in two worlds: An integrated Spanish/English biliteracy approach* (3rd ed.). Boston, MA: Allyn & Bacon.

Reyes, I. (2006). Exploring connections between emergent biliteracy and bilingualism. *Journal of Early Childhood Literacy, 6*(3), 267–292.

Reyes, E., & Azuara, P. (2008). Emergent biliteracy in young Mexican immigrant children. *Reading Research Quarterly, 43*(4), 374–398.

Reyes, M. de la Luz. (2001). Unleashing possibilities: Biliteracy in the primary grades. In M. de la Luz Reyes & J. J. Halcon (Eds.), *The best for our children: Critical perspectives on literacy for Latino students* (pp. 96–121). New York: Teachers College Press.

Reyes, M. de la Luz, & Halcon, J. J. (2001). *The best for our children: Critical perspectives on literacy for Latino students.* New York: Teachers College Press.

Teale, W. H., & Sulzby, E. (1989). Emergent literacy: New perspectives. In D. S. Strickland & L. M. Morrow (Eds.), *Emergent literacy: Young children learn to read and write* (pp. 1–15). Newark, DE: International Reading Association.

Valdés, G. (1992). Bilingual minorities and language issues in writing: Toward profession-wide responses to a new challenge. *Written Communication, 9*(1), 85–136.

Venezky, R. L. (1999). *American English orthography.* New York: Guilford Press.

Vernon-Feagans, L., Hammer, C. S., Miccio, A., & Manlove, E. (2001). Early language and literacy skills in low-income African American and Hispanic children. In S. B. Neuman & D. K. Dickinson (Eds.), *Handbook of early literacy research* (pp. 192–210). New York: Guilford Press.

Volk, D., & de Acosta, M. (2001). Many differing ladders, many ways to climb: Literacy events in the bilingual classroom, homes, and community of three Puerto Rican kindergartners. *Journal of Early Childhood Literacy, 1*(2), 193–224.

Vygotsky, L. S. (1978). *Mind and society.* Cambridge, MA: Harvard University Press.

Vygotsky, L. S. (1997). *The collected works of L. S. Vygotsky. Vol. 4. The history of the development of higher mental functions* (R. W. Rieber, Ed.; M. J. Hall, Trans.). New York: Plenum Press.

Walsh, C. E. (1991). *Pedagogy and the struggle for voice: Issues of language, power, and schooling for Puerto Ricans.* New York: Bergin and Garvey.

Wertsch, J. V. (1998). *Mind as action.* New York: Oxford University Press.

Whitmore, K. F., & Crowell, C. G. (1994). *Inventing a classroom: Life in a whole language learning community.* York, ME: Stenhouse Publishers.

Whitmore, K. F., Martens, P., Goodman, Y., & Owocki, G. (2004). Critical lessons from the transactional perspective on early literacy research. *Journal of Early Childhood Literacy, 4*(3), 291–325.

PART I
Emergence of Biliteracy
The Preschool Years

PRESCHOOL VIGNETTE

Thoughts from an expectant bilingual mother:

> My husband and I are bilingual/biliterate in Chinese and English; I simultaneously acquired Chinese and English when I was growing up in China. My husband learned Chinese while living and working in Beijing as an English teacher for four years. We met in America while I was a graduate student, fell in love, and I have lived in America ever since. We are pregnant with our first child and I don't know what language we should speak at home. If we speak only English our child will not be able to communicate with my family. If we speak only Chinese, our child will not be able to communicate with my husband's family. If we speak both Chinese and English at home I am afraid our child will get confused and her language and literacy development will suffer. Since Chinese and English do not share the same orthography, I wonder if our child will be confused even further? I don't know what to do. Please help!

Thoughts from a preschool teacher of bilingual children:

> I believe that being bilingual and biliterate is beautiful. In most parts of the world bilingualism and biliteracy are viewed as a resource. My many years living in Mexico taught me that language and culture are interwoven. I know that my students come to school with Spanish language and literacy knowledge that they can use to understand English. English is the language that I am required to use in my classroom because students must be prepared to enter English-only classroom environments in kindergarten. In my heart I know that allowing children to utilize their

Spanish language in my classroom while they are acquiring English language proficiency will provide the necessary scaffold they need in order to become proficient language and literacy users in both Spanish and English. I just wish society would recognize and value these resources. It would help if I had some research to support my intuitive feelings that students' home languages and cultures are resources that will support the English learning process.

Language and literacy learning are natural processes in the early years of child development. Children observe peers, family, friends, and teachers as they engage in language and literacy events and eventually begin to join in as active users and constructors. At present, there is an extensive body of scientific research that illustrates the early literacy development in monolingual children. In contrast, there is little research on young developing bilingual and biliterate children despite the growing body of evidence illustrating the advantages of bilingualism and biliteracy. Fortunately for the expectant mother and the preschool teacher, many dedicated researchers are deliberately working to build a knowledge base related to their questions and issues. The authors of this section begin to fill an important void by presenting research that answers key questions and addresses prominent issues regarding the early bilingual and biliteracy development of children in home and school contexts. Some of these questions include: How exactly does exposure to two languages in the primary years impact a child's language and literacy development in both languages? What is the role of supportive caregivers in this process? How does context inhibit or facilitate biliteracy development? How do children make sense of different writing systems? Does a child develop skills equally in both languages? Are there cognitive benefits of learning two languages? If yes, what are they? What can caregivers and teachers do to support the development of emerging bilinguals?

The questions and issues presented above are complex and multifaceted. They require deep thought and reflection. Before learning the answers to the above questions, pause and reflect on your own language and literacy experiences. To begin this process you will create your own literacy narrative. It doesn't matter if you are monolingual, bilingual, or multilingual; it will be a beautiful story because it's yours.

Take a minute and think about your earliest memories learning language at home? What about literacy? Who were the characters? How did they support and scaffold your emergent literacy experiences? How did these experiences change as you entered school? What do you remember about your language and literacy development? With your narrative in mind it is now time to enter into the world of emerging bilinguals. How does becoming bilingual and biliterate in the earlier years compare to your narrative? How are the tools caregivers and teachers use to support students' emerging bilingual and biliteracy skills similar or different than your own? Embrace the journey and be prepared to come back equipped to answer the questions posed by the expectant mother and preschool teacher at the beginning of this vignette and the multiple others who approach you with the same questions.

Key Questions to Think About as You Read the Preschool Year Section
How does exposure to two languages in the primary years impact a child's language and literacy development in both languages? Are young children able to simultaneously acquire, organize, manipulate, and sort out the similarities and differences present in two languages? Is this process different for children who are learning languages with different orthographies? Does exposure to language and literacy practices in two languages interfere with the learning process?

2

SUPPORTING THE EARLY DEVELOPMENT OF BILITERACY

The Role of Parents and Caregivers

Eurydice Bouchereau Bauer and Dumisile Mkhize

Introduction

Parents' role in supporting the language development of young bilinguals has been captured in seminal work of Leopold (1949), Grosjean (1989) and more recently Caldas (2006), to name a few. Research has shown that young children by the age of three differentiate between their two languages (Buckwalter & Lo, 2002; Kenner, 2004), are aware of their interlocutors (Lee, 2003), and are not confused by the use of their two languages (Bauer, 2000; Bauer & Montero, 2001). The last decade has given rise to increased interest in the development of young children's biliteracy development and their active role in the process. Some researchers have documented the emergent biliteracy development of their children (e.g., Bauer, 2000; Caldas, 2006; Schwarzer, 2001) and have shown some of the strategies/skills the children develop in the process of becoming biliterate. What is often underexplored is how the parents and or caregivers scaffold the development of these young bilinguals' strategies and skills. In this chapter we describe how members of one family scaffolded their literacy interactions with a simultaneous bilingual child and the impact of those scaffolded interactions on the child's emergent biliteracy development. Understanding the role of caregivers in shaping young bilinguals' biliteracy development is important if we are to understand what young bilinguals bring with them to school.

Clearly one of the skills that young bilinguals bring to school is their language. In order to understand how students use their languages, it is important to appreciate how the languages were learned in the home. In particular, it is important to discern how the caregivers indirectly and directly convey to children what is permissible and not permissible in the children's language use, thereby shaping its development. The following dialogue illustrates a shared reading session with

Elena (the focal child), an English/German bilingual, and her German caregiver, Birgit. In this conversation, Birgit and Elena are discussing a German text, *Kleine Grosse Schwester*, about a girl who becomes a big sister.

BIRGIT: Wo tragt sie denn den Baby Bruder? [Where does she carry the baby brother?]

ELENA: In Haus! [Into the house!]

BIRGIT: Und wo liegt er da? Weisst du wo er da drin liegt? Wie man das nennt? [And what is he in? Do you know what he is in? What that's called?]

ELENA: (looks at picture) In 'ne Tasche! [In a bag.]

BIRGIT: In einer Tragetasche, genau. [In a carrying bag, right.]

ELENA: Sie is – sie is *not supposed to* nehm a Tasche, *is supposed to* nehm *a seat!* [She is not supposed to take a bag; she's supposed to take a seat!]

BIRGIT: Ja, das ist verschieden, manche haben eine Tasche, manche haben solchen Sitz. [Yes, that varies. Some have a bag, and some have a seat like that.] (Age: 3:2)

As the excerpt shows, Elena seemed to be questioning the content of the text. Her understanding of the world told her that the adult portrayed in the story should use a [car]seat and not a bag to carry the child. To express this view, she switched to English, using the phrase "not supposed to" although the conversation was in German. In keeping with typical interactions, the adult continued with the conversation and overlooked the code-switch. Instead, the adult remained focused on the meaning that she and Elena were constructing of the text.

The conversation between Elena and Birgit is typical of contexts where literacy is viewed as the negotiation of meaning with the text, the world, and other participants (Dworin, 2003; Reyes, 2001; Reyes & Azuara, 2008). In these contexts the focus is on the construction and co-construction of meaning in sociocultural contexts (Vygotsky, 1978). In the case of simultaneous bilingual and biliterate children, and as highlighted by this example, the interplay between their languages facilitates the construction of meaning.

In this chapter we explore how the context, adults, and Elena's use of her two languages supported her in becoming biliterate and bilingual in English and German. We agree with other scholars that providing simultaneous bilingual and biliterate children with adult scaffolds enhances biliteracy development in these children (Moll et al., 2001; Reyes, 2006, Reyes & Azuara, 2008; Reyes & Costanzo, 2002). We also subscribe to the view that biliteracy and bilingualism need to be understood from a bilingual perspective (Garcia, 2000; Gort, 2006; Grosjean, 1989; Kenner et al., 2004). Focusing solely on one of the bilinguals' languages will provide us with a partial view of what these children can do.

This chapter, therefore, adds to the research that focuses on what emerging simultaneous bilingual and biliterate children know and can do in both languages and how adults and caregivers support this process. We examine how

Elena used English and German as she experimented with reading and writing. The focus is on the strategies she used and how she used them within and across the two languages. Attention was given to the transfer of skills and knowledge during her literacy learning. We contend that the fact that Elena saw literacy as an activity which is not tied to a given language enhanced her ability to transfer the skills and knowledge across the two languages. Importantly, throughout the chapter we highlight the role that the adults played in enhancing Elena's development of literacy in two languages. Specifically we asked: how did Elena's social context and her interaction with bilingual adults influence and shape her biliteracy development in English and German? At the end of the chapter, we provide lessons that can be learned from Elena's early literacy development in two languages.

Literature Review

While previous research on emerging literacy focused on monolingual children (Clay, 1972; Ferreiro & Teberosky, 1982; Teale & Sulzby, 1986), some recent studies have focused on how emergent bilingual and biliterate children develop literacy in their two languages (Kenner, 2004; Kenner et al., 2004; Reyes & Azuara, 2008). The bilingual perspective adopted in these studies reveals that emerging bilingual and biliterate children display literacy behavior that is a result of their bilingual and bicultural contexts. From this perspective, children's languages are viewed as resources (Dworin, 2003; Hornberger, 1989; Reyes & Costanzo, 2002). Similarly, their sociocultural contexts and knowledge are valued (Moll et al., 2001; Pérez, 2004; Reyes, 2006). Children are not forced to choose one language and culture in favor of the other.

Several studies on emerging bilingual and biliterate children have shown that, similar to monolingual children, bilingual and biliterate children benefit from literacy-rich contexts (Buckwalter & Lo, 2002; Reyes & Azuara, 2008; Roberts, 2008). In these contexts, adults use both languages to develop children's emerging understanding of texts such as knowledge about book handling, directionality of print, and one-to-one correspondence between sound and letter. For example, Buckwalter and Lo found that a five-year-old Chinese preschooler who was exposed to multiple literacy activities in Chinese at home and in English at home and his daycare center came to understand basic emergent literacy principles in both languages. In this environment the adults supported the child's learning of these principles by providing him with multiple opportunities to explore texts written in both languages.

Not only do exposure and adult support help bilingual and biliterate children to grasp emergent literacy concepts, but these factors also enhance children's learning of letter–sound relationships in meaningful contexts (Araujo, 2002; Lesaux & Siegel, 2003; Guerrero & Sloan, 2001; Reyes & Azuaru, 2008). In fact, some studies have found that when bilingual and biliterate children learn phonemic awareness and phonics within literacy-rich contexts, including contexts where multiple storybooks are used, they learn to manipulate and distinguish sounds in both their languages (Buckwalter & Lo, 2002; Kenner et al., 2004). Sometimes this occurs despite differences in the writing systems across the two languages (Bialystok et al., 2005; Kenner, 2004). For example, Buckwalter and Lo's study revealed how five-year-old Ming understood that Chinese characters provided him with a different kind of information than the letters in English words (also see Yaden & Tsai in this volume for a discussion of early writing in Chinese and English). However, although Ming worked with adults on a regular basis to develop his English and Chinese literacy skills outside school, the specific role of the adults in shaping Ming's strategies and skills are not explored.

The studies cited above suggest that developing literacy in two languages does not lead to confusion. In fact, some scholars have argued that literacy development in both languages may provide students with cognitive benefits, particularly because bilinguals have been found to have heightened cognitive flexibility and metalinguistic awareness (Bauer, 2000; Bauer & Montero, 2001; Bialystok, 2001; Reyes & Azuara, 2008; Roberts, 2008). For example, Roberts found that when Hmong and Spanish preschool children participated in home storybook reading in two languages they were able to use both of their linguistic resources to learn English vocabulary. There was no negative influence of storybook reading in L1 and L2 on the acquisition of English vocabulary by the children as children made significant gains in learning the English vocabulary. Reyes and Azuara obtained similar results. Spanish–English bilingual preschoolers in their study were aware that Spanish and English look differently in writing even though both languages use letters; as a result, they were not confused when reading in these two languages. These findings provide a better understanding of what young children can do across their languages. What is needed is a better understanding of how the adults shape children's behaviors and development through interactions in regard to each of their respective languages.

Although bilingual and biliterate children are able to distinguish their languages and keep them apart, they also understand that their languages cannot be entirely separated. This is particularly evident when children switch between their languages during conversations and literacy learning (Gort, 2002, 2006; Moll et al., 2001; Reyes, 2001). A strong research base demonstrates that children's code-switching behaviors are not random but purposeful and systematic (Bauer, 2000; Bauer & Montero, 2001; Gort, 2002, 2006). For example, in a study of a two-way bilingual immersion program in two elementary schools, Pérez (2004) found that code-switching among early bilinguals occurred the most in oral language communication. Importantly, during instruction, the teachers encouraged the students to code-switch by adopting what they called a "Say It in Any Language" strategy. In this respect, the teachers supported students' maximum use of their linguistic resources. If students can be encouraged and scaffolded to use their languages as resources as they complete school tasks, one has to wonder how simultaneous bilinguals interact with print in the home environment and the role of the adults in the process. Do parents and caregivers provide similar types of scaffolds to their children?

We do know that when adults acknowledge children's languages, this supports the transfer of skills and knowledge across children's two languages in a bidirectional way rather than a unidirectional one (Dworin, 2003; Reyes, 2001; Reyes & Costanzo, 2002; Toloa et al., 2009). In a study of biliteracy development in English and Spanish of second grade children, Reyes found that bidirectional transfer occurred even in a monolingual environment. This transfer occurred in part because the teachers allowed the children to use both their languages as they explored literacy learning in their language of schooling. Evidently, the children's ability to transfer literacy skills across their languages was enhanced by the teacher. That is, the adults encouraged the co-existence of the two languages.

Furthermore, when children's languages and sociocultural experiences are recognized as legitimate sources of knowledge, this creates what some scholars have called the third space (Gutierrez et al., 1997; Moje et al., 2004). In this space knowledge of all members of the learning community is important. In bilingual and biliterate children, this enhances the development of bicultural and bilingual identities beyond their linguistic development (Manyak, 2001, 2008; Moll et al., 2001; Reyes, 2001). For example, in Moll et al.'s study on the writing practices of Spanish kindergartners and third graders, third grade students helped one another to write a bilingual text that reflected their bilingual and bicultural identities. Through their writing, the third graders reflected on the negative attitude of the larger community toward immigrants. In this respect, not only did the students come to appreciate their bilingual and bicultural identities, but they also enhanced their critical thinking skills. The authors contended that the students' introspections were the result of the supportive context created by the adults in which both languages were nurtured.

In sum, the studies discussed here show that in order for bilingual and biliterate children to benefit from their dual language and literacy skills, adults need to provide children with literacy-rich contexts in which they have ample opportunities to explore their bilingual and biliterate skills and identities. Importantly, adults should allow and encourage children's attempts to experiment with their languages in varied contexts. In the process of children's explorations, adults should scaffold children's development. In the present study, we examine the role of parents and caregivers in shaping the biliteracy development of a simultaneous bilingual.

Method

This study is presented as a qualitative case study because this approach allows the researcher to describe a phenomenon in detail, exploring its richness and complexities as experienced by participants in their social contexts (Dyson & Genishi, 2005; Erickson, 1987; Stake, 2005). Using this approach, we were able to more deeply explore how the adults shaped and supported Elena's literacy in her two languages.

Context of the Study

The data for the study reported here are part of a larger ethnographic case study of Elena, a bilingual and biliterate child, over a period of four years (ages two to six). The goal at the onset of the study was to capture Elena's bilingual and biliteracy development as shaped by her interactions with English and German caregivers during literacy, play, and other daily activities in the home. This chapter is based on data collected over a two-year period, age 2:1–3:11 (all ages given in years:months). During this time, Elena actively engaged in multiple literacy activities, language activities, and play as she explored her literacy and language skills in English and German with multiple participants.

Participants

The key participants in this study were Elena and her parents – Robert and Eurydice (the first author). Robert, her father, is German and Eurydice is Haitian American. Another participant was Elena's German-speaking caregiver who took care of her when both parents were at work. Robert and Eurydice followed the *une-personne une-langue* rule (Ronjat, 1913). Robert spoke to Elena only in German, and Eurydice spoke to her only in English. At the request of Elena's parents, Elena's caregiver spoke to her only in German.

Robert and Eurydice saw this longitudinal study as an attempt to understand Elena's development as a bilingual and biliterate child. To minimize the intrusion of the study into Elena's life and that of other adults, data were collected around (already occurring) routine home activities, instead of situations specifically created for the purpose of this study. However, because Eurydice and her husband were interested in the emergence of Elena's bilingualism and biliteracy development, this led to specific discussions about Elena's ownership of the two languages, her biliteracy, and the possible impact of this study on her overall development. These conversations invariably affected the perceptions of the adults' roles, especially the parents, and their interactions with Elena.

Data Collection

The findings reported here are drawn from videotaped and audiotaped observations of Elena's literacy, language, and play interactions during English and German reading sessions between the ages of 2:1 and 3:11. One day a week, the entire day was audiotaped using wireless microphones. All videotapes and audiotapes were catalogued. For this analysis, we chose those texts Elena read frequently. In some cases Elena asked an adult to read the texts to her and in other situations the adults chose the text to be read. The English texts discussed in this chapter are: *Dr. De Soto, Hard to be Six, The Three Little Pigs, Tip was Tim's Dog,* and *White, Black, Just Right.* The German texts used are: *Einkaufen mit Mama (Shopping with Mommy), Kleine Grosse Schwester (Little Big Sister), Miranda und der neue Teddy (Miranda and Her New Teddy [Bear]),* and *Wer Kommt mit in den Kindergarten (Who Will Come to the Kindergarten).*

Data Analysis

Each transcript of Elena's reading sessions was read, reread, and coded for how Elena approached the reading events, her specific actions, strategies, and miscues. The adults' actions and/or input were also coded for how they supported Elena's emergent biliteracy and bilingual development. Each of the transcript sections that was coded was then charted across the various books. Major themes were then pulled from the chart and are presented in the next section of the chapter.

Findings

Our analysis of Elena's biliteracy development in both German and English revealed that this was a complex process that involved the interplay between different factors in terms of the contexts and participants. Specifically, three themes emerged from the data and are presented below. Although there were several examples representing each theme, the length limitations placed on this chapter allow us to present just a few.

Using Context to Develop Vocabulary and Background Knowledge

Storybooks are great resources for parents to help young bilingual children develop vocabulary (Biemiller & Boote, 2006; Collins, 2005; Roberts, 2008). Quality children's literature provides adults and children with opportunities to have extended discussion around vocabulary that extends beyond a quick definition of a word. As a result, parents have an opportunity to create and extend background knowledge that will assist the child across both languages. For example, when Elena and her father were reading *Dr. De Soto,* an English text about a mouse who is a dentist that Elena insisted hearing in German, Elena's father provided Elena with a detailed explanation about what a dentist is and does.

German Transcript

DAD: Weisst du was der Mann, weisst du was der ist, die Maus? (points at the cover)
[Do you know what the man, do you know what he is, the mouse?]

ELENA: Nee. [No.]

DAD: Er ist ein Zahnarzt. Ja, wenn man, wenn man Aua hat im Mund, dann geht man zum Zahnarzt und dann macht er das wieder in Ordnung. (looks over to her while he is explaining) [He is a dentist. Yes, when one, when one has a booboo in the mouth, then one goes to a dentist and he makes everything alright again.]

DAD: (points at something on the first page) Siehst du, er kuemmert sich um die Zaehne, der Zahnarzt. (turns pages, looks over at Elena) [See, he is taking care of the teeth, the dentist.]

DAD: (reads) Doktor de Soto, Zahnarzt. (looks over to her) [Doctor De Soto, dentist.]

ELENA: A scheini. (Schwein) [A pig.]

ELENA: Warum, warum hat der daui (aui)? [Why, why does he have booboo?]

DAD: Weil in seinem Mund die Zaehne weh tun, ganz arg. Siehst du, deswegen hat er ja einen Wickel um den Kopf. [Because the teeth in his mouth are hurting, very badly. Do you see, that is why he has a scarf around his head.] (Age: 3:4)

In this shared reading episode, Elena and her father are not engaged in a simple task of defining the word dentist. Instead, their conversations serve two purposes. First, the conversation serves as an opportunity to build background knowledge about the concept of dentists relieving tooth pain. Second, the interaction serve as an opportunity for Elena to question her father about the text (e.g., why does he have a booboo?).

In a subsequent dialogue, Elena's father expanded on the above points and highlighted for her what happens when one does not take care of his teeth. These teachable moments, which were not previously planned by her father, provided both of them with opportunities to discuss dental health issues.

German Transcript

DAD: Ja. Wenn man die Zaehne immer gut putzt, dann bleiben sie schoen weiss und ganz, aber wenn man sie nicht gut putzt, dann werden sie braun und dann gehen sie kaputt. [Yes. When one always brushes one's teeth well, then they stay nicely white and complete, but when you don't brush them well, then they get brown and then they break.] (Age: 3:4)

In addition to using detailed explanations, the adults also provided Elena with ample opportunities for exploring synonyms. It was a typical pattern to have adults either provide synonyms for unfamiliar vocabulary words found in text, or to have Elena provide the synonym herself. This is important because knowing synonyms can broaden children's vocabulary. For example, in the following conversation, based on the English text, *The Three Little Pigs*, Elena's mother provided another word for angry.

MOM: (reads) The first little pig peered out of the window. When he saw the big bad wolf he said, no indeed I won't let you in, not by the hair of my chinny chin chin. That made the wolf cross.
MOM: (looks at Elena) That means angry. (Age: 3:5)

Although Elena did not go on to use the word "cross" in the reading session, the data show that with each reading, her mother highlighted for her that cross meant angry. One can speculate that these repeated exposures to low frequency words, along with adult provided synonyms, are creating the base from which Elena would later build her understanding of text as she reads for meaning.

Although the adults used synonyms for low frequency words, they needed to go beyond synonyms for discussing unfamiliar expressions. The example below shows that the adults also used gestures to help Elena understand the meaning of the words she did not know. Gestures allowed her to visualize what was being discussed without a great deal of adult explanation. In the example below, when Elena and Birgit were discussing the book, *Wer Kommt mit in den Kindergraten*, Birgit demonstrated to Elena what it means to blow a kiss. Not only did the gestures help Elena to know the meaning of this expression, but it also enhanced her comprehension of the text.

BIRGIT: "'Du Bloedmann!, schreit Lena. 'Ohne Kuss bleibst du fuer immer ein Frosch!' 'Ist mir doch egal', sagt Tilo, 'ich spiel nicht mehr mit.' – 'Wir werfen ihm Kusshaende zu', kichert Sara." ["'You idiot!, Lena yells. 'Without a kiss, you'll be a frog forever!' – 'I don't care', Tilo says, 'I'm no longer playing'. – 'We could blow him kisses', Sara laughs."]
BIRGIT: Weisst du was ein Kusshand ist? [Do you know what blowing someone a kiss means?]
ELENA: Um um. (meaning no)
BIRGIT: (demonstrates) /?/ eine Kusshand. Wenn man auf die Hand küsst ... (repeats demo; Elena tries it herself) und dann dem nächsten zublast. [(demonstrates) /?/ blowing a kiss. If you kiss your hand ... (repeats demo) and then blow the kiss to someone else.]
BIRGIT: (reads) "'dann ist er auch erloest.' – 'Au ja', sagt Lena. Sie pusten ihm beide Kusshaende zu und das Spiel ist aus. Sie packen die Klamotten zurueck in die Kiste und laufen nach draussen zum Spielen." ["'that should free him too.' – 'Good idea!' Lena says. They blow him kisses, and the play is over. They put the costumes back in the box and run outside to play."] (Age: 3:10)

Using picture storybooks did not simply provide the adults with an opportunity to help Elena learn words in her two languages, but it also helped her to categorize her knowledge of the words. For example, in the German text *Einkaufen mit Mama*, the vocabulary words and pictures are organized under larger headings (e.g., bakery). Across two pages, the child sees numerous items that can be found in a bakery and other common places in a community. During these interactions, Elena's German interlocutors would ask Elena to locate items that can be found in a bakery, a drugstore, etc. In addition to helping Elena learn to categorize items found in a particular context, the book did an excellent job capturing the context in culturally relevant ways. In the U.S., we have bakeries and supermarkets, but the way products are displayed, the types of products, and the general structure of the place can be different in different countries. Through the use of texts such as *Einkaufen mit Mama*, Elena was learning key vocabulary, categorization of key vocabulary and culturally relevant representation of these items in Germany. Therefore the use of culturally authentic text and discussion of these texts with adults supported Elena's understanding of target vocabulary and its cultural representation.

A good way to describe the way in which the adults interacted with Elena is multimodal. The data revealed that the adults used a variety of different techniques to keep Elena on task and to scaffold her learning. One of the ways that the adults supported vocabulary development was through many forms of gentle cueing. For example, in the excerpt below, Birgit and Elena engaged in a discussion of what can be found in a bakery. Birgit helped Elena remember the name of the person who works in a bakery by using a song known to both of them. The song that Birgit sang was a popular German children's rhyme about a baker.

ELENA: Aber dis ist Brot! (points) [But this is bread]

BIRGIT: Ja, aber was ist das denn für ein Laden, wenn's Brot gibt und Semmeln zum Kaufen ...Wer macht denn die Sachen? [Yes, but what kind of store is this where there are breads to be sold ...Who bakes these things?]

BIRGIT: Wie heisst der Mann? (humming "Backe Backe Kuchen") Der auch Kuchen bäckt? [What do we call the man? (humming the German song, trying to elicit "baker")

BIRGIT: (singing) Backe, backe Kuchen, der...

ELENA: (humming the song)

BIRGIT: der...?

ELENA: (singing) Kuchen war er backen...

BIRGIT: (singing) Backe, backe Kuchen, der...

ELENA: Backe Kuchen, der Bäcker backt Kuchen.

BIRGIT: Genau, der Bäcker backt den Kuchen.

ELENA: Uhu, ich hab ein /dach/ davon

ELENA: (singing, making up words) Backe, backe Kuchen, der Bäcker hat de Kuchen's /rau/ so – so die /bute/ war /kollo/ (laughing) in die /kollkum/ (Age: 3:10)

There is a playful element to the above interaction. Singing familiar rhymes made it easier for Elena to retrieve the German information she was looking for and apply it to the book interaction. By periodically pausing as she sang, the adult helped to scaffold Elena's learning as well as to create an inviting environment for the interaction. The adult also modeled ways of connecting what she already knew (the nursery rhyme in German) to the text at hand. In the context of this study, singing a relevant song not only facilitated Elena's learning of vocabulary, but it also made it fun and enjoyable.

The examples briefly discussed here show that it is important for adults to use rich contexts and a variety of approaches in order to aid children in learning vocabulary. When appropriate, adults used text to build broader concepts (e.g., dentist) to help Elena organize her emerging knowledge. Other times the adults provided her with a synonym for low frequency words when it was clear she already understood the word/idea at hand (angry/cross). Interactions with texts also gave the adults an opportunity to teach expressions that Elena may not have been familiar with (e.g., blowing a kiss). These varied experiences collectively supported Elena's language development across her two languages.

Shaping Personal Connections through Socially Cultivated Acts

Studies have shown that students who can make personal connections to the text are better engaged in the text they are reading (Manyak, 2008; Moll et al., 2001). Although it is well accepted in the literacy field that students should be encouraged to make meaningful connections to text, how children learn this is less discussed and how very young bilinguals navigate and learn how to accomplish this is even less understood. In this section of the chapter, we discuss how Elena was socialized in her bilingual home to develop the skill of personal connection. A central element in the scaffolding of Elena's engagement with text was the type of text used by the parents. As a child growing up bilingually and biculturally, Elena had access to texts that reflected her personal family dynamics. These texts provided Elena with the opportunity to reflect on who she is and where she fits in the larger context of her immediate world. In the excerpt below, we see Elena's attempts to see herself in the text. At the heart of these interactions is Rudine Sims Bishop's (1982) notion that books serve as a mirror to reaffirm one's life. Throughout the interaction below, we see Elena's insistence that she is in the book.

MOM: (reading) Mama's face is chestnut brown, her dark brown eyes are bright as bees. Papa's face turns pink in the sun, his blue eyes squinch-up when he smiles. My face, I look like both of them. A little dark, a little light.

MAMA AND PAPA SAY: Just…

ELENA: Right. (she turns the page) Now, that's mommy, daddy, and Elena. (she points at the picture of the family)

MOM: Ya. Mommy, Daddy, and Elena.
MOM: Ya. It does look like our family. Does it look like our family? (Age: 3:4)

One way to assist children in their development of comprehension is to guide them in understanding the character's feelings and actions. Elena's mother's question regarding whether or not the family in the text resembles her own served to reinforce the fact that Elena should be trying to make personal connections. In addition, Elena's mother reinforced her testing her identity via the protagonist in the text because she did not negate Elena's observation. Elena was never told this could not be a possibility. This approach to interacting with text was reinforced regardless of who she was reading with or the language she was using. In the example below, Elena and her father read the book *Kleine Grosse Schwester*. Throughout the interaction the adult relinquished control and allowed Elena to take over the reading when she wanted.

ELENA: Ich moechte, dass du liest. [I would like you to read.]
DAD: (reading) "Ich weiss noch wie es frueher war, vor langer, langer Zeit. Da gab es nur" ["I know how it was a long, long time ago. There was only"]
ELENA: (emergent reading) Papa, Papa – Mama, Mama – Elena, Elena (pointing at the pictures)
DAD: Uhum (reads) "gab es nur Mama, Papa und mich." ["there was just mama, papa and me"] (Age: 3:2)

These interactive reading sessions illustrate how both parents supported Elena in taking on the role of reader. They allowed her to complete sentences and to pretend to be the character in the text. Because both adults welcomed Elena's personal connections, they invariably sent her the message that this way of interacting with text was permissible. Although Elena repeatedly introduced herself in texts that paralleled her life, her parents modeled how to make connections with text that did not involve injecting herself in the text as the protagonist. In the following example, Elena is reading *Hard to be Six* with her mother, a story about a six-year-old girl. Elena's mother drew Elena's attention to the illustrator of the text by connecting it to her name.

ELENA: Two people. There are two names [reference to the name of the illustrator]
MOM: Oh, yeah, Cheryl is her first name, and Hannah is a girl's name, but here it is only one person. Her first name is Cheryl, just like your first name is Elena. And her last name is Hanna, just like your last name is Bauer. That's her whole name. Cheryl Hanna. So it's one person. (Age: 3:8)

Elena was confused by the name of the illustrator because to her it sounded like two first names. Her mother clarified for her the illustrator's name, but made the point even clearer by using Elena's name. In addition to making a general connection around names, the interaction also highlighted for Elena the concept of first and last name. This kind of explicit attempt to link information from the text with one's own life served as a continual model for Elena.

Similarly, when reading the text *Kleine Grosse Schwester*, Birgit helped Elena to make the connection between the baby brother in the book and her baby brother, Christopher.

BIRGIT: Uhum. Manchmal bist du klein, da darfst du noch nicht alles machen, da muss man aufpassen, aber fuer den Christopher bist du die (raises voice and waits) grosse Elena, die grosse Schwester. Na, jetzt schaun wir mal, was da passiert. (opens book) [Uhum, Sometimes you're little, there are things you can't do yet and we have to watch you, but for Christopher (her brother) you are the big Elena, the big sister. So, let's see, what happens.] (Age: 3:10)

In the above excerpt, Birgit accomplished two goals as she interacted with Elena. First she set the stage for the reading by helping Elena connect with the content of the text before it is read. Elena, like the protagonist in the text, is a big sister to a little brother. She also invited Elena and modeled for her how to wonder about a text by stating "let's see what happens next." These types of modeling set the stage for Elena to take up and practice what she observed.

Early Efforts to Support Elena's Word Reading Within and Across the Two Languages

As the above examples show, long before Elena was able to read in conventional ways, the adults in her life worked to broaden her vocabulary across both languages, allowed her to make use of both of her languages as resources, and supported her efforts to make meaningful connections to text. As Elena's interest in reading actual text emerged the adults modified their interactions in ways that scaffolded her literacy development.

During the beginning of a shared reading event, for example, Elena picked up the book *Miranda und der neue Teddy*. She then announced to her mother that she knew how to read the name of one of the characters because she watched her father read the name in the book. She also showed her mother how her father read the name *Frau Hoffmann* (Mrs. Hoffmann). Her mother then asked her:

MOM: Can you show me *Frau Hoffmann's* name?
ELENA: (leafs through the pages, then points to *Frau Hoffmann's* picture). This one is her.
MOM: That's her.
MOM: Can you find her name?
ELENA: (searching) H-h-h-h-h- see, here's the /

MOM: How did you know it says Hoffmann?

ELENA: I saw it when daddy was reading.

MOM: How was he reading it? Show me how he was reading it so that you saw it.

ELENA: He read it like this. (opens the book) He was reading a little faster, he read *de Hoffmann* (stresses "Hoffmann") *mit de Teddy sitzen on de — on de Stuhl.* (Age: 3:11)

Elena and her dad had read the above text numerous times. At about three-and-a-half, Elena showed a keen interest in letters and their sounds in text. Her father recognized this interest and incorporated a playful element in his reading with her. This was especially true with texts that were not very long. The excerpt below captures this playfulness and also reveals the source of Elena's previous remark about her ability to locate *Frau Hoffmann*'s name. The following example provides evidence that the knowledgeable other played a significant role in helping Elena to start breaking the code.

DAD: Und wo steht "Kaufhaus"? [And where does it say "Kaufhaus?"]

ELENA: /k/ (searching and making the sound of the letter)

DAD: k-k-k-k-k. – Jawohl. [Yeah, that's right!] (when Elena finds the right word)

DAD: (reads) "Sie steht in der Spielwaren-Abteilung vor den Teddys." Wo steht "Teddys? " ["She is standing in front of the teddy bears in the toy department." Where does it say "teddy bears? "]

ELENA: t-t-t-t-t-t-t (points to the "t" in the word "steht")

DAD: Da ist ein "t," aber das kommt ganz am Ende. "Sie steht in der Spielwaren Abteilung vor den..." (points to each word) [That's a "t," but it's at the end. "She is standing in front of the..."]

ELENA: "t!"

DAD: Teddys!

ELENA: "T" – Teddys. [/t/ "t" – teddys] (Age: 3:7)

This excerpt confirms that Elena and her dad were involved in interactions that were focused on identifying letters and their sounds in words. From this excerpt we also see Elena's dad helping her identify letter sounds at the beginning of words versus at the end of words. This game of hide and seek seems to be in part reinforcing Elena's understanding of letter sounds in German (many are identical to English), placement of letter sounds, and, to a lesser extent, using the letter sound and some visual cues from the word. The fact that Elena could locate "Frau Hoffmann" with her mother long after her interaction with her dad ended indicates that she might be using a combination of initial sounds along with some visual cues. There were other words with the initial sounds /f/ and /h/ on the page, yet she did not attend to them. Although Elena was inclined to be very playful with locating initial letter sounds, she was perhaps on some level also attending to some other element of the written text. Given the relationship between German and English (both Indo-Germanic languages), it is not surprising that the adults would help her see the positive relationships between the languages as well as the differences that may create temporary challenges.

In their interactions with her, the adult helped Elena address when to sound out a high frequency word in English and/or in German. In this featured episode, Elena is reading an early reader entitled *Bow-Wow*. This text had short sentences and the vocabulary was controlled.

ELENA: (as Elena came across the word "was" in the book she was reading, she started sounding it out) /w/ /a/ /s/ *was* (German pronunciation) (appears to be questioning the word, checks the spelling again) /w/ /a/ /s/ was.

MOM: When you see that word what do you normally say?

ELENA: *Was* (German pronunciation)

MOM: You sounded this word out in German. How would you say it in English?

ELENA: Was? (English pronunciation)

MOM: Yeah, was. (Age 3:06)

It is clear from this example that Elena knew the German pronunciation of the high frequency word *was*. She also sensed its use in the English reading context was incorrect. The adult's role in this context was to highlight for Elena what she had done – decode the word in German. The adult scaffolded Elena's next attempt by asking her to think about how she would say the same word in English. That level of scaffolding was sufficient for Elena to arrive at the English pronunciation of the word. Through these types of interactions, Elena learned that some words that look exactly alike in both languages must be treated differently.

Lessons Learned

How did Elena's social context and her interaction with bilingual adults influence and shape her biliteracy development in English and German?

The analysis of Elena's case revealed that one of the main contributing factors to the development of her literacy in the two languages was the supportive and nurturing context of the home. As indicated by the examples discussed in this chapter, the adults in Elena's life nurtured her literacy learning by encouraging her to construct knowledge about what it means to learn to be literate in the two languages. Similar to other studies on bilingual and biliterate children (Dworin, 2003; Moll et al., 2001; Reyes & Costanzo, 2002; Reyes & Azura, 2008), Elena's active participation in her becoming biliterate was aided by the literacy-rich environment with supportive adults who scaffolded her learning through social interactions. Elena was supported in her varied interactions with the adults in her life to explore her two languages beyond the printed word. In particular, the adults supported her attempts to connect her bicultural personal experiences to texts. Promoting this behavior legitimized her bicultural identity and unleashed her potential for bilingualism and biliteracy (Reyes, 2001).

We also found that integrating different modes of literacy – reading, acting out, and talking about text – aided Elena in her exploration of literacy. The adults modeled this multimodal way of exploring encounters with text. Evidently, Elena's use of different approaches to learning shows that when children are encouraged to explore several modes of literacy, they become engaged literate people. For bilingual children, the process of becoming biliterate is not simply distributed between languages, but it is also distributed among the different modes as "children with a variety of 'embodied knowledges'" (Kenner, 2003, p. 105) learn possible communicative strategies.

Another factor that contributed to Elena's biliteracy development was play. The types of play that the adults introduced to Elena were at the time of their introduction appropriate and supported her language and literacy development. For instance, in the example cited in this chapter, Elena sang playfully with her *German caregiver* as she was learning vocabulary. Not only did play become a tool for extending Elena's zone of proximal of development (Vygotsky, 1978), but it also made her learning an enjoyable and fun experience. Other studies have reported similar findings in bilingual and biliterate children (Lee, 2003; Reyes, 2001). Lee, in a study of native Korean-speaking kindergartners and native English-speaking kindergartners in a two-way immersion program, reported that play enhanced the development of English in younger emergent bilingual kindergarten girls who engaged in imaginary talk compared to the boys who spent most of their time in action games. Evidently, this suggests that children should be exposed to situations where they can explore learning in a relaxed and fun way.

In sum, Elena's biliteracy development points to the role of supportive environment where adults are active in engaging and scaffolding emergent bilingual children's encounters with literacy. Furthermore, in this environment the child is an active participant who is actively constructing her understanding of literacy in her two languages.

Implications

Although this study was a multiyear in-depth qualitative study, there are limitations to transferring this family's experiences to other families. Nevertheless, this family's effort to raise a bilingual and biliterate child can provide insights and possible directions for caregivers, preschool educators and parents to consider. The findings from this study highlight the significance of supportive contexts in facilitating emergent biliteracy development in younger children. Parents/ caregivers of bilingual preschoolers play an important role in shaping their literacy and language development. Across the various examples provided in this chapter, the texts used play a central role. Below are some suggestions for pre-school teachers and caregivers of young bilinguals.

1. Select children's books that support learning age appropriate topics that provide opportunities to discuss words and ideas that are unfamiliar or only partially understood. When books are well selected, children and parents engage in genuine in-depth discussions around book topics that result in increasing the child's conceptual understanding of their world and the necessary vocabulary.

2. Do not over-rely on lengthy discussions. Activities that involve locating synonyms for low frequency words are an important way for children to broaden their vocabulary. As students have more exposure to certain words, caregivers and/or teachers should encourage children using the words.

3. Act out vocabulary or expressions that are unfamiliar to the child. Unusual expressions will be much more memorable using this technique than giving a verbal explanation.

4. Select texts with a variety of formats. Books such as *Einkaufen mit Mama* provide preschoolers with opportunities to categorize their knowledge of certain concepts. Texts that visually describe the experiences of immediate importance to the child allow them to reaffirm and explore the issue. The books should reflect opportunities to explore personal experiences to develop age-appropriate background knowledge. Going back and forth among these books keeps children's interest and reinforces the variety of experiences we can gain through books.

5. Be aware of when the child is ready to explore certain literacy events. In the case of Elena, she signaled she was ready to "play" with letters and sounds in both of her languages. The adults responded by supporting her in ways that maintained her interest.

6. Set a tone in the interactions that makes it permissible to openly talk about the relationship between the two languages. In the case of Elena, her caregivers used language like "You sounded it out in German" and "How would you say that in English?" It should be a normal part of bilingual adult–child interactions to say things like "in English we say...., but in German [or what ever the language might be] we say..." or "the sounds are similar, but they look different when we write them." These kinds of interactions build on the metalinguistic skills that young bilinguals have.

Many of these suggestions can be applied to teachers working in a preschool context with young bilinguals. In cases where teachers do not know the children's language, they may solicit the help of parents or paraprofessionals. The goal is to immerse children in print-rich environments that are appropriate in order to support their biliteracy development across their languages.

Future Research

This study suggests that there is a need for understanding literacy development in emergent biliterate children who are learning their languages simultaneously. Studies that examine biliteracy development in the home and outside the home are needed. This study revealed that parents and caregivers shape the way children come to understand and engage in literacy. Future research should examine this issue across different language pairs in order to better understand the influence of various languages on the overall process. Do bilingual children hold a uniform view of book interactions regardless of their languages? In addition, studies with a focus on bilingual preschool children should seek to understand their metalinguistic development and the role of literacy in shaping it. Most importantly, we need to understand these children using a bilingual lens that takes into account the socio-cultural context of their experiences.

References

Araujo, L. (2002). The literacy development of kindergarten English-language learners. *Journal of Research in Childhood Education, 16*(2), 232–247.

Bauer, E. B. (2000). Code-switching during shared and independent reading: Lessons learned from a preschooler. *Research in the Teaching of English, 35*(1), 101–130.

Bauer, E. B., & Montero, K. (2001). Reading versus translating: A preschool bilingual's interpretation of text. *National Reading Conference Yearbook, 50*, 115–126.

Bialystok, E. (2001). *Bilingualism in development: Language, literacy, and cognition.* Cambridge: Cambridge University Press.

Bialystok, E., McBride-Chang, C., & Luk, G. (2005). Bilingualism, language proficiency, and learning to read in two writing systems. *Journal of Educational Psychology, 97*(4), 580–590.

Biemiller, A., & Boote, C. (2006). An effective method for building meaning vocabulary in primary grades. *Journal of Educational Psychology, 98*(1), 44–62.

Buckwalter, J. K., & Lo, Y. H. G. (2002). Emergent biliteracy in Chinese and English. *Journal of Second Language Writing, 11*(4), 269–293.

Caldas, S. J. (2006). *Raising bilingual-biliterate children in monolingual cultures.* Clevedon, UK: Multilingual Matters.

Clay, M. (1972). *Reading: The patterning of complex behavior.* Auckland, New Zealand: Heinemann Educational Books.

Collins, M. F. (2005). ESL preschoolers' English vocabulary acquisition from story reading. *Reading Research Quarterly, 40*(4), 40–41.

Dworin, J. E. (2003). Insights into biliteracy development: Toward a bidirectional theory of bilingual pedagogy. *Journal of Hispanic Higher Education, 2*(2), 171–186.

Dyson, A. H., & Genishi, C. (2005). *On the case: Approaches to language and literacy research.* New York: Teachers College Press.

Echevarria, J., Vogt, M. E., & Short, D. J. (2008). *Making content comprehensible for English learners: The SIOP model* (3rd ed.). Boston, MA: Pearson, Allyn Bacon.

Erickson, F. (1986). Qualitative methods in research on teaching. In M. Wittrock (Ed.), *Handbook of research on teaching* (pp. 119–161). Washington, DC: American Educational Research Association.

Ferreiro, E., & Teberosky, A. (1982). *Literacy before schooling*. Portsmouth, NH: Heinemann.

Garcia, G. E. (2000). Bilingual children's reading. In M. L. Kamil, P. B. Mosenthal, P. D. Pearson, & R. Barr (Eds.), *Handbook of reading research* (pp. 813–834). Mahwah, NJ: Lawrence Erlbaum Associates.

Gort, M. (2002, April). A preliminary model of bilingual writing development for Spanish-dominant and English-dominant students: Portraits from dual-language classrooms. Paper presented at the annual meeting of the *American Educational Research Association*, New Orleans, LA (ERIC Document 475741).

Gort, M. (2006). Strategic codeswitching, interliteracy, and other phenomena of emergent bilingual writing: Lessons from first grade dual language classrooms. *Journal of Early Childhood Literacy, 6*(3), 323–354.

Grosjean, F. (1989). Neurolinguists, beware! The bilingual is not two monolinguals in one person. *Brain and Language, 36*(1), 3–15.

Guerrero, M., & Sloan, K. (2001). When exemplary gets blurry: A descriptive analysis of four exemplary K-3 Spanish reading programs in Texas. *Bilingual Research Journal, 25*(1 & 2), 173–201.

Gutierrez, K., Baquedano-Lopez, P., & Turner, M. G. (1997). Putting language back into language arts: When the radical middle meets the third space. *Language Arts, 14*(5), 368–378.

Hornberger, N. (1989). Continua of biliteracy. *Review of Educational Research, 59*(3), 271–296.

Kenner, C. (2003). Embodied knowledges: Young children's engagement with the act of writing. In C. Jewitt & G. Kress (Eds.), *Multimodality literacy* (pp. 88–106). New York: Peter Lang.

Kenner, C. (2004). *Becoming biliterate: Young children learning different writing systems*. Stoke-on-Trent, England: Trentham.

Kenner, C., Kress, G., Al-Khatib, H., Kam, R., & Tsai, K. C. (2004). Finding the keys to biliteracy: How young children interpret different writing systems. *Language and Education, 18*(2), 124–144.

Lee, S. Y. (2003). Contexts of language use in a two-way immersion program: Examining dimensions and dynamics of language and literacy practices. Unpublished doctoral dissertation, University of California, Berkeley.

Leopold, W. (1949). *Speech development of a bilingual child: A linguist's record, Vol 4: Diary from age 2*. Evanston, IL: Northwestern University Press.

Lesaux, N., & Siegel, L. (2003). The development of reading in children who speak English as a second language (ESL). *Developmental Psychology, 39*(6), 1005–1019.

Manyak, P. C. (2001). Participation, hybridity, and carnival: A situated analysis of a dynamic literacy practice in a primary-grade English immersion class. *Journal of Literacy Research, 33*(3), 423–465.

Manyak, P. C. (2008). What's your news? Portraits of a rich language and literacy activity for English-language learners. *Reading Teacher, 61*(6), 450–458.

Moll, L., Saez, R., & Dworin, J. (2001). Exploring biliteracy: Two student case examples of writing as a social practice. *Elementary School Journal, 101*(4), 435–449.

Pérez, B. (2004). *Becoming biliterate: A study of two-way bilingual immersion education*. Mahwah, NJ: Lawrence Erlbaum Associates.

Reyes, I. (2006). Exploring connections between emergent biliteracy and bilingualism. *Journal of Early Childhood Literacy, 6*(3), 267–292.

Reyes, I., & Azuara, P. (2008). Emergent biliteracy in young Mexican immigrant children. *Reading Research Quarterly, 43*(4), 374–398.

Reyes, M. L. (2001). Unleashing possibilities: Biliteracy in the primary grades. In J. J. Halcon & M. de la Luz Reyes (Eds.), *The best for our children: Critical perspectives on literacy for Latino students* (pp. 96–121). New York: Teachers College Press.

Reyes, M. L., & Costanzo, L. (2002). On the threshold of biliteracy: A first grader's personal journey. In L. D. Soto (Ed.), *Making a difference in the lives of bilingual/bicultural children* (pp. 145–156). New York: Peter Lang.

Roberts, T. A. (2008). Home storybook reading in primary or second language with preschool children: Evidence of equal effectiveness for second-language vocabulary. *Reading Research Quarterly, 43*(2), 103–130.

Ronjat, J. (1913). *Le développement du langue observé chez un enfant bilingue.* Paris: Champion.

Schwarzer, D. (2001). *Noa's ark: One child's voyage into multiliteracy.* Portsmouth, NJ: Heinemann.

Sims Bishop, Rudine. (1982) *Shadow and substance: Afro-American experience in contemporary children's fiction.* Urbana, IL: National Council of Teachers of English.

Stake, R. E. (2005). Qualitative case studies. In N. Denzin & Y. Lincoln (Eds.), *The Sage handbook of qualitative research* (pp. 443–466). Thousand Oaks, CA: Sage.

Teale, W., & Sulzby, E. (1986). Emergent literacy as a perspective for examining how young children become writers and readers. In W. H. Teale & E. Sulzby (Eds.), *Emergent literacy: Writing and reading* (pp. vii–xxc). Norwood, NJ: Ablex Publishing.

Toloa, M., McNaughton, S., & Lai, M. (2009). Biliteracy and language development in Samoan bilingual classrooms: The effects of increasing English reading comprehension. *International Journal of Bilingual Education and Bilingualism, 12*(5), 513–531.

Vygotsky, L. (1978). *Mind in society.* Cambridge, MA: Harvard University Press.

3

LITERACY PRACTICES AND LANGUAGE USE AMONG LATINO EMERGENT BILINGUAL CHILDREN IN PRESCHOOL CONTEXTS

Lucinda Soltero-González and Iliana Reyes

Preschool teachers are facing the challenge of serving the nation's growing number of students from culturally and linguistically diverse backgrounds in an increasingly restrictive climate that dismisses native language instruction. In the U.S. over two million of these children attend pre-kindergarten through grade 3 classrooms (Abedi et al., 2004). Although the number of English-language learners (ELLs) entering pre-kindergarten continues to grow, the early literacy development of these children has not been thoroughly investigated (but see Kenner et al., 2004; Reyes, 2006; Reyes & Azuara, 2008; Soltero-González, 2008, 2009).

In spite of extant research evidence on the advantages of bilingualism and biliteracy (e.g., August & Shanahan, 2006; Dworin, 2003; Pérez, 2004; Reyes, 2001), 87 percent of the ELL students enrolled in public schools are in English medium programs (National Center for Education Statistics [NCES], 2006). Additionally, anti-bilingual education initiatives have been approved in three states (i.e., Proposition 227 in California, 1998; Proposition 203 in Arizona, 2000, and Question 2 in Massachusetts, 2003), restricting the implementation of native language instruction. Given that most bilingual children are instructed in English-only settings across the U.S., there is a critical need for research in pre-school classrooms that explores how children's home language could be tapped to improve their literacy learning.

The study we present in this chapter contributes to the discussion of the early literacy development of young Spanish-speaking children in English-medium school environments (also see Riojas-Cortez, 2000; Soltero-González, 2008, 2009). The implications of our study underscore the importance of building on the language and cultural resources children bring from home into the classroom to support English-language and literacy development.

We examine the ways in which young Spanish-speaking children use their home language in their preschool classroom to learn about forms (conventions) and functions (uses) of written language in English. This study is part of the Emergent Literacy and Language Development in Latino Children project (ELLD), a longitudinal study that examines the language and biliteracy practices at home and in the classroom for first- and second-generation immigrant Mexican children and their families. Findings from the ELLD project indicate that young bilingual children actively construct knowledge about the uses of language and literacy from observation, interactions, and conversations about print in their homes and communities before they enter school (see Reyes, 2006 and Reyes & Azuara, 2008, for further details). Unique to this student population is that children make use of resources available to them in both languages as they make sense of print, even when English is the main medium of instruction at school. This study focused on the following research questions:

1. What do emergent bilingual children come to know about literacy and its uses in English-medium preschool classrooms?
2. How do emergent bilingual children use the home language to participate in literacy practices within such contexts?

A Conceptual Framework for Understanding Emergent Biliteracy

Biliteracy Development from a Sociocultural Perspective

We draw on a sociocultural perspective to examine the literacy learning of young Spanish-speaking children (Dworin & Moll, 2006; Moll, 1990; Pérez, 2004; Reyes, 2001; Vygotsky, 1978). From this perspective, literacy is viewed as a meaning-making process that is embedded in the social contexts of home, community, and school. The interaction of children with peers and adults as they participate in literacy practices plays a central role in the development of emergent literacy. Furthermore, we recognize the importance of validating the wealth of literacy knowledge and linguistic resources that children bring to school from their homes and communities (Heath, 1983).

Within this theoretical perspective, the construct of hybridity (de la Piedra, 2006; Gutiérrez et al., 1999) has been helpful in understanding the unique learning experiences of bilingual children. The ability to draw from a variety of linguistic and cultural resources as well as use them competently in specific contexts defines hybrid language practices (Gutierrez et al., 1999). The work of Gutierrez et al. in school and after school settings describes how "these hybrid language practices fostered language and literacy development" (1999, p. 291).

Code-switching in particular has been identified as an ability that bilinguals use strategically to process information across-languages (Escamilla et al., 2009b; Reyes & Ervin-Tripp, 2004; Zentella, 1997). Several studies have challenged the strict separation of languages for language arts instruction. These studies show how effective literacy practices that promote the strategic use of two languages enhance the meaning-making process and foster biliteracy development (Gutiérrez et al., 1999; Martínez-Roldán & Sayer, 2006; Moll & Díaz, 1987). They also demonstrate how bilinguals utilize their two languages deliberately "to access and manipulate resources for intellectual and academic purposes" (Moll & Dworin, 1996, p. 238) when instruction supports bilingual literacy (Dworin, 2003; Moll et al., 2001; Pérez, 2004). Children's dispositions toward the development of "spontaneous biliteracy" (Reyes, 2001) even when they are only receiving instruction in their dominant language has also been revealed in these studies.

Additionally, several scholars have documented how young children represent and communicate meaning "multimodally" by integrating different kinds of symbolic systems including drawing, drama, music, mathematics, movement, and talk (Dyson, 1990; Genishi et al., 2001; Kress, 1997; Medd & Whitmore, 2000; Rowe, 1994). Understanding how early literacy develops when children are exposed to more than one language and script (orthographic system) during preschool or earlier is critical for all educators in the U.S. given the increasing number of children from culturally and linguistically diverse backgrounds entering school.

In short, the overwhelming findings of the studies described above are that children can learn to read and write in two languages concurrently without becoming confused or delayed in some way, and instead they experience cognitive benefits. Also, *hybridity* and *multimodality* are important aspects of the literacy development in young children who speak a language other than English.

A Bilingual Perspective to Early Biliteracy Development

Our study is also framed within a bilingual orientation (Dworin, 2003; Escamilla, 2000; Valdés, 1992). This view explicitly refutes the common assumption of monolingualism as the norm and emphasizes the importance of taking a bilingual lens that recognizes the interplay of languages in bilinguals (Dworin & Moll, 2006). A bilingual is not simply "two monolinguals in one person" (Grosjean, 1989), but rather "bilinguals have special linguistic resources beyond what monolinguals in either of the languages have, and [they] are able to employ these resources strategically and with great sensitivity to contextual factors" (Martínez-Roldán & Sayer, 2006, p. 296). In line with this bilingual perspective, we adopt the term *emergent bilingual* (Reyes, 2006) instead of English-language learners to emphasize the potential that these children have to become bilingual and biliterate in environments where their home language is viewed as a "resource" to learn English instead of viewing it as a "problem" (Ruiz, 1988).

Recent studies have investigated writing development in school-age bilingual children (Dworin, 2003; Escamilla et al., 2009b; Gort, 2006; Kenner et al.,

2004; Moll & Dworin, 1996; Moll et al., 2001; Reyes, 2001). However, the early literacy development of preschool bilingual children has received little attention. A few studies have been conducted with young children in the contexts of the home (Bauer, 2000; Kendrick, 2003; Reyes et al., 2007), school (Riojas-Cortez, 2000; Soltero-González, 2008, 2009), and in both settings (Reyes, 2006; Reyes & Azuara, 2008).

As part of another study within the ELLD project, Reyes and Azuara (2008) administered tasks and interview questions to young children at the beginning of the preschool year. The purpose of these tasks was to explore how the participant children develop concepts about print (Clay, 1989) (e.g., directionality for reading, concept of word, letter identification), book-handling skills (e.g., knowledge of book parts, page turning, and directionality of print), and hypotheses about how written language in Spanish and English works (e.g., letter sound relationships, spelling patterns, punctuation). The data suggest that emergent bilingual children, like their monolingual counterparts, acquire book-handling skills and use contextual cues to derive meaning from environmental print before they receive formal instruction (Goodman & Altwerger, 1981). The study also supports previous research with monolingual children which indicates that young children hypothesize about how to read and write and derive meaning from print long before they enter school (Ferreiro & Teberosky, 1982; Goodman, 1990; Martens, 1996; Rowe, 1994; Whitmore et al., 2004).

Reyes and Azuara's study provides three important findings that are unique to emergent bilinguals. First, exposure to print in two languages appears to facilitate the development of metalinguistic awareness (the ability to reflect on and manipulate aspects of language), which confirms results from previous research studies (Bauer, 2000; Bialystok, 1997; Gort, 2006; Kenner et al., 2004). Second, the children perceived themselves capable of reading and writing in both languages. Finally, the researchers conclude that variability in the literacy development in each language is expected in bilinguals (Dworin, 2003; Kenner et al., 2004), given the patterns of language use in their immediate sociocultural contexts (family, community, school). These findings are important because they provide insights about the emergent literacy knowledge that bilingual children may develop and, more importantly, their dispositions toward bilingualism and biliteracy. A direct teaching implication from these findings is the importance of building on, rather than neglecting, the important role of children's home language in their learning of a second language.

The study we describe here utilizes a sociocultural and a bilingual perspective to examine emergent bilingual children's literacy practices in preschool contexts. Our analysis of these literacy practices underscores how the children's use of their home language supported their early literacy development and exploration of English literacy functions within an all-English classroom. We conclude our chapter with teaching implications and future research directions.

Students, Teachers, and the Preschool Classrooms

We conducted this study in two preschool classrooms in a southern Arizona school district. The classroom teachers, both European-American women, were committed to the education of Latino children and this motivated them to participate in the study. They each had more than ten years of teaching experience in preschool. The teacher at Saguaro Preschool,[1] Ms. Vásquez, was bilingual, although nonnative Spanish speaker, and lived in Mexico for 20 years. Ms. Vásquez's classroom had a total of 18 children and all of them were Spanish-dominant speakers when they entered preschool. The teacher at Nopal Preschool, Ms. Lewis, had a bilingual endorsement and a fair command of Spanish, although she did not consider herself bilingual. Ms. Lewis also had 18 students in her classroom, 14 of which spoke Spanish as their first language; two children were monolingual English speakers, and the other two were Spanish–English simultaneous bilinguals who were learning rapidly to speak, read, and write in English.

All children in both classrooms were of Mexican descent, either recent immigrant or U.S. born, and qualified for free or reduced-price lunch. Most of the children were just turning five years old when we started the study. Spanish was the dominant language used at home (in most cases the only language used by parents and adults).

Teachers expressed their beliefs about the importance of native language maintenance for second-language acquisition; however, the development of oral language and early literacy skills in English was the main focus in both classrooms. The teachers' beliefs in favor of bilingualism were challenged by the perceived necessity of immersing children in English as a way to help them more easily transition into kindergarten where English must be the sole language of instruction due to the state-mandated English-only policy. In these classrooms, Spanish was used solely as a means of getting students started while they develop control of English. The use of Spanish was not banned; however, no attempt was made to explicitly foster Spanish literacy development.

Methodological Elements of the Study

We employed a case study methodology (Dyson & Genishi, 2005), which included qualitative research procedures such as ethnographic field notes, video, and audio recordings of interactions among the participants, recorded conversations and interviews of the teachers and parents, as well as students' writing samples.

Classroom observations were conducted one day per week for at least three hours each visit during a full academic year. Data collection focused on capturing children's participation in literacy practices, language use, and peer interaction in six classroom contexts:[2] circle time, story time, journal time, learning centers (including dramatic play in the housekeeping area), lunch time, and free choice time. In total, we collected field notes from 50 classroom observations, and transcriptions of 40 hours of audio- and video-recorded classroom interaction as well as interviews with the students, teacher, and parents. We were particularly interested in identifying which children learned what uses of literacy, in what language, and in what contexts as they progressed in their preschool year. We also focused on the participation structures in which such early literacy learning and language use occurred (child–child and teacher–child events).

We used literacy events as the basic unit of analysis. Literacy events were defined as children's construction and interpretation of texts that could be oral, written, drawn, dramatized, or, as was most often the case, multimodal (a combination of any of those symbol systems) productions (Rowe, 1994; Soltero-González, 2008).

Reading, Writing, and Language Use in the Classroom

Although teacher–child interaction is crucial in children's literacy learning, we focus mainly here on peer interaction to examine children's uses of language and explorations of written language during literacy events. In the early part of the year, most conversations among children were in Spanish. As the year progressed, the children's control of English increased; however, they continued using Spanish and code-switching, or alternations between Spanish and English, became frequent. Thus, peer interactions revealed a lot more about language use in both Spanish and English than the interactions of the students with the teacher. Four salient themes emerged from our observations in the two classrooms, which we illustrate in the following examples.

Using the Home Language as a Meaning-Making and Representational Tool

Although English was the language of instruction in the classroom, children continued using Spanish not only for social interaction and communicative purposes but also as a meaning-making and representational tool (i.e., to construct and represent meaning) that served academic purposes. Of importance in our study is that these uses of language were observed in events that gave children room for choice and were not directly guided by the teachers.

The following vignettes illustrate those findings. The first event took place in Ms. Lewis' classroom during learning centers time, near the end of March. The children were drawing a geometric shape as part of another figure. Ms. Lewis encouraged children to use lots of details because they were going to dictate a story to accompany their drawings and make a book out of it. Adalberto, who at the beginning of the school year was a monolingual Spanish speaker, decided to use a triangle as the body of a tiger. By the end of the year, he was able to produce formulaic phrases as well as more sophisticated language structures in English to communicate with Ms. Lewis, but Spanish continued to be the language he preferred to use with his peers.

Vignette 1

(Translations from Spanish to English are indicated in parentheses) [Additional information is described in brackets]

1. ADALBERTO: Look, *éste es un tigre* (Look, this is a tiger)
2. MS. LEWIS: Oh look! Is that your tiger?
3. ADALBERTO: *Yo los he visto pero yo vi un león que luego se quería brincar.* [Now he is talking to the researcher]
4. *Yo fuí al zoológico y luego unos tigres negros que tenían muchos negros*
5. *así. Y luego, luego que aquí había un lago y se cuelgaban de arriba.* (I've seen them but I saw a lion that wanted to jump out. I went to the zoo and then some black tigers that had black like this. And then, then that there was a lake here and they hung from up there).
6. RESEARCHER: *¿En dónde lo viste?* (Where did you see it?)
7. ADALBERTO: *En un zoológico, había agua y no quieren que se bajen porque se ahogan.*
8. *Y ahí hay un hoyo. Y luego se caen y por eso y ahí duermen y ahí comen.* (At the zoo, there was water and they don't want that the tigers go down because they drown. And then they fall down and that's why they sleep there and they eat there.).

After he received instructions from Ms. Lewis to add more background details to his drawing, Adalberto continued the conversation with the researcher about his experience at the zoo. When he finished, he showed his work to Ms. Lewis so she could write down his words on the page:

1. ADALBERTO: [showing his drawing to Ms. Lewis] Tiger.
2. MS. LEWIS: You made a tiger out of your triangle! Tell me, what is your tiger doing?
3. ADALBERTO: Uh, is eating grass.
4. MS. LEWIS: My tiger is eating grass [writes it down] And you did the grass right there!

Although a dynamic oral narrative in Spanish emerged while Adalberto was drawing, which he shared with the researcher who is Spanish–English bilingual, his dictation to Ms. Lewis was merely a one-word label in English ("Tiger"). When Ms. Lewis specifically asked him what the tiger was doing to encourage him to elaborate on the meaning of his drawing he responded, "Is eating grass." Clearly, these words left out the rich narrative he created in Spanish. Because this was the only point of contact between Adalberto and Ms. Lewis, she could only observe the product (the drawing of a tiger) but not the process he went through for the construction of the story. During this process, Adalberto used Spanish to access prior knowledge (i.e., a visit to the zoo), which served as a springboard for constructing a story that he was supposed to dictate in English. Additionally, combining talk in Spanish with drawing and movement enabled him to express his ideas more clearly than he was able to do through drawing alone and in his English dictation to Ms. Lewis.

This event illustrates the multimodality of literacy. That is, literacy not only involves written forms of language but also other symbol systems such as oral language, drawing, movement, music. Furthermore, it shows the important role of children's home language and background knowledge in their literacy development in English (August & Shanahan, 2006; Escamilla et al., 2009a; Genesee et al., 2006). Adalberto's oral narrative in Spanish included a rich description of the setting, characters, actions, and events in the story, clearly a use of language that served literacy-related purposes. Unfortunately, these existing language competences in Spanish were overlooked and untapped by the classroom literacy practices. They were not seen as a foundation or building blocks for the acquisition of literacy in English. The language use restrictions inadvertently limited opportunities to help children make connections between oral and written language in Spanish and apply that knowledge to the teaching of English literacy. We also observed that few opportunities to expand children's oral language in English through modeling, scaffolding, and rehearsing were provided during teacher–child interactions.

Vignette 2

This episode shows a shared reading event about insects that involved the whole group in Ms. Vásquez's classroom. The two boys featured in the dialogue, like most of the children in the two classrooms, started preschool speaking Spanish as their primary language. The event occurred in April, and even when English dominated the teacher's discourse, the children's use of Spanish as a resource for learning is evident.

1. TEACHER: Bugs, bugs, bugs, I love bugs
2. CHILDREN: I love bugs [all repeated in unison]
3. TEACHER: Grasshoppers that go hup hup hup [teacher gestures insects jumping]
4. ALEXIS: *Chapulines* (grasshoppers)
5. TEACHER: Yes, *chapulines* ... (grasshoppers)
6. SERCAN: *Chapulines chapulines* (grasshoppers, grasshoppers)

7. *Así le dicen a mi papá* (that's my dad's nickname)
8. ALL: Bugs bugs bugs, I love bugs! [said in unison]
9. TEACHER: Bees zzzzzzz
10. CHILDREN: zzzzzz
11. TEACHER: Buzzing by flowers that smell so good
12. SERCAN: *Son abejas . . . abejas*
13. TEACHER: *Son abejas . . .* see he has a happy face

Although there was no direct encouragement to use the home language during this reading event, Ms. Vásquez acknowledged when children used Spanish to make sense of the text (see lines 5 and 13). Using the home language as well as picture cues helped children to monitor their understanding of the story. Additionally, Sercan used Spanish to connect the story to a personal experience (i.e., his father's nickname being *chapulin)*; however, this comment went unnoticed (line 7).

Despite English being the medium of instruction in both classrooms, children drew upon their home language to construct knowledge and make personal connections with books. While their bilingualism and early biliteracy continued to spontaneously develop, these competences were not recognized in the official curriculum and the children's use of the home language as a resource for their academic development was dismissed (Moll et al., 2001; Reyes, 2001).

Using Code-Switching and Bilingual Strategies During Reading

As children gained greater control of English, the use of hybrid language practices (Gutiérrez et al., 1999) that included code-switching and bilingual strategies (e.g., returning to Spanish to discuss a text in English, translating key concepts) became more frequent. They used the two languages, separately or together, for a wide range of functions (Grosjean, 1989) in their everyday interactions at school. However, they were not encouraged as part of the classroom literacy practices. Instead, children were expected to use English in their interaction with the teachers, and the curriculum focused on the development of discrete literacy skills (letter identification, sight words, letter–sound relationships, etc.) exclusively in English.

Vignette 3

The following event occurred at the end of October during free choice time, on a day when Dariana's mother was volunteering in Ms. Lewis' classroom. Both Ms. Lewis and Dariana's mother reported that from the beginning of the school year, Dariana communicated successfully in both languages. During our classroom visits we observed her constantly engaging in literacy-related activities with both adults and peers.

The event consisted of Dariana and her mother reading together *The Very Busy Spider* by Eric Carle.

1. MOTHER, DARIANA: [Mother is reading. Dariana is looking at the pictures] "Baa! Baa!" [they both said in unison]
2. MOTHER: "Bleated the sheep. Want to run in the meadow?"
3. "The spider didn't answer. She was very busy spinning her" . . .
4. DARIANA: WEB!
5. MOTHER: " 'Neigh! Neigh!' said the horse. Want to go for a ride?"
6. "The spider didn't answer. She was very busy spinning her web."
7. DARIANA: Sewing his WEB [exaggerated rising intonation when saying "web"]
8. MOTHER: Spinning her web.
9. *Ahí lo está haciendo así.* (She is making it right there.)[points to the web]
10. DARIANA: *Mami cuando ya cuando ya hagas una poquita* voice *y es el* [unaudible]
11. *dices,* she was busy doing his WEB. [exaggerated rising intonation] (Mummy when you make a little voice and it is [unaudible] you say, she was busy doing his WEB.)

The beginning of the interaction (lines 1–8) happened in English. Later, Dariana tried to modify the way in which her mother read "spinning her web" by using an exaggerated rising intonation when saying "web" (line 7) and substituting "spinning" for "sewing" with which she seemed to be more familiar. Despite her emphasis on a change of intonation, Dariana's mother ignored it and instead repeated the phrase as it appeared in the book. This is when Dariana switched to Spanish and explicitly asked her mother to modify her tone of voice and read that phrase in a certain way ("making a little voice," lines 10–11). In relation to language use, the event reveals a kind of discourse tradition that both mother and child drew upon to create a more intimate environment that captured some aspect of the experiences they shared. Returning to Spanish was a sign of their shared cultural identity (i.e., Mexican-American), which permitted the alternated use of two languages. The use of both languages, both separately and together, permeated the entire literacy event for different functions. The following interaction happened after Dariana and her mother had finished reading the book:

1. MOTHER: *¿Por qué no jugó con los animales? Por qué no . . . espérate. ¿Por qué no jugó el spider con los animals?* (Why didn't it play with the animals? Why didn't . . . hold on. Why did the spider not play with the animals?)
2. DARIANA: *Porque estaba haciendo su . . .* spinning his web (because it was making its . . . spinning his web).

Dariana's utterance *"porque estaba haciendo su ...* spinning his web," reveals her ability to pull out words from her lexical repertoire in the two languages to make sense out of an English text. Code-switching, defined in the literature as the "bilinguals' use of both languages in a conversational turn" (Reyes & Ervin-Tripp, 2004, p. 320), is certainly a sign of Dariana's development as a bilingual speaker in a community where a bilingual mode of speaking is the norm. The use of both English and Spanish as resources to co-construct meaning (Moll et al., 2001) with her mother is remarkable given that in her classroom she had only received literacy instruction in English.

Using Writing to Build Friendships in the Classroom

While some of the children's literacy engagements mirrored their classroom instructional practices (practicing letter identification, writing their names in their work, copying words, etc.), others were spontaneous (e.g., writing notes to their friends, playing at literacy) and clearly driven by social functions that were meaningful to them. In the context of spontaneous engagements with literacy, children's attempts to use written language served "social-interactional" purposes (Taylor & Dorsey-Gaines, 1988). The following event illustrates how children used print to build and maintain relationships with friends in their classroom.

Vignette 4

While other children were engaged in different activities during free choice time in Ms. Lewis' classroom, Araceli gave Sofia, her best friend, a birthday letter. In September, when the school year started, both girls were Spanish dominant. By the beginning of the spring semester they had gained a fair control of English. Although they spoke English in most of their interactions with Ms. Lewis and during whole group activities such as story time and circle time, they continued speaking Spanish with their peers. The following event occurred in February. The dialogue was initiated by Araceli who also engaged the researcher in the conversation:

ARACELI: [Araceli shows a birthday card to the researcher] *Mira lo que le mandé a Sofia, porque era su su sus su cumpleaños* (Look what I sent to Sofia because it was her her her her her birthday).

RESEARCHER: *Vamos a ver. ¿Tú sabes qué dice ahí?* [pointing to the phrase "Best friends" written in the front of the envelope] (Let's see. Do you know what it says there?)

ARACELI: *Mmm ... para Sofia* (Mmm ... to Sofia) [Sofia takes the envelope and both girls smile at each other].

ARACELI: *Yo te lo hice* (I made it for you).

Inside the envelope there was a commercial card with English print and a hand-written letter whose text was in Spanish. Sofia took them out of the envelope, opened the handwritten folded letter and using invented reading she read it as follows:

SOFÍA: *Sofía y Araceli jugamos mucho mucho y siempre es mi amiga* (Sofia and Araceli play a lot and she is always my friend) [child continues looking at the letter]

After reading the handwritten letter, Sofia opened the birthday card and pretended she was reading it:

SOFÍA: *Querida Sofía, te quiero mucho por tu cumpleaños que me distes un pastel. Te quiero mucho* (Dear Sofia, I love you so much for your birthday that you gave me a cake. I love you very much).
ARACELI: *Sofía, ¿te gustó?* (Did you like it?)
SOFÍA: *¡Sí!* (Yes!)

As Dyson (1990) reminds us, "To understand the contribution of peer talk, we must first consider how children use symbols as social tools with their friends" (p. 54).

It is apparent from the dialogue above that Sofia and Araceli saw written language as a "social tool," or a means for building relationships. As the author of the card, Araceli was not only trying to communicate a message to her friend, but to express the importance of their friendship. The event also shows that she was exposed to print in Spanish and English at home and in her community as well as to social uses of writing that were relevant to her own life. Sofia's invented reading of both cards was based on what she expected the message in a birthday card to be as well as on her knowledge of the format and function of a letter, which presumably were motivated by a view of literacy as a "social tool."

Although the girls were not able to read conventionally yet, they showed emergent awareness of form (letter discourse and format) and functions of written language (expression of feelings, friendship). This is an example of the emergent knowledge about literacy that young children acquire as a result of living in a literate environment and that they bring into the classroom. Given that the discourse and format typical of a letter are similar in Spanish and English, emergent bilingual children like Sofia and Araceli could benefit from instruction that explicitly makes cross-language connections for children (Escamilla et al., 2009a). This type of instruction has the potential to effectively support children's development of metacognitive and metalinguistic knowledge in their two languages, the similarities and differences between them, and support their English literacy development.

Using the Home Language to Explore Sound–Symbol Relationships

Another important finding from our study is that children spontaneously showed interest in exploring sound–symbol relationships in Spanish even when their literacy instruction had been only in English, as it is illustrated in the event below. This early literacy behavior was commonly seen in children's dialogs about the letters in their own names and in the names of friends and family members in the context of child-initiated activities. While reading and writing their own name served personal and social functions in the classroom (e.g., identifying their work, selecting the learning center in which they chose to work, reading the birthday calendar), it provided them opportunities to explore speech–print relationships.

Vignette 5

It was near the end of February and the children in Ms. Lewis' classroom were getting ready for lunch. Dariana and Damon were sharing a table with two other children and they engaged in a conversation about the letters in their names:

1. DAMON: *Yo se cual es la "ka." El Gabriel es la "ka."* (I know which one is the "kah." Gabriel is the "kah" [he pronounces the letter /k/ using Spanish phonetic].
2. ANA: *La mía es ésta* (Mine is this one) [pretending to draw an /a/ with her finger on the table].
3. ALICIA: *Como la mía* (Like mine).
4. DAMON: *Las mías son la "de," la "e," ah no, la "o" y un palito, la "eme" y*
5. *la "u" y un palito, ésta* [making the /n/ with his finger on the table] (My letters are the "deh," the "eh," oh no, the "oh" and a stick, the "eh-meh" and the "oo" and a stick, this one [letters <d>, <e>, <o>, <m>, <v> in Spanish].
6. DARIANA: *Es la "ene"* (It's the "eh-neh") [letter <n> in Spanish].
7. DAMON: *¿La "ene?"* (The "eh-neh?").
8. DARIANA: *Sí* (Yes).

After that conversation, all the children started looking for "their letters" on a letter puzzle printed in their milk bottles. Damon, one more time, identified "his" letters using Spanish letter names as he found them in the letter puzzle: *"la 'de,' la 'o' con un palito, la 'eme' y la 'ene'"* (the "deh" the "oh" with a stick, the "eh-meh" and the "eh-neh").

In the previous dialogue, Dariana and Damon were negotiating knowledge about sound–letter relationships and letter names as they learned the conventional spelling of their names. Damon realized that the letters in his name (for which he used English pronunciation) did not match his knowledge of the Spanish alphabet. He perceived a discrepancy between the sound and the graphic representation of the letter <a>. The mismatch that Damon perceived is understandable because the long vowel sound for the letter <a> in English corresponds to two different phonemes and graphemes in Spanish (/e/ and /i/). Although he recognized the letter <a> in reciting his ABCs in English, when trying to spell out his name using Spanish phonology he said the first sound he heard (/e/). Then he corrected himself and referred to the letter <a> as an "o" and a "stick" ("*la 'o' y un palito*").

He resolved the perceived discrepancy through a symbolic invention (i.e., adding a "stick" to a letter that he knows, in this case the letter <o>, turns it into a different letter). Later on he applied the same logic to the letter <n> which he described as an "'oo' and a stick" (he is perceiving an inverted <u>). Dariana, who was sitting next to him, taught him the name of that letter in Spanish (line 6).

To summarize, this example illustrates how through play young children act as "cultural agents" (Moll et al., 2001) for each other in their explorations of written language. The joint participation of less-experienced and more-experienced literacy users as well as their ability to pull from their linguistic repertoires expanded their knowledge of sound–symbol relationships and letter naming in both languages. Another important finding that emerged from our study is that young bilingual children demonstrate metalinguistic awareness, "the general ability to manipulate language as a formal system" (Gort, 2006, p. 348). The children in this study demonstrated an early development of abstract knowledge about relationships between sounds and letters, mostly in Spanish, without formal instruction in that language. Although an examination of this competence is beyond the scope of this analysis, it is important to emphasize that this finding is consistent with research that has documented the emergence of metalinguistic awareness in young developing bilinguals (Bauer, 2000; Bialystok, 1997; Gort, 2006; Kenner et al., 2004; Reyes & Azuara, 2008). This aspect merits further investigation.

Lessons Learned

The previous vignettes describe the literacy practices and language use of young emergent bilingual children within all-English preschool classrooms. Through a series of episodes we describe how children's English-language development was enhanced as a result of being able to use Spanish in the classroom. Using their home language did not delay the acquisition of English. Instead, it became a scaffold to learn English and to participate in school literacy practices. It is important that teachers in all-English classrooms realize that supporting the *use of the home language* facilitates more sophisticated understandings of English literacy.

Our observations also indicate that in their explorations and uses of literacy, children like Adalberto experience drawing, reading, writing, movement, and talk as interconnected processes (Dyson, 1990; Genishi et al., 2001; Taylor & Dorsey-Gaines, 1988). This suggests that the literacy practices of young emergent bilinguals are *multimodal* (Genishi et al., 2001; Kress, 1997). Literacy instruction that acknowledges and purposefully incorporates *multiple symbol systems* is pedagogically sound (Dyson, 1990; Medd & Whitmore, 2000) as it creates the "possibility of more intellectual challenge and success for young literacy learners" (Whitmore et al., 2004).

The use of *hybrid language practices* was identified as an important aspect in the language and literacy development of emergent bilingual children. For children like Dariana and Sercan, who demonstrated a greater control of English than their peers, accessing their linguistic resources in both languages helped them more fully participate in school literacy events in English. Their bilingualism fueled spontaneous biliteracy development even when the preschool curriculum overlooked its intellectual potential and benefits for academic growth. These hybrid practices provided children with opportunities to connect their home language and literacy experiences with school literacy practices in ways that were relevant to their lives (de la Piedra, 2006).

Code-switching and *bilingual strategies* such as using Spanish to make sense of and discuss an English text enhanced rather than inhibited children's English literacy learning. By drawing from their linguistic repertoires in two languages (alone or simultaneously), children were able to make connections with their background knowledge and experiences as well as to construct and share new meanings regardless of their level of English competence. Based on these findings, we have come to believe that the use of explicit teaching to help children use their two languages strategically and make cross-language connections (August & Shanahan, 2006; Escamilla et al., 2009b) is an effective method to support second-language literacy. While we recognize that emergent bilingual children may make these connections spontaneously, direct instruction that attends to the similarities and differences between languages allows for a more efficient use of instruction time. It also facilitates the acquisition of English literacy – by building on children's existing language competencies, while strengthening children's native language (Genesee et al., 2006).

Another important lesson learned is that young emergent bilingual children, like their monolingual peers, actively construct knowledge about the uses and functions of written language (Dyson, 1990; Goodman, 1990; Taylor, 1993; Teale, 1986) through social interaction. While learning to participate in school literacy practices, *interaction with peers in the home language* allowed them to learn about and experience uses of literacy for both *social* and *academic purposes*. As a result of being able to use Spanish, children experienced literacy as a means to demonstrate how much they cared for each other and build friendships. Through interactions with peers and adults who shared their home language and cultural background, children's understanding about the forms and functions of written language was expanded.

Sound–symbol relationships in Spanish were the subject of children's explorations during play-based activities and conversations about the letters in their own names. An important lesson from our observations is that children's interest in exploring letter–sound correspondence in Spanish did not disappear as the year progressed, even though literacy instruction was provided only in English. Early literacy studies with monolingual children have shown that when children discover the function and need for writing their name, they become more aware of the conventions of print (Dyson, 1990; Martens, 1996; Taylor & Dorsey-Gaines, 1988). For the emergent bilingual children in our study, awareness of print conventions included explorations about letter–sound relationships and letter identification in two languages during games or conversations about their names.

Pedagogical Implications

The episodes described in this chapter point to different possibilities in the literacy instruction for young emergent bilingual children in all-English instruction environments, which we summarize as follows:

1. The home language is a source of support and not a source of interference in the learning of English. Regardless of the language of instruction, children need and use their native language to construct and represent meaning as well as to access prior knowledge. Therefore, even in English-medium classrooms, it is a good idea to allow the use of the home language because it facilitates the acquisition of English literacy.

   A way in which teachers can encourage children to use their home language to support English literacy development is using the language experience approach. This method has been widely used with young children and more recently has been incorporated into ESL instruction (Peregoy & Boyle, 2005). Preschool teachers of emergent bilinguals can implement it by having students draw and dictate their stories. When possible, teachers should allow children to dictate their stories in their home language; paraprofessionals, older bilingual students, and parents can help with children's dictation when teachers do not speak the children's home language. Encouraging children to tell their own stories in the home language helps them to develop literacy and reaffirm their identity. These children-created stories can be used to model functional reading and writing, speech–print connections in both languages, and reading fluency (Escamilla et al., 2009a). We know from previous research studies that the academic skills and background knowledge students develop in their home language can be applied to learning to learning to read and write in a second language (August & Shanahan, 2006; Cloud et al., 2009; Cummins, 1981); therefore, children will not have to learn those skills all over again during English literacy instruction.

2. Instruction that incorporates multiple symbol systems as integrated processes not only supports literacy acquisition but also higher order thinking abilities. Teachers can scaffold these processes for young emergent bilinguals by modeling how to make predictions and represent them symbolically as they listen to a story. One example would be using the Directed Listening-Thinking Activity (DL-TA) (Peregoy & Boyle, 2005). This activity can be adapted for emergent bilingual children by asking them to draw their predictions about what will happen next in the story and share them with partners in whichever language they choose. The teacher can then provide children with the oral and visual support to express their ideas in English, helping them to gradually expand and refine their vocabulary and language structures in English. Through activities like DL-TA, children become actively involved in the reading process and, as the year progresses, they may get better at making predictions through more sophisticated language structures, which can also enhance their reading comprehension skills.

3. Children's hybrid language practices are also an important aspect of learning to read and write in a second language. Supporting the strategic use of hybrid language practices such as code-switching, bilingual reading strategies, and cross-language connections (talking about similarities and differences between the two languages) enhances the construction of knowledge and second-language learning. Recent research syntheses suggest the need for programs that support second-language literacy through direct instruction to make cross-language connections (August & Shanahan, 2006; Genesee et al., 2006). Helping children to make explicit connections between their home and second language and allowing them to use their home language to access background knowledge are scaffolds to learning English. One way to create these connections is through the use of strategies like "preview–review" in the home language to make sense of books in English (Ulanoff & Pucci, 1999; Peregoy & Boyle, 2005). Another strategy is the use of cognates (Herrera et al., 2010) as part of reading and writing activities.

4. Given the importance of the social context in literacy acquisition and learning in general (Moll, 1990; Vygotsky, 1978), interactive learning or collaborative approaches should be present in any literacy program for emergent bilinguals (Genesee & Riches, 2006). Collaborative group work provides opportunities for children to receive the support of more capable peers or adults, which allows them to work within their zone of proximal development and do more than they could do independently (Vygotsky, 1978). In addition, comprehension and production language abilities are enhanced because children with a higher control of English (English learners or native English speakers) provide good models for emergent bilinguals, thus

stretching their learning of English. Teachers should purposefully design learning environments that promote collaborative learning where children jointly explore a wide variety of literacy functions. Riojas-Cortez (2000) suggests sociodramatic play as an avenue to motivate children to exercise a "literate use of language," which is necessary for the development of early literacy skills and active participation in school literacy practices. While teacher–mediated activities are important to provide modeling and guidance for children, play-based activities promote social interaction and the possibility for children to act as mediators for each other's learning.

Future Research Directions

Research designed to examine the role of the first language in early literacy development can contribute to the discussion of how to support English literacy development while maintaining the language and cultural resources that emergent bilinguals bring to the classroom. There is a great need for further research that explores the dynamics of early biliteracy along with the existing constraints *and* bilingual resources available in the classroom. In order to better understand the literacy learning of the young bilingual child as a whole, a shift from a monolingual view to a bilingual view is critical. A monolingual view of language and literacy development is problematic because it privileges monolingualism as the norm from which to understand bilingual and biliteracy development. Also, under this view, students from culturally and linguistically diverse backgrounds are seen in deficit terms and the potential benefits of bilingualism and biliteracy are neglected. A bilingual orientation, in contrast, offers a view of diversity and bilingualism as supporting not only emergent bilinguals' learning but as enriching all children's learning. It would be very useful if such research studies are based on ethnographic and qualitative traditions in order to examine the day to day classroom interaction, language use, and literacy practices that support native language instruction and value it as a scaffold to learning English.

Notes

1. We use pseudonyms for all the participants and research sites.
2. Due to space limitations, we do not include examples of each classroom context in this analysis.

References

Abedi, H., Hofstetter, C. H., & Lord, C. (2004). Assessment accommodations for English-language learners: Implications for policy-based empirical research. *Review of Educational Research, 74*(1), 1–28.

August, D., & Shanahan, T. (2006). *Developing literacy in second-language learners: Report of the National Literacy Panel on Language-Minority Children and Youth.* Mahwah, NJ: Lawrence Erlbaum & Assoc.

Bauer, E. B. (2000). Code-switching during shared and independent reading: Lessons learned from a preschooler. *Research in the Teaching of English, 35*(1), 101–130.

Bialystok, E. (1997). Effects of bilingualism and biliteracy on children's emerging concepts of print. *Developmental Psychology, 33*(3), 429–440.

Clay, M. (1989). Concepts about print in English and other languages. *Reading Teacher, 42*(4), 268–276.

Cloud, N., Genesee, F., & Hamayan, E. (2009). *Literacy instruction for English language learners. A teacher's guide to research-based practices.* Portsmouth, NH: Heineman.

Cummins, J. (1981). The role of primary language development in promoting education success for language minority students. In *California State Department of Education Schooling and Language Minority Students: A theoretical framework* (pp. 3–49). Los Angeles: Evaluation, Dissemination, and Assessment Center, California State University.

de la Piedra, M. T. (2006). Literacies and Quechua oral language: Connecting sociocultural worlds and linguistic resources for biliteracy development. *Journal of Early Childhood Literacy, 6*(3), 383–406.

Dworin, J. E. (2003). Insights into biliteracy development: Toward a bidirectional theory of bilingual pedagogy. *Journal of Hispanic Higher Education, 2*(2), 171–186.

Dworin, J., & Moll, L. C. (2006). Guest editors' introduction. *Journal of Early Childhood Literacy, 6*(3), 234–240.

Dyson, A. H. (1990). Symbol makers, symbol weavers: How children link play, pictures and print. *Young Children, 45*(2), 50–57.

Dyson, A. H., & Genishi, C. (2005). *On the case: Approaches to language and literacy research.* New York: Teachers College Press.

Escamilla, K. (2000). Bilingual means two: Assessment issues, early literacy and two language children. In *Research in literacy for limited English proficient students* (pp. 100–128). Washington, DC: National Clearinghouse for Bilingual Education.

Escamilla, K., Geisler, D., Hopewell, S., Sparrow, W., & Butvilofsky, S. (2009a). Using writing to make cross-language connections from Spanish to English. In C. Rodriguez (Ed.), *Achieving literacy success with English language learners: Insights, assessment, and instruction* (pp. 141–156). Worthington, OH: Reading Recovery Council of North America.

Escamilla, K., Soltero-González, L., Butvilofsky, S., Hopewell, S., & Sparrow, W. (2009b). *Transitions to biliteracy: Literacy squared* (pp. 7–27). Boulder, CO: The BUENO Center for Multicultural Education.

Ferreiro, E., & Teberosky, A. (1982). *Los sistemas de escritura en el desarrollo del niño.* México: Siglo XXI.

Genesee, F., Lindholm-Leary, K., Saunders, W., & Christian, D. (Eds.). (2006). *Educating English language learners: A synthesis of research evidence.* Cambridge: Cambridge University Press.

Genesee, F., & Riches, C. (2006). Literacy instruction issues. In F. Genesee, K. Lindholm-Leary, W. Saunders, & D. Christian (Eds.), *Educating English language learners: A synthesis of research evidence* (pp. 109–176). Cambridge: Cambridge University Press.

Genishi, C., Stires, S. E., & Yung-Chan, D. (2001). Writing in an integrated curriculum: Prekindergarten English language learners as symbol makers. *Elementary School Journal, 101*(4), 399–416.

Goodman, Y. M. (1990). Discovering children's inventions of written language. In Y. M. Goodman (Ed.), *How children construct literacy: Piagetian perspectives* (pp. 1–11). Newark, DE: International Reading Association.

Goodman, Y. M., & Altwerger, B. (1981). *Print awareness in preschool children: A study of the development of literacy in preschool children* (Occasional Paper No. 4). Tucson, AZ: University of Arizona, College of Education, Program in Language and Literacy, Arizona Center for Research and Development.

Gort, M. (2006). Strategic codeswitching, interliteracy, and other phenomena of emergent bilingual writing: Lessons from first grade dual language classrooms. *Journal of Early Childhood Literacy, 6*(3), 323–354.

Grosjean, F. (1989). Neurolinguists, beware! The bilingual is not two monolinguals in one person. *Brain and Language, 36*(1), 3–15.

Gutiérrez, K., Baquedano-Lopez, P., & Tejada, C. (1999). Rethinking diversity: Hybridity and hybrid language practices in the third space. *Mind, Culture, and Activity, 6*(4), 286–303.

Heath, S. B. (1983). *Ways with words: Language, life, and work in communities and classrooms.* Cambridge, MA: Cambridge University Press.

Herrera, S. G., Perez, D. R., & Escamilla, K. (2010). *Teaching reading to English language learners: Differentiated literacies.* Boston. MA: Allyn & Bacon.

Kendrick, M. (2003). *Converging worlds: Play, literacy, and culture in early childhood.* Bern: Peter Lang AG.

Kenner, C., Kress, G., Hayat, A., Kam, R., & Tsai, K. (2004). Finding the keys to biliteracy: How young children interpret different writing systems. *Language and Education, 18*(20), 124–144.

Kress, G. (1997). *Before writing: Rethinking the paths to literacy.* London: Routledge.

Martens, P. (1996). *I already know how to read: A child's view of literacy.* Portsmouth, NH: Heinemann.

Martínez-Roldán, C. M., & Sayer, P. (2006). Reading through linguistic borderlands: Latino students' transactions with narrative texts. *Journal of Early Childhood Literacy, 6*(3), 293–322.

Medd, S. K., & Whitmore, K. F. (2000). What's in your backpack? Exchanging funds of language knowledge in an ESL classroom. In P. Smith (Ed.), *Talking classrooms: Shaping children's learning through oral language instruction* (pp. 42–56). Newark, DE: International Reading Association.

Moll, L. C. (Ed.). (1990). *Vygotsky and education: Instructional implications and applications of socio-historical psychology.* New York: Cambridge University Press.

Moll, L. C., and Díaz, S. (1987). Explaining the school performance of minority students. *Anthropology and Education Quarterly, 18*(4), 300–311.

Moll, L. C., & Dworin, J.E. (1996). Biliteracy development in classrooms: Social dynamics and cultural possibilities. In D. Hicks (Ed.), *Discourse, learning and schooling: An interdisciplinary perspective* (pp. 221–246). Cambridge, MA: Cambridge University Press.

Moll, L. C., Sáez, R., & Dworin, J. E. (2001). Exploring biliteracy: Two student case examples of writing as a social practice. *Elementary School Journal, 101*(4), 435–449.

National Center for Education Statistics (2006). *The condition of education 2006: Indicator 7: Language minority school age children.* U.S. Department of Education: Institute of Education Sciences. Retrieved May 10, 2008 from: http://nces.ed.gov/pubsearch/pubsinfo.asp?pubid=2006071.

Peregoy, S. F., & Boyle, O. F. (2005). *Reading, writing, and learning in ESL: A resource book for K-12 teachers* (4th ed.). Boston, MA: Pearson Education.

Pérez, B. (2004). *Becoming biliterate: A study of two-way bilingual immersion education.* Mahwah, NJ: Lawrence Erlbaum Assoc.

Reyes, I. (2006). Exploring connections between emergent biliteracy and bilingualism. *Journal of Early Childhood Literacy, 6*(3), 267–292.

Reyes, I., & Azuara, P. (2008). Emergent biliteracy in young Mexican immigrant children. *Reading Research Quarterly, 43*(4), 374–398.

Reyes, I., & Ervin-Tripp, S. (2004). Code-switching and borrowing: Discourse strategies in developing bilingual children's interactions. *The proceedings of the Second International Symposium on Bilingualism at the University of Vigo.* Vigo: Universidade de Vigo.

Reyes, I., Alexandra, D., & Azuara, P. (2007). Home literacy practices in Mexican households. *Cultura y Educación, 19*(4), 395–407.

Reyes, M. L. (2001). Unleashing possibilities: Biliteracy in the primary grades. In M. L. Reyes & J. J. Halcón (Eds.), *The best for our children: Critical perspectives on literacy for Latino students* (pp. 96–121). New York: Teachers College Press.

Riojas-Cortez, M. (2000). Mexican American preschoolers create stories: Sociodramatic play in a dual language classroom. *Bilingual Research Journal, 24*(3), 295–308.

Rowe, D. W. (1994). *Preschoolers as authors: Literacy learning in the social world of the classroom.* Cresskill, NJ: Hampton Press.

Ruiz, R. (1988). Orientations in language planning. In S. L. McKay & S. C. Ling Wong (Eds.), *Language diversity: Problem or resource?* (pp. 3–25). New York: Newbury House/ Harper & Row Publishers.

Soltero-González, L. (2008). The hybrid literacy practices of young immigrant children: Lessons learned from an English-only preschool classroom. *Bilingual Research Journal, 31*(1 & 2), 75–93.

Soltero-González, L. (2009). Preschool Latino immigrant children: Using the home language as a resource for literacy learning. *Theory into Practice, 48*(4), 283–289.

Taylor, D. (1993). *From the child's point of view.* Portsmouth, NH: Heinemann.

Taylor, D., & Dorsey-Gaines, C. (1988). *Growing up literate: Learning from inner-city families.* Portsmouth, NH: Heinemann.

Teale, W. (1986). Home background and young children's literacy development. In W. Teale & E. Sulzby (Eds.), *Emergent literacy: Writing and reading* (pp. 173–206). Norwood, NJ: Ablex.

Ulanoff, S. H., & Pucci, S. L. (1999). Learning words from books: The effects of read aloud on second language vocabulary acquisition. *Bilingual Research Journal, 23*(4), 409–422.

Valdés, G. (1992). Bilingual minorities and language issues in writing: Toward profession wide responses to a new challenge. *Written Communication, 9*(1), 85–136.

Vygotsky, L. S. (1978). *Mind in society: The development of higher psychological processes.* Cambridge, MA: Harvard University Press.

Whitmore, K. F., Martens, P., Goodman, Y. M., & Owocki, G. (2004). Critical lessons from the transactional perspective on early literacy research. *Journal of Early Childhood Literacy, 4*(3), 291–325.

Zentella, A. C. (1997). *Growing up bilingual.* Cambridge, MA: Blackwell.

4

LEARNING HOW TO WRITE IN ENGLISH AND CHINESE

Young Bilingual Kindergarten and First Grade Children Explore the Similarities and Differences between Writing Systems

David Yaden, Jr. and Tina Tsai

Introduction

While Mandarin Chinese and English are the two most commonly spoken languages in the world, in the 2000 census (U.S. Census Bureau, 2003a, 2003b) the Chinese language rose notably to the rank of the third most commonly spoken language in the United States after English and Spanish, an almost 100% increase in Chinese speakers in a single decade. Based on these statistics, it can be concluded that there is a significant English/Chinese bilingual and biliterate population in the United States that should be better understood. In addition, there is the practical need for more understanding of English/Chinese biliteracy development for educators who work at schools in Chinese-speaking communities, educators who work at Chinese schools teaching Chinese literacy to Chinese American children, or educators in Asian countries where Chinese and English play prominent roles in schools and society.

Additional reasons for studying early English/Chinese reading and writing development relate to the acquisition of biliteracy itself. Theoretical and empirical explorations of the phenomenon of biliteracy (cf. Bialystok, 1997; Hornberger, 2003; Hornberger & Skilton-Sylvester, 2003) and multiliteracy (Cope & Kalantzis, 2000) have only just begun to gain momentum following the establishment of a broad body of research on bilingualism in the past few decades (see Garcia, 2002). Although there is a widely quoted literature on bilingual children's reading of Chinese (e.g., Bialystok, 1997; Chen et al., 2003; 2004; Shu & Anderson, 2003; Shu et al., 2000), studies on the *simultaneous* development of English and Chinese writing by young children are much less well known (see Buckwalter & Lo, 2002; Chan & Louie, 1992; Chan & Nunes, 2001; Tsai, 2007 for exceptions). In addition, there is the issue of just how "phonetic" information is represented in Chinese characters and, subsequently, learned by children (Bialystok, 1997; Chen et al., 2003) which, in turn, is a part of the larger debate as to whether Chinese is viewed as logographic (see Chan & Louie, 1992; Chen et al., 2003) or syllabic (cf. DeFrancis, 1989).

Finally, most of the research on early writing of mono- or bilingual children has focused on the *figurative* aspects of early writing (cf. Bloodgood, 1999; Burns & Casbergue, 1992; Defior & Serrano, 2005; Hildreth, 1936; Levin et al., 2005; Levin & Bus, 2003; Sulzby, 1985) as opposed to how children *conceptualize* both the symbols and processes they use to represent what they want to mean in their writing (cf. Adi-Japha et al., 1998; Brenneman et al., 1996; Luria, 1998). Thus, the present study draws particularly upon the clinical methodology developed by Vygotsky and colleagues (Luria, 1998; Vygotsky, 1997) in the 1920s and more recently by Ferreiro and Teberosky (1982) to elicit children's thinking about what they are writing during the actual process.

In summary, then, the general purpose of the present study was to study in detail the ways in which 11 kindergarten and first grade bilingual children learning both English and Chinese literacy "figure out" these very different writing systems. In order to help us do this, we also drew on work using *microgenetic* approaches (e.g., Granott, 2002; Siegler & Crowley, 1991) which provide insight into tracking the moment-by-moment processes such as would be used by children in writing either words or sentences. This methodological design will be discussed shortly.

In the following chapter we, first of all, give a brief description of the Chinese system of writing. Second, we review pertinent work with young Chinese/English bilingual children learning to read either Chinese or English followed by an outline of our particular methods for this study. Next we discuss our results, related both to the children's performances in English writing as well as to their responses to the same tasks in Chinese. Finally, we present some graphical depictions of selected children's patterns of conceptual understanding in both languages. In the last section, then, we offer some interpretations of our findings and suggest some possible applications for research and practice.

Selected Chinese Syllabic and Phonetic Principles

The main Chinese writing system is composed of characters or graphemes, called /zì/ (字), which is "the fundamental contrastive unit of writing in Chinese" (Rogers, 2005). A standard estimate is that there are 50,000 characters found in the dictionary. Further, each /zì/ represents a syllable in the spoken Chinese languages (Chen et al., 2004; Rogers, 2005); and, unlike English, in most Chinese dialects changing the tone changes the meaning of the word (diacritical marks in the chapter represent the four tones of Chinese – high level, rising, low then rising, and falling: e.g., /mā/, /má/, /mǎ/, /mà/.) For example, /bìng/ (病) with a falling tone means "sick, sickness," in contrast, (bīng) (冰) with a high level tone means "freeze, cold."

However, like and more so than English, Chinese is highly homophonous with similar sounding words having different meanings depending upon the context. Thus, /bīng/ (兵) with the high level tone can also mean "soldiers; a force; an army," or "arrow-quiver" (挧). Similarly, /bǐng/ (芮) with a falling then rising tone can mean "bright, shining" or "plate" (鉼). Interestingly, both English and Chinese are considered to have "deep" orthographies (cf. Das et al., 2009) that is, the association between the linguistic unit and grapheme is more irregular than in Spanish or Indonesian, for example.

The most common type of Chinese character is the semantic–phonetic compound, usually composed of usually two /zì/ in which one part of the character relates to the pronunciation of the whole character and the other to its meaning (estimates of semantic-compound frequency range from 72% to over 90%, see Chen et al., 2003; DeFrancis, 1989, respectively). It is important to note here that the "phonetic" radical or part of the character only provides a general clue to overall pronunciation of the character and is not representative of a subsyllabic or phonemic linguistic unit. To further complicate matters, the "phonetic" radical can provide either full, partial, or no information about the overall pronunciation of the character; and sometimes there is no "phonetic part," as in semantic–semantic compound /zì/ (字) itself. Thus, Ku and Anderson (2001) found that contextual support was more helpful in incidental learning of new characters during reading than phonetic regularity, pointing to the importance of context that children must use to determine the conventional pronunciation of characters.

Studies of Young Children Interpreting Chinese Writing

As mentioned earlier, several studies have examined facets of the process involved in reading and pronouncing Chinese characters (e.g., Bialystok, 1997; Chen et al., 2003). However, we found far fewer studies which asked children to write in Chinese and even fewer who asked them to interpret that writing. One such study conducted by Chan and Louie (1992) in Hong Kong with 60, three- to five-year-old children required them to draw a picture of themselves and write their name below it in order to investigate whether they could differentiate drawing from writing, match characters with syllables, use multiple units within a character, and segment conventionally. While children did not interpret their writing in this study, by analyzing the complexity of the characters produced, Chan and Louie (1992) concluded that even the youngest children demonstrated implicit knowledge of the differences between drawing and writing, had an awareness of the graphic structure of Chinese characters and made connections from the stroke patterns to the speech units in their names.

In a further study, Chan and Nunes (1998, 2001) created three categories of pseudo characters with either illegal stroke patterns or illegal graphic (i.e., non-stroke-like) features and asked 100, five- to nine-year-old children to judge which characters might have been written by a child "from another planet" learning to write Chinese. Again, while the researchers did not probe children for their reasoning about which characters were "illegal," they concluded that even without explicit instruction on the positioning of stroke patterns within characters children demonstrated intuitive knowledge of what could be a legitimate Chinese character or not.

However, we found only one study that addressed emerging English/Chinese biliteracy specifically. Buckwalter and Lo (2002) conducted a 15-week case study using semi-structured literacy activities and interviews in the home of a five-year-old boy (Ming) recently arrived from Taiwan only five months earlier with his parents who were full-time graduate students in the U.S.. While Ming's parents spoke Chinese to him at home, he was placed in an English-speaking daycare from 9:00a.m. to 5:00p.m. Over the 15 weeks of the study, the researchers read books to the boy in Chinese and English and engaged him in a variety of board and card games, writing activities, trips around the neighborhood in which pictures of environmental print were taken, and book making in which Ming dictated sentences to be written under the photographs of places and signs in the neighborhood.

From their study, Buckwalter and Lo (2002) determined that Ming was acquiring both "foundational emergent literacy awareness" which applied to both languages and scripts as well as "surface level emergent literacy awareness" in which script specific knowledge was applied to either English or Chinese. As an example of the latter, according to the researchers, Ming understood that Chinese characters were not "sources of phonetic information" as were letters (p. 284). In addition, he was observed paying attention to the parts of characters to determine their meaning. In contrast, in his English writing development, Ming demonstrated a quick movement from a prephonetic level to letter name writing, commonly observed stages among young children learning to write English (cf. Temple et al., 1982). Thus, Buckwalter and Lo concluded that even without formal instruction, Ming incorporated without confusion knowledge about two differing orthographic systems.

Socio-Psychogenetic Perspectives for Studying Biliteracy Development: Studies across Various Languages and Scripts

Ferreiro and Teberosky's (1979/1982) study of children's thinking about the processes of learning to write is the seminal study on investigating the developing conceptual understandings children form about writing systems. While currently, there are no studies in Chinese early writing comparable to Ferreiro and Teberosky's studies in Spanish, subsequent research with children learning to write English, Hebrew, Italian, Korean, and Japanese using very similar or identical methods has corroborated their findings that children move through increasing levels of more conventional understanding related to how scripts represent both sound and meaning, regardless of whether the script is alphabetic or consonantal (see Kato et al., 1998; Kwak, 2006; Manning et al., 1993, 1995; Pontecorvo & Zucchermaglio, 1988; Tolchinsky & Teberosky, 1998; Tolchinsky Landsmann & Levin, 1985, 1987; Vernon & Ferreiro, 1999; Yaden & Tardibuono, 2004). In addition, children's use of figurally or graphically correct letters or forms does not automatically indicate a conventional understanding of them. Descriptions of these levels from Ferreiro and Teberosky (1982) are provided in Table 4.1.

The Clinical Interview or Inquiry Method

The study methodology primarily used in the psychogenetic approach is the *clinical interview* used both by Piaget (1955/1977b) and by Vygotsky (1987, 1997), a method which has been suggested by the National Research Council

TABLE 4.1 Ferreiro and Teberosky's levels of writing conceptualizations

Level	Writing conceptualizations
Level 1	Children reproduce what they identify as basic writing form. This manifests in scribbles or letter-like forms. Children conceptualize writing globally or as connected and do not realize that writing represents speech nor that it can be broken down. There is a level of what Piaget calls *nominal realism* – children expect the writing to somehow reflect the object it represents in a quantifiable way (e.g., size) but not figural (e.g., picture representation).
Level 2	The central hypotheses that children have about writing at this level is that writing must have some objective differences in order to represent or "mean" different things. A manifestation of this concept is that children write with variation in characters. Minimum quantity principle: children conceptualize writing as having a minimum quantity of characters, usually 3+.
Level 3	The central hypothesis that children have about writing at this level is what is commonly known as the syllabic hypothesis: each letter, written character/grapheme is thought to represent a single syllable.
Level 4	This level is the transition from the syllabic hypothesis to the alphabetic hypothesis. Children will try to analyze writing and speech beyond the syllable and assign one phoneme to each grapheme though the correspondence will not be complete nor conventional (i.e., some phonemes and/or graphemes will be unaccounted for in the interpretation).
Level 5	The milestone of this level is the conceptualization of written language as directly corresponding to spoken language in what is commonly known as the alphabetic principle. Though not completely conventional in its written manifestation, they do understand that sound values smaller than the syllable can correspond to writing.

Source: Ferreiro and Teberosky, 1982.

(Bowman et al., 2001) as a powerful method for understanding children's cognitive processes. The clinical interviewer elicits children's writing through various tasks (see Table 4.2) and, then, through a series of questions and or manipulations to the text which the children wrote, or by writing new text with certain distinctive features (such as no spacing between words), attempts to engage the children in further conversation about the forms, meaning, and processes used in the writing at hand. The data used in analysis, then, comprises both the children's writing performances as well as their talk about those performances. Ferreiro and Teberosky (1982, p. 21) have described their *inquiry method* as:

> Following the general approach of Piagetian genetic psychology, all tasks involve an interaction with the child and the object of knowledge (in this case, written language) in the form of a problem to be solved. From this interaction, a dialogue develops between child and interviewer, a dialogue with the purpose of exposing the mechanisms of child thought. The experimental design includes situations of interpreting the alphabetic code as it appears in the daily world and situations of graphic production. In all the proposed tasks we introduce conflictive (or at least potentially conflictive) elements whose solution requires real reasoning on the part of the child.

While various descriptive and quantitative analyses can be done with aspects of the writing sample, the primary analysis of data is qualitative, conceptual, and deductively based upon psychogenetic principles first outlined by Piaget (1977a, 1955/1977b) and later by Ferreiro and Teberosky (1982) as they apply to literacy. In brief, these principles (paraphrased) are that (a) reading cannot be reduced strictly to deciphering, in other words, simply decoding letters to sound; (b) writing is not merely copying a model or developing skill to reproduce conventional graphic shapes. Writing is, first and foremost, a conceptual task where children put into play their hypotheses about the meaning of graphic representation; and (c) progress in literacy does not come about primarily through advances in deciphering and copying. Learning to write is an active construction on the part of the child whose existing knowledge is continually restructured both by internal and external influences (pp. 20–21).

To this methodology and analytic procedure, we have added some additional characteristics drawn from microgenetic studies of children's learning (e.g., Granott & Parziale, 2002; Siegler, 1996) which we describe in the next section.

Applying a Socio-Psychogenetic and Microgenetic Approach to the Study of Biliteracy

Setting and Participants

The research site from which children for this study were recruited was a small private after-school Chinese program that provides Chinese language instruction to students from kindergarten to eighth grade. The surrounding working-class to upper-middle-class suburban city located within a large metropolitan area has a population of a little over 50,000 and a racial make-up that is predominantly White (41%) and Asian (36%) (U.S. Census Bureau, 2003a).

Participants in this study were 12 young Chinese American children, ages four to six years, who during a screening process were found to not have a stable concept of the alphabetic principle for English or the phonetic principle for Chinese. As one child's data was incomplete due to scheduling conflicts, the final sample included two first grade children and nine kindergartners, three girls and eight boys. Although each child had varying degrees of language and literacy ability in the two languages of Chinese and English, all had had exposure to and instruction in both languages and could converse in both. Environmental print in the neighborhood within which these children reside included a mixture of Chinese, English, and Spanish writing, and instruction at the public schools where the students attended was conducted all in English.

In addition, all children received Chinese literacy instruction, either at the research site or at home, and all but one child had family members who spoke Mandarin Chinese at home. The child whose home language was not Mandarin attended the Chinese program and faculty, staff, and classmates always spoke Mandarin Chinese to him. Chinese literacy instruction at the research site occurred for one hour a day, five days a week.

Study Procedures and Tasks

Inquiry interview. During the initial clinical interview, the children were asked to complete 11 writing tasks each in English and Chinese (see Table 4.2). For each writing task, the children were asked to use a finger as they interpreted/ read their own writing. In addition, for each writing task, the researcher

TABLE 4.2 English and Chinese writing tasks

English	*Chinese*
Child's name	Child's name
Family member 1 name	Family member 1 name
Family member 2 name	Family member 2 name
Mom	媽媽
Dad	爸爸
Dog	狗
Baby	寶貝
Toad	蟾蜍
Map	地圖
Duck	鴨
Dad kicks the ball.	爸爸踢球.

covered one half and then the other half of the writing with white paper and asked the child to read the part of the writing that was visible. This required the children to interpret parts of English words and parts of Chinese characters. Manipulations such as these have been employed by Ferreiro and Teberosky (1979/1982) as well as other researchers to elicit children's reasonings about their writing.

Finally, one of us (Tsai) began with the list of English and Chinese writing tasks, but changed the order of tasks based on the child's comfort and preferences. For example, all tasks could be completed in English followed by Chinese or vice versa; or sometimes there was alternation between English and Chinese tasks during a session. Also, children often spontaneously produced writing or requested to write English and Chinese words that were not on the original task list. These children's writings and their interpretations of them were included in the analysis when appropriate.

Microgenetic factors in the study design. The microgenetic method has three central properties: (a) making multiple observations over the course of change; (b) ensuring a high density of observations relative to change; and (c) intensive trial-by-trial analysis aimed at studying qualitative and quantitative characteristics of change (Siegler & Crowley, 1991). In following these guidelines, each of the 11 children participated in ten clinical interviews in addition to their initial screening interview, for a total of at least 11 clinical interview sessions per child over a three-month period between late September 2006 and early January 2007. One to two interviews were held with each child per week. Interview sessions lasted from 15 to 60 minutes, and all were videotaped.

Our interview procedures differed importantly from other socio-psychogenetic studies (see e.g., Ferreiro & Teberosky, 1982; Manning et al., 1993) in the following three ways. First of all, the inquiry/clinical interviews were repeated several times a month, rather than at only one point in time. Second, judgments about the children's reasonings during writing were done task-by-task, rather than making a general judgment across all writing samples. And, finally, often the interviewer wrote the word conventionally first and then asked the child to produce his/her sample. This latter strategy, adopted from other microgenetic studies (Siegler & Crowley, 1991), is designed to actually provide a prompt for change such as would occur in the natural environment where a child often receives a correction from a caregiver for an unconventional graphic response or is shown a specific model of adult writing to follow (cf. also Ferreiro & Teberosky, 1982, on similar techniques).

Findings

Given the constraints of the present chapter, the following discussion of findings will be of necessity limited to certain portions of the entire corpus. After a brief description of some general characteristics of the data collection, and a definition of an *Instance of Conceptual Evidence* (ICE), the primary unit of analysis, some select examples of Levels 1–3 of the conceptualization scheme of Ferreiro and Teberosky in both languages (see Table 4.1) will be illustrated. However, the main focus shall be upon (a) the children's understanding of English and Chinese from Level 3 on, and (b) patterns in their development of understanding both English and Chinese when viewed over the three months of the data collection period.

Overview of Data Collection

A total of 56 hours of video footage of children interpreting their own Chinese and English writing formed the corpus of data with the interview time ranging between four and seven hours per child. For the ten sessions, a necessary modification occurred around the third and fourth sessions. Due to the marked fatigue that the children exhibited in completing the 11 tasks in English and 11 tasks in Chinese, the number of writing tasks was reduced from 11 per language to five per language (see Table 4.3 for the tasks continued). However, tasks were not limited to these as the children sometimes preferred to do one of the omitted tasks from the original list or, when a child declined one task, a task from the list of omitted tasks was offered as an alternative.

Further, there were instances when children either chose certain writing tasks over others or spontaneously composed or requested to compose writing outside of the clinical interview writing tasks. For example, one child wrote "Godzilla kicks the helicopter" instead of the predetermined "Dad kicks the ball" task. Another child opted to write 媽媽, 我喜歡你 (Mom, I like you) instead of 爸爸踢球 (Dad kicks the ball). This sort of flexibility and adaptation for the child was necessary to keep the child's attention and participation in the interview activities. The goal was to capture as much evidence of self-reported conceptual knowledge about their writing as possible.

Definition of Instances of Conceptual Evidence

As opposed to previous studies of children's writing development in which a child was given a general "level" for a clinical interview session (e.g., Yaden &

TABLE 4.3 Reduced number of writing tasks used in the study

English	Chinese
Child's name	Varies by child
Mom	媽媽
Dog	狗
Baby	寶貝
Dad kicks the ball.	爸爸踢球.

Tardibouno, 2004), each clinical interview session was analyzed on a trial-by-trial basis and performance on each task was given a conceptual categorization score (i.e., 1–5, see Table 4.1). To do this, children's interpretations of their own writing were analyzed into ICE, which became the basic unit of analysis. An ICE was defined as evidence of a conceptual understanding of the writing system (Chinese or English) through the child's interpretation of his/her own writing with a further manipulation of the child's text by the interviewer.

For example, when a child wrote and read his/her own name in English conventionally, the researcher then covered half of his/her name and asked the child to interpret it again. If the child read that *part* of the name as his/her full name, this subsequent interpretation would be termed a Level 1 ICE. In other words, the child most likely, at that moment, understood the English writing system as "global" representation system – that part of the name can still represent the whole spoken name. Although the children produced a variety of responses that could be considered *conceptual evidence* as defined in this study, only children's interpretations of their own writing are included in the results. In the present study, a total of 3,418 ICEs were categorized, 1,689 in English (average per child = 154); 1,729 in Chinese (average per child = 157). A portion of judgments of ICE level was also verified through consultation with others familiar with the methodology.

Conceptual Development Concerning Written English, Levels 1–3

English Level 1

Generally, children at this first level interpreted English words as wholes – as pictures rather than linguistic representations. An example of a child demonstrating Level 1 was seen in an interview session with Frank (pseudonym) who was asked to write the word "Mom" (Figure 4.1).

When asked to interpret what he wrote, he promptly replied, "Mom." When part of the word was covered and only "Mo" of "Mom" was visible, he indicated "Mom" for the two letters showing. In other words, part of the word was enough to represent the rest of the word – a key characteristic of Level 1 conceptualization.

English Level 2

For Level 2, the central hypothesis that children have about writing is that it must have some objective differences in order to "mean" or not mean different things. For example, Andrea gave very clear evidence of the *minimum quantity principle* (cf. Ferreiro & Teberosky, 1982) in the following illustration. First, the child wrote the word "Love" with conventional letters and spelling (Figure 4.2).

FIGURE 4.1 Frank writes "Mom" during session conducted in English.

RESEARCHER: What does that say? [indicating written text "Love"]
ANDREA: Love?
RESEARCHER: Okay, good, and what … can you read with your finger? Show where it says "love" with your finger.
ANDREA: Love. [child points to conventionally written "Love"]
RESEARCHER: Can you read that now? [researcher shows "Lov" text of "Love"]
ANDREA: No.
RESEARCHER: No? Why can't you read it?
ANDREA: That's because it's very short.

FIGURE 4.2 Andrea writes "Love" during session conducted in English.

English Level 3

A Level 3 conceptualization means that the child understands that each letter, written character/grapheme, or other part represents a single syllable. This is known as the syllabic hypothesis, and it is one of the key findings of Ferreiro and Teberosky's (1982) research that supports the idea that children actively construct their understandings of written language.

Use of the syllabic hypothesis to interpret English writing was demonstrated by Bill in his final interview. He requested the word "Ultraman" to be written by the researcher. He then wrote "Ultraman" as well with conventional script (see Figure 4.3). When asked to read it, he interpreted his writing as "Ul-tra-boy" and pointed syllabically, once for each syllable. When asked to read the part "Ult" of "Ultraman," he interpreted his writing as "Ni-tro," also with syllabic pointing.

Conceptual Development Concerning Written Chinese, Levels 1–3

Chinese Level 1

These children's concepts about written Chinese were similar to their concepts about written English discussed earlier, at least as applicable to levels 1–3. For example, Katrina provided an example of a Level 1 understanding for Chinese writing when she wrote the Chinese word 爸爸 (bà bà, father) which consists of the characters shown in Figure 4.4. When asked to interpret only the first character 爸 of the two identical characters that make up the Chinese word for father, she tapped twice in the same place with her finger and said the whole word "bàbà," assigning the entire utterance to just one of the characters.

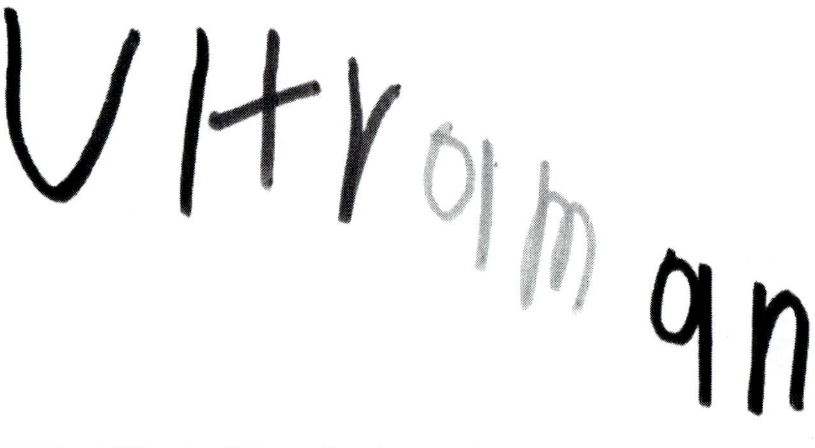

FIGURE 4.3 Bill writes "Ultraman" on his own after asking the researcher to write it first.

FIGURE 4.4 Katrina writes 爸爸 (bàba, father) during session conducted in Chinese.

Chinese Level 2

Five-year-old Eric provided an example of the conceptual understanding that the part is not enough to represent the whole, that an objective difference necessitates a different interpretation. In this example Eric declined to write the standard clinical interview task, 爸爸踢球 (Bàbà tī qiú, Dad kicks the ball). Instead, he requested the Chinese word 機器人 (Jī Qì Rén, robot). Figure 4.5 shows the child's tracing of the researcher's writing. After he had traced the researcher's writing of the three-character Chinese word, he interpreted it as

FIGURE 4.5 Eric's tracing over the researcher's writing of "robot" 機 器 人 (Jī Qì Rén) after declining to write the sentence "Dad kicks the ball" in Chinese.

"robot" in English. However, when asked to interpret just the first character of the three, 機 (Jī), Eric promptly said that he did not know what it said. Although he gave unconventional English interpretations of the characters, reading 機器人 as "robot" in English, his response of "I don't know" when asked to interpret just the first character suggests an understanding that the part cannot represent the whole, that the objective difference (one character versus three) cannot have the same meaning interpretation.

Chinese Level 3

With each Chinese character representing exactly one syllable, the strongly established presence of the syllabic hypothesis in these data is a direct result of this conventionality. As an example, Alice demonstrated a conventional, syllabic reading of a two-character Chinese word, 寶貝 (baǒbei) or "baby" (see Figure 4.6).

RESEARCHER: [Researcher writes "寶貝]
ALICE: [pronounces "Baǒbei" and engages in drawing for awhile]
ALICE: [Child writes 寶貝]
RESEARCHER: Can you read what you wrote?
ALICE: "Baǒbei" [child points syllabically/conventionally to each character as she interprets it]

Summary of Findings for Conceptualization Levels 1–3 for Chinese and English

In this study, we were able to support the first three levels of conceptual development (see Table 4.1) as defined by Ferreiro and Teberosky (1982) as

FIGURE 4.6 Alice writes 寶貝 (Baǒbei, baby) at the researcher's request during session conducted in Chinese.

being demonstrated in our sample by young Chinese/English bilingual and emerging biliterate children. Some children as of yet had not linked any linguistic unit (syllable or word) with the script they were writing (Level 1), although some had begun to realize that objective differences in the scripts indicated that the meaning of the writing had changed (Level 2). Finally, several children in the study indicated awareness of the syllabic hypothesis (Level 3) in that letters or clusters of letters (although unconventional in the sound/letter association) in English represented syllables in words just as single /zì/ or characters in Chinese represented syllables (or words in many cases) in Chinese.

It is, however, at levels 4 and 5 of Ferreiro and Teberosky's conceptual scheme that the divergence in knowledge about the respective scripts begins to emerge. These differences are taken up in the following section.

Findings Regarding Phonetic Representations in English Words and Chinese Characters

English Level 4
At Level 4 children try to analyze writing and speech beyond the syllable and assign one phoneme to each grapheme, although the correspondence will not be complete or conventional, and some phonemes and/or graphemes will be unaccounted for in the interpretation. Clarice provided evidence of this level in her interpretation of her own writing of "Mommy" as shown in Figure 4.7. Although initially interpreting "MoMMy" as "Mom," when only part of the text was showing, she produced a phonemic sounding of the first two letters.

RESEARCHER: Can you write "mom?"
CLARICE: [child writes "MoMMy"]
RESEARCHER: What does that say? [researcher shows the entire word "MoMMy"]
CLARICE: Mom.
RESEARCHER: Mom. Can you read with your finger?

FIGURE 4.7 In response to researcher's request to write "mom," Clarice writes "Mommy" during a session conducted in English.

CLARICE: Mom. [child points at the text once]
RESEARCHER: What does that say? [researcher shows "MoM" of "MoMMy"]
CLARICE: /Moh/. [short o sound]

Although this is not a totally alphabetic or conventional interpretation, it is definitely a step away from the syllabic hypothesis and toward the alphabetic principle.

English Level 5

Although the conceptualization is not completely conventional just yet, children at this level begin to assign sounds to individual letters and are reasonably accurate in interpreting the texts that they have written. Alex, who consistently performed a stable concept of the alphabetic principle for the English language throughout all of the interview sessions, provided many examples of Level 5 concepts. One example is illustrated in Figure 4.8.

ALEX: [child writes "yum"]
RESEARCHER: Yum. What about this? [researcher shows "um" of "Yum"]
ALEX: Um.
RESEARCHER: Can you show me with your finger?
ALEX: [child points once to text that is showing, "um" of "Yum"]

Reasoning about Phonetic Principles in Chinese, Levels 4 and 5

In our study, we found a few children who undertook a more careful analysis of the internal construction of the character itself and recognized other characters embedded within the character they wrote. The phonetic principle in Chinese involves determining the syllabic pronunciation of another smaller, stylized

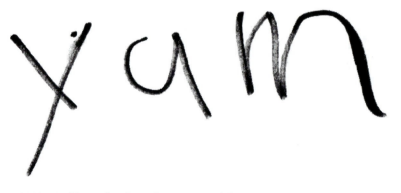

FIGURE 4.8 Alex writes "yum" unprompted during a session conducted in English.

character which gives a clue (regular only in about 25% of the instances) to the pronunciation of the overall character (see Chen et al., 2003; DeFrancis, 1989, for specific discussions of this principle).

While some children were able to detect other characters within the semantic–phonetic compounds they were writing, they usually could not make a connection between the name/sound that they assigned to the part and the pronunciation of the whole character's total conventional sound value.

Chinese Level 4

An example of what has just been described was demonstrated by David in his writing and interpretation of the Chinese word 媽媽 (/Mā/ /mā/) or "Mom." He traced over the researcher's writing (Figure 4.9) and then conventionally interpreted each embedded character. When he was asked to interpret the left half only of the character 媽 (/Mā/), he assigned it the character name /Nú/ (female), a conventional interpretation of 女. For the right half of the second 媽 (Mā), he assigned the character name /Mǎ/ (horse), a conventional interpretation of 馬 which shares a similar syllable structure, but with a different tone.

Both of these interpretations of the parts of the character are conventional for each of the embedded characters. However, the right half of this character, 馬 /Mǎ/, serves as a fairly regular phonetic clue to the entire character's sound value, 馬 (Mǎ), despite the tonal difference. Thus, although the child recognized that the parts can be interpreted, he did not make a connection between these pronunciations and the interpretation of the entire character.

FIGURE 4.9 David traces the characters which comprise the kanji for "mom" in Chinese 媽媽 (Mā mā).

Chinese Level 5

It is possible that the few examples of the interpretation of Chinese *zì* at this level are actually interferences from English reading instruction since they involve assigning a character onset and rime features which cannot be associated with the stroke patterns of Chinese characters. Gerard provided a clear example of this level of conceptualization (Figure 4.10).

RESEARCHER: Can you write the word goǔ?
GERARD: [child writes a mostly conventional 狗 (Dog)] Like this? Show me.
RESEARCHER: Do you want me to write it bigger? [researcher writes 狗]
GERARD: [child writes mostly conventional 狗 again]
RESEARCHER: Can you read that please? What does it say?
GERARD: /Goǔ/.
RESEARCHER: What does that say? [researcher covers the right half of 狗]
GERARD: /guh/
RESEARCHER: What does that say? [researcher covers the left half of 狗]
GERARD: /Où/.

While these are not conventional interpretations of the left and right halves of the character 狗 (Goǔ) for the Chinese word for dog, this interpretation shows a more advanced understanding of the Chinese writing system in that the child was searching for cues within the character which would result in its overall pronunciation. Thus, by assigning the onset to one half of the character and the rime to the other, Gerard demonstrated that he was also linking them to the possible interpretation of the whole even though such subsyllabic units cannot be derived from the internal structure of the semantic-compound character.

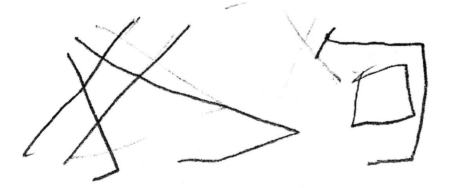

FIGURE 4.10 Gerard writes 狗 (Goǔ, dog) at researcher's request during session in Chinese.

Patterns of Biliterate Understanding Across Languages

One of the benefits of employing a microgenetic design (see Siegler, 1996; Granott & Parziale, 2002) is the possibility of capturing patterns of growth across brief periods of time where change is happening. One major view of development shared by Piaget (1977a,b), Vygotsky (1987, 1997) and other developmentalists (e.g., Thelen & Smith, 1994; van Geert, 1994; Siegler, 1996; Bronfenbrenner, 1979, 2005) is that development is not a lock-step, linear process, but is in fact dynamic and nonlinear.

Subsequently, in this study, we were particularly interested in how the knowledge gained about one language related to the conceptualizations of the written system in the other. To this end, we graphed the ICEs task-by-task for each session held with the child over the three-month period, so we could compare their understandings of both English and Chinese. In doing so, we discovered that there were at least four major patterns (cf. Granott & Parziale, 2002) across the two languages. The depicted graphs are exemplars of the performances of other children not illustrated.

Pattern 1: Backward Transitions (Chinese) and Punctuations After Stability (English)

In Figures 4.11 and 4.12, Frank shows a "backward transition" (Granott, 2002) in Chinese after the first two sessions from level 3 and 4 judgments (syllabic or word interpretation of whole composite characters or their embedded

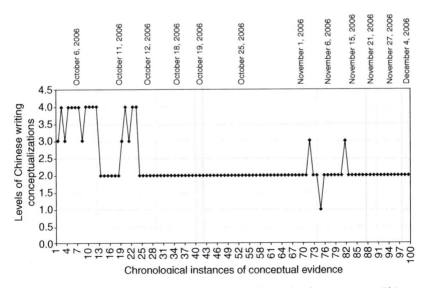

FIGURE 4.11 "Backward transitions" from higher to lower level reasonings in Chinese.

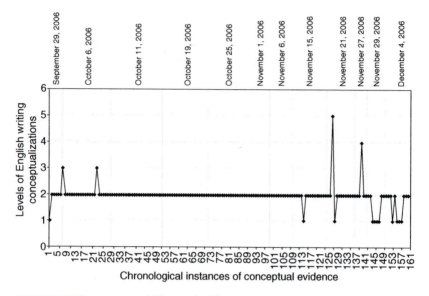

FIGURE 4.12 Long-term stability marked by ending punctuations or variance in reasoning levels in English.

semantic and phonetic components) to a less sophisticated level 2 interpretation of objective differences such as the number of strokes or characters used to represent a word. This pattern of responding remained stable through the end of the study with only a few instances of higher level reasoning in analyzing characters.

Pattern 2: Stability in One Language, Variation in the Other

For Bill, his knowledge of Chinese (Figure 4.13) has stabilized solidly at a level 3 where all characters and their parts were assigned a conventional interpretation, regardless of the overall pronunciation of the character. In English (Figure 4.14), however, his conceptualization varies widely back and forth between interpreting English written strings as visual logos (level 1) and as symbols which have some syllabic or phonemic components (levels 3 and 4).

Pattern 3: Ordered Fluctuations

Alice's graphs (Figures 4.15 and 4.16) show what Granott (2002) has termed "ordered fluctuations" in the sense that the variations are regularly constrained – in this case, between two levels in Chinese and three levels in English. Thus, the child's reasoning varies regularly between poles, and not irregularly (cf. Figure 4.14).

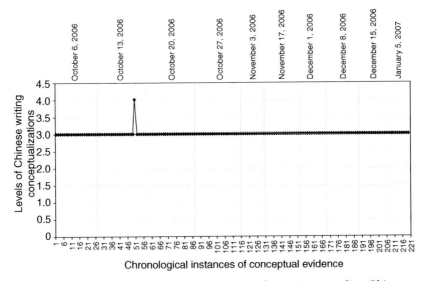

FIGURE 4.13 Long-term stability with no change of reasoning regarding Chinese.

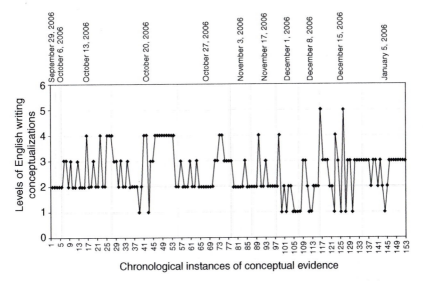

FIGURE 4.14 Regular and substantial variation in reasoning levels in English.

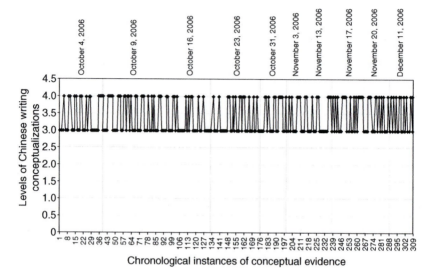

FIGURE 4.15 Tightly ordered fluctuations between two levels of reasoning in Chinese.

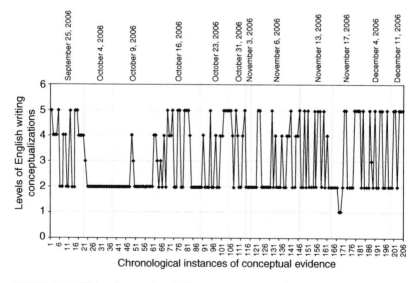

FIGURE 4.16 Wide, but ordered fluctuations across four levels of reasoning in English.

Pattern 4: Substantial Variation in Both Languages

Finally, to complicate matters, Harry's patterns (Figures 4.17 and 4.18) indicate maximum variation across all levels of conceptualization. According to developmental theory (Bronfenbrenner, 2005), one could reasonably predict that there

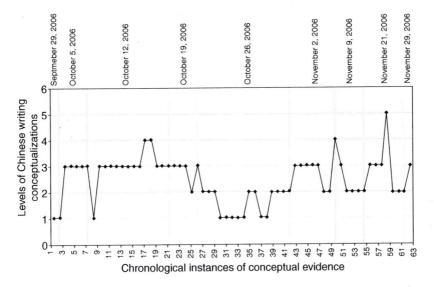

FIGURE 4.17 Wide, but spaced and periodic variation in reasoning levels over three months concerning Chinese.

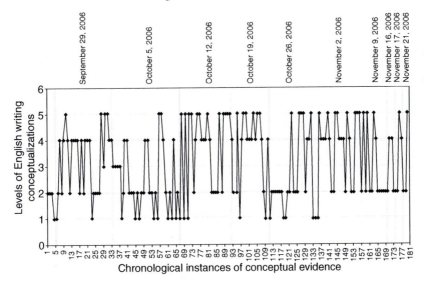

FIGURE 4.18 Wide, irregular, and densely clustered variation in reasoning about English.

should occur some plateaus, stabilizing around certain conceptualisations – but our research design fell short of following him to see these features emerge.

Discussion

The best way we know to begin a discussion of how to interpret our findings and of what import they may have for the field is to begin with an extended statement by Vygotsky (1997, p. 99) on the complexity of literacy growth among young children from his essay "On the Prehistory of Written Language" written in approximately 1929.

> But a positive picture of [child development] is possible only if we radically change our representation of child development and take into account that it is a complex dialectical process that is characterized by complex periodicity, disproportion in the development of separate functions, metamorphoses or qualitative transformation of certain forms into others, a complex merging of the process of evolution and involution, a complex crossing of external and internal factors, a complex process of overcoming difficulties and adapting.

For us, the graphs in the preceding section show the complexity of which Vygotsky speaks, and suggest some initial interpretations. First of all, while children's biliteracy knowledge about diverse scripts such as Chinese and English does not necessarily mirror each other, there seems to be a general tendency for the variation appearing in the home language to also appear in the second language (see Figures 4.13 and 4.14, for an exception) slightly magnified (see Figures 4.11 and 4.12; 4.15–4.18).

Second, young children, for the most part, operate with several, seemingly conflicting knowledge levels about the nature of scripts and what they represent all at once for long periods of time similar to what Siegler (1996) found in investigating children's math knowledge. Particularly, in the cases of Alice (Figures 4.15 and 4.16) and Harry (Figures 4.17 and 4.18), both children demonstrate wide variations in knowledge of both Chinese and English consistently over the three-month period even though the tasks were the same each session. This phenomenon of consistent variation in knowledge, learning strategies, or other aspects of human functioning has been a finding in the microgenetic literature which challenges the conventional wisdom that humans use only those strategies with the highest possible success rates (cf. Granott & Parziale, 2002, for several examples across fields). Thus, in truth, it is the *variation* in human behavior which is adaptive and normal, not necessarily the stability (see also Thelen & Smith, 1994).

A third interpretation of our findings we believe results in a methodological correction of the procedures of prior socio-psychogenetic research (cf. Katoet et al., 1998; Manning et al., 1995; Pontecorvo & Zucchermaglio, 1988; Tolchinsky

& Teberosky, 1998), procedures which collect data usually at one time only and average the conceptual ratings across several tasks and sessions. We will elaborate further on this procedural issue in the upcoming and final section.

Implications

For Educators

Often the fear of parents and educators is that learning two or more languages and writing systems leads to confusion for a learner, especially if that learner is a young child. In our study, however, we did not find such confusions (cf. also Buckwalter and Lo, 2002). In fact, our evidence indicates that application of concepts from one language to another was appropriate for where Chinese and English were similar (levels 1–3) and differed when the scripts demanded a different approach (levels 4–5).

Thus, first of all, educators of young bilingual and emerging biliterate children need to be aware, at least, of some of the differences and similarities of the languages and scripts children bring to the classroom. Whether this professional development is accomplished by personal study or formal education, it must be acquired; otherwise children's frequent unconventional writing performances will only be judged by the dominant language of the teacher – only half of the story. Without such professional knowledge at hand, children's emerging metalinguistic awareness about language will be mistaken only for error rather than for the creative, discovery process it is.

Second, educators should know that young children's application of their knowledge of both first- and second-language scripts will *vary normally* and *situationally* with the task at hand (cf. Sulzby 1985). As the more experienced literacy user, the teacher must strive to understand children's understandings of the writing systems they are mastering in order to provide the best adaptive pedagogical support for conceptual development.

Third, in this study, we did not find that providing a model first of adult conventional writing initially changed the children's reasonings about their own writing. In a general sense, this procedure is meant to highlight the differences between *development* and *learning* (cf. Thelen & Smith, 1994; van Geert, 1994), the former construct envisioned as changing more slowly and being related to a broad network of macro and micro influences needed for change (cf. Bronfenbrenner, 1979, 2005) while the latter, complex in its own right, is more situational. Therefore, teachers should not be surprised if yesterday's instruction does not appear in today's performance. Conceptual change takes time and is interwoven with frequent practice with the language.

Finally, and related to the prior point, Siegler (1996) found that children do not so much drop old strategies of learning for new ones as much as they only slowly abandon strategies which work less frequently – thus keeping at hand at all times a wide portfolio, as it were, of understandings about written language which can be applied selectively. Thus, teachers should not be surprised when children apply earlier strategies as oftentimes these earlier, first established strategies are called upon when tasks get more difficult.

For Researchers

It was clear from this study that children exhibited a range of understandings even in a single session when asked to interpret various names or words that they wrote (cf. Yaden, 2009). Therefore, averaging responses across tasks as is normally done in psychogenetically oriented studies (e.g., Kato et al., 1998; Kwak, 2006; Manning et al., 1993) on early literacy results in three related problems: (a) information is lost about the child's range of knowledge in different writing tasks; (b) the resulting categorization of level of conceptual knowledge is only partially representative; and (c) averaged concept scores obscure the fact that young children's knowledge about written language is highly situational, depending upon the production task required, or the actual written array to be interpreted and the child's prior experience with it and similar texts. Thus, we found that incorporating microgenetic design principles (Granott & Parziale, 2002) along with those of the clinical/inquiry method allowed much more specificity and accuracy, we believe, in interpreting children's writing performances both within and across languages.

Last, one principle of microgenetic change is that wide variation in response often presages a more dramatic phase shift to more sophisticated levels of understanding of the task at hand (Siegler, 1996). While we closely studied these children for three months as they were involved in both intensive Chinese and English literacy instruction, this period of time was not long enough to capture any dramatic changes in the nature of their reasonings, although trends were definitely noted. It is possible, then, that we studied them in the period just before these substantial increases in knowledge became a regular part of their response patterns.

Thus, studying young children provides an interesting dilemma for researchers since change may happen very quickly over a few hours even, or not be evident over several weeks or months. Capturing the actual time of developmental change in literacy growth, then, is a complex design issue involving both knowledge of the domain to be studied as well as knowledge of appropriate design principles to be employed so that the targeted changes are revealed.

While all research designs and methods have flaws, given that early literacy and biliteracy growth is a developmental phenomenon, it is our view that it is best studied by developmental methods (cf. Bronfenbrenner, 2005) be they experimental or interpretive. Thus, longitudinal research is potentially more revealing than cross-sectional, and multiple measurements over time, at shorter time intervals, are more informative than infrequent ones with longer periods in between. That children continually are learning, developing, and exploring their world is beyond dispute. It is our theory and research methodology which needs to rise in complexity to investigate that learning.

References

Adi-Japha, E., Levin, I., & Solomon, S. (1998). Emergence of representation in drawing: The relation between kinematic and referential aspects. *Cognitive Development, 13*, 25–51.

Bialystok, E. (1997). Effects of bilingualism and biliteracy on children's emerging concepts of print. *Developmental Psychology, 33*, 429–440.

Bloodgood, J. W. (1999). What's in a name? Children's name writing and literacy acquisition. *Reading Research Quarterly, 34*, 342–367.

Bowman, B. T., Donovan, S., & Burns, M. S. (2001). *Eager to learn: Educating our preschoolers.* Washington, DC: National Academy Press.

Brenneman, K., Massey, C., Machado, S. F., & Gelman, R. (1996). Young children's plans differ for writing and drawing. *Cognitive Development, 11*, 397–419.

Bronfenbrenner, U. (1979). *The ecology of human development.* Cambridge, MA: Harvard University Press.

Bronfenbrenner, U. (2005). *Making human beings human.* Thousand Oaks, CA: Sage.

Buckwalter, J. K., & Lo, Y. G. (2002). Emergent biliteracy in Chinese and English. *Journal of Second Language Writing, 11*, 269–293.

Burns, S. M., & Casbergue, R. (1992). Parent–child interaction in a letter-writing context. *Journal of Reading Behavior, 24*, 289–312.

Chan, L., & Louie, L. (1992). Developmental trend of Chinese preschool children in drawing and writing. *Journal of Research in Childhood Education, 6*, 93–99.

Chan, L., & Nunes, T. (1998). Children's understanding of the formal and functional characteristics of written Chinese. *Applied Psycholinguistics, 19*, 115–131.

Chan, L., & Nunes, T. (2001). Explicit teaching and implicit learning of Chinese characters. In L. Tolchinsky (Ed.) *Developmental aspects in learning to write* (pp. 33–53). Dordrecht, The Netherlands: Kluwer.

Chen, X., Shu, H., Wu, N., & Anderson, R. C. (2003). Stages in learning to pronounce Chinese characters. *Psychology in the Schools, 40*, 115–124.

Chen, X., Anderson, R. C., Li, W., Hao, M., Wu, X., & Shu, H. (2004). Phonological awareness of bilingual and monolingual Chinese children. *Journal of Educational Psychology, 96*, 142–151.

Das, T., Kumar, U., Bapi, R. S., Padakannaya, P., & Singh, N. C. (2009). Distinct reading routes for deep and shallow orthographies in simultaneous biliterates: A functional imaging study. *NeuroImage, 47*, S39–S41.

Defior, S., & Serrano, F. (2005). The initial development of spelling in Spanish: From global to analytical. *Reading and Writing, 18*, 81–98.

DeFrancis, J. (1989). *Visible speech: The diverse oneness of writing systems.* Honolulu: University of Hawaii Press.

Ferreiro, E., & Teberosky, A. (1982). *Literacy before schooling* (K. Goodman, Trans.). Exeter, NH: Heinemann Educational Books. (Originally published 1979.)

Garcia, G. E. (2002). Bilingual children's reading. In D. Pearson & R. Barr (Eds.), *Handbook of reading research* (pp. 813–834). Mahwah, NJ: Erlbaum.

Granott, N. (2002). How microdevelopment creates macrodevelopment: Reiterated sequences, backwards transitions, and the Zone of Current Development. In N. Granott & J. Parziale (Eds.), *Microdevelopment: Transition processes in development and learning* (pp. 213–242). New York: Cambridge University Press.

Hildreth, G. (1936). Developmental sequences in name writing. *Child Development, 7*, 291–303.

Hornberger, N. H. (2003). Continua of biliteracy. In N. H. Hornberger (Ed.), *Continua of biliteracy: An ecological framework for educational policy, research, and practice in multilingual settings* (pp. 3–34). Tonawanda, NY: Multilingual Matters Limited.

Hornberger, N. H., & Skilton-Sylvester, E. (2003). Revisiting the continua of biliteracy: International and critical perspectives. In N. H. Hornberger (Ed.) *Continua of biliteracy: An ecological framework for educational policy, research, and practice in multilingual settings* (pp. 35–67). Tonawanda, NY: Multilingual Matters Limited.

Kato, Y., Ueda, A., Ozaki, K., & Mukaigawa, Y. (1998). Japanese preschoolers' theories about the "Hiragana" system of writing. *Linguistics and Education, 10*, 219–232.

Kwak, J. (2006). The writing development of Korean heritage children. Unpublished doctoral dissertation. University of Southern California, Los Angeles.

Levin, I., & Bus, A. G. (2003). How is emergent writing based on drawing? Analyses of children's products and their sorting by children and mothers. *Developmental Psychology, 39*, 891–905.

Levin, I., Both-DeVries, A., Aram, D., & Bus, A. (2005). Writing starts with own name writing: From scribbling to conventional spelling in Israeli and Dutch children. *Applied Psycholinguistics, 26*, 463–477.

Luria, A. R. (1998). The development of writing in the child. In M. K. de Oliveira & J. Valsiner (Eds.), *Literacy in human development* (pp. 1–56). Stamford, CT: Ablex.

Manning, M., Manning, G., Long, R., & Kamii, C. (1993). Preschoolers' conjectures about segments of a written sentence. *Journal of Research in Childhood Education, 8*, 5–11.

Manning, M., Manning, G., Long, R., & Kamii, C. (1995). Development of kindergarteners' ideas about what is written in a written sentence. *Journal of Research in Childhood Education, 10*, 29–36.

Piaget, J. (1977a). *The development of thought: Equilibration of cognitive structures* (A. Rosin, Trans.). New York: Viking. (Original work published 1975.)

Piaget, J. (1977b). Formal thought from the equilibrium standpoint. In H. E. Gruber & J. J. Voneche (Eds.), *The essential Piaget* (pp. 820–831). New York: Basic Books. (Original work published 1955.)

Pontecorvo, C., & Zucchermaglio, C. (1988). Modes of differentiation in children's writing construction. *European Journal of Psychology of Education, 3*, 371–384.

Shu, H., & Anderson, R. C. (2003). Role of radical awareness in the character and word acquisition of Chinese children. *Reading Research Quarterly, 32*, 78–89.

Shu, H., Anderson, R. C., & Wu, N. (2000). Phonetic awareness: Knowledge of orthography–phonology relationships in the character acquisition of Chinese children. *Journal of Educational Psychology, 92*, 56–62.

Siegler, R. S. (1996). *Emerging minds: The process of change in children's thinking.* New York: Oxford University Press.

Siegler, R. S., & Crowley, K. (1991). The microgenetic method. *American Psychologist, 46*, 606–620.

Sulzby, E. (1985). Kindergarteners as writers and readers. In M. Farr (Ed.), *Advances in writing research. Vol. 1: Children's early writing development* (pp. 127–199). Norwood, NJ: Ablex.

Temple, C., Nathan, R., & Burris, N. (1982). *The beginnings of writing*. Boston, MA: Allyn and Bacon.

Thelen, E., & Smith, L. (1994). *A dynamic systems approach to the development of cognition and action*. Cambridge, MA: MIT Press.

Tolchinsky, L., & Teberosky, A. (1998). The development of word segmentation and writing in two scripts. *Cognitive Development, 13*, 1–24.

Tolchinsky Landsmann, L., & Levin, I. (1985). Writing in preschoolers: An age-related analysis. *Applied Psycholinguistics, 6*, 319–339.

Tolchinsky Landsmann, L., & Levin, I. (1987). Writing in four- to six-year-olds: Representation of semantic and phonetic similarities and differences. *Journal of Child Language, 14*, 127–144.

Tsai, T. (2007). A microgenetic analysis of English/Chinese early writing development. Unpublished doctoral dissertation. University of Southern California, Los Angeles.

U.S. Census Bureau. (2003a). *Census 2000 summary file 1 (SF 1) 100-Percent Data*. Washington, DC: U.S. Department of Commerce.

U.S. Census Bureau. (2003b). *Language use and English-speaking ability: 2000*. Washington, DC: U.S. Department of Commerce.

Vygotsky, L. S. (1987). *The collected works of L. S. Vygotsky. Vol. 1. Problems of general psychology* (R. W. Rieber & A. S. Carton, Eds.; N. Minick, Trans.). New York: Plenum Press.

Vygotsky, L. S. (1997). *The collected works of L. S. Vygotsky. Vol. 4. The history of the development of higher mental functions* (R. W. Rieber, Ed.; M. J. Hall, Trans.). New York: Plenum Press.

Yaden, D. B., Jr. (2009, December). Reintroducing development into theories of the acquisition and growth of early literacy: Developmental science approaches and the cultural-historical perspective of L.S. Vygotsky. Paper presented at the annual meeting of the National Reading Conference, Albuquerque, NM.

Yaden, D. B., Jr., & Tardibuono, J. M. (2004). The emergent writing development of urban Latino preschoolers: Developmental perspectives and instructional environments for second-language learners. *Reading and Writing Quarterly, 20*, 29–61.

PART II

Biliteracy Development in Early Elementary School

SCHOOL AGE VIGNETTE

Thoughts of a first grade teacher:

Mrs. Cervantas is a bilingual/biliterate Spanish and English woman who has taught in a mainstream English classroom for 7 years at Hope Elementary. She is a dedicated, hard-working teacher committed to creating learning conditions that validate students' cultural and linguistic resources. Through the utilization of a variety of ESL techniques, such as allowing code-switching, Mrs. Cervantes creates a classroom environment where students' bilingual status is nurtured and they grow academically. Despite her success, Mrs. Cervantes believes she can do more. Being an avid reader of professional literature on literacy and bilingual instruction and avid "kidwatcher," she wants to explore further ways to help her students. Let's listen in to the conversation between Mrs. Cervantes and her principal to gain insights into her thinking.

MRS. CERVANTES: Mr. Proto, I am concerned that in the process of my students becoming successful English readers and writers my bilingual students are losing their opportunity to become fully bilingual and biliterate. In my classroom I only assess their English reading and writing knowledge, disregarding their native language as a possible resource that will help them acquire literacy in English. Further, when they are reading aloud or producing a written product, I use a monolingual perspective to assess their work. What I mean is that I only look to see if their work is correct according to the grammar, syntax, and lexicon of English. In an article I recently read it reported that children may utilize knowledge of their first language to help them process information in their second language. If this is true then what I consider an error in writing may be a child's attempt to approximate skills based in their first language understanding. This would not be an error, rather a sign that they are transferring knowledge from their first language to English. If they are transferring information from their first language to English then I wonder in what ways my English instruction is impacting their literacy development in their first language? I am not sure about any of this. Maybe when they use their first language it actually interferes with learning in English. Maybe they need to have paired instruction in English and Spanish to help facilitate biliteracy. I don't know anymore. I have so many questions and I want all of my students to excel and become beautiful bilingual/biliterate citizens. I have been thinking in enrolling in the bilingual certification program at the local university. Mr. Proto what should I do?

MR. PROTO: Mrs. Cervantes, thank you for sharing your thoughts with me. I highly respect what you do for our students. You raise some really important questions that we need to be asking ourselves as a school. If you are willing to enter the bilingual certification program I will continue to talk with you about what you are learning and use this information to have whole staff discussions about what type of instructional programming should be in place. You can use this experience as your professional learning goal for the year.

MRS. CERVANTES: Thank you, Mr. Proto. I really think we can tailor our instruction to help all students become bilingual and biliterate.

Societal attitudes towards bilingualism vary. Being bilingual or multilingual is the expected norm in many countries throughout the world; however, in the United States monolingualism predominates. In a country of individuals who speak myriad languages with similar and different typographical structures to English, researchers have tried to document the most effective programming models and the types of literacy instruction that will facilitate students' academic growth. Students enter school at different stages of bilingual development. Some students are simultaneous bilinguals (learning two languages at the same time) and others are sequential bilinguals (learning one language, than a second). Given students' varied processes for acquiring bilingualism, school personnel like Mrs. Cervantes and Mr. Proto, along with researchers, have questions about how to facilitate biliteracy in reading and writing. Some of these questions include: Do bilinguals keep their languages separate or do they strategically utilize both languages? If strategic, what do students do? Does a student's literacy knowledge in their first language help or interfere with learning to read and write in a second language? What is the role of code-switching, code-mixing, and linguistic borrowing in students' writing development? What role does second-language oral language development have on students' reading in their second language? Are students able to transfer knowledge bidirectionally from their L1 to L2 and L2 to L1? What role do individual student experiences and instructional context have on a student's biliteracy development? What processes do bilinguals use when revising their writing? What is the impact of utilizing culturally compatible texts on students' biliteracy development?

Answering the questions above will help educators and researchers determine the most effective and efficient literacy practices for students learning English as an additional language. If students are able to transfer knowledge from their first language to the second then teachers will not have to replicate the teaching of certain literacy processes such as phonological awareness. This will allow more time for helping a student make meaning from written text and write text focused on meaning. Before reading the chapters that follow, stop and think about the bilingual students you know in grades kindergarten through grade 3. Based on these students, how would you answer the questions posed above? Now enter the pages that follow and learn what Mrs. Cervantes and Mr. Proto need to know to make informed decisions about the programming at Hope Elementary. Given what you learn, what would you recommend they do?

5

EVALUATION AND REVISION PROCESSES OF YOUNG BILINGUALS IN A DUAL LANGUAGE PROGRAM

Mileidis Gort

Writing enables us to explore and articulate our thoughts, and, as such, is a complex, cognitive function. Writing is also a social act. Effective writing requires one to make frequent and appropriate assessments of the draft in process in order to evaluate the relative quality of the text. During revising, writers solve composing problems and take corrective action when their writing is not meeting expectations. Therefore, the ability to evaluate and act to modify writing is an important skill that influences the rest of the composing process.

Writing process research has provided considerable evidence of the occurrence and frequency of evaluation acts in the revision process of English speakers (e.g., Calkins, 1994; Graham & Harris, 1996; Graves, 1994, Murray, 2004) and English-language learners in English-as-a-Second-Language contexts (e.g., Raimes, 1985; Samway, 1993; Urzua, 1987; Zamel, 1982, 1983). In contrast, little is known about the processes that young bilingual children apply when evaluating and revising their writing in bilingual situations. An investigation of the composing and revising strategies of emergent bilinguals may provide insights into the relationship between bilingual development, biliteracy learning, and metalinguistic awareness. Such research can inform educators about ways to modify writing instruction to help bilingual learners engage in evaluation and revision more effectively.

This chapter presents selected examples from case studies of the writing and revising processes and strategies of six emergent bilingual/biliterate first graders from English and Spanish backgrounds as they composed stories in Spanish and English in a Writing Workshop (WW) context. The term *emergent bilingual* is used here to describe children who potentially could develop two languages and biliteracy if supported in their immediate environments, including home, school, and community. The chapter begins with a brief review of the literature that informed this work. Next, relevant aspects of the classroom setting, the teachers, and the students are described to provide an orientation to the research context. Findings related to strategies and behaviors that assist first grade emergent Spanish/English bilinguals to clarify, tune, reshape, expand, and recognize incongruence in their writing, as well as the role of students' bilingualism (including their language use) in the writing and revising process, follow. The chapter concludes with a discussion of implications of the findings for educators and researchers.

Research on Bilingual Children's Writing

Over the past several years, there has been growing interest in the phenomenon of biliteracy, that is, "literate competencies in two languages, developed to varying degrees, either simultaneously or successively" (Dworin, 2003, p. 29). This interest has been fueled by a number of factors, among them the growing recognition of the utility of literacy ability in more than one language by both native and non-native English speakers (Lindholm-Leary, 2001) and the understanding that biliteracy is associated with academic achievement and participation in society outside of school for the increasing numbers of bilingual students in the U.S. (Ovando et al., 2003).

What We Know About Young Bilinguals' Writing Process

A small but growing body of research on bilingual literacy development suggests that students' biliterate abilities represent a special form of literacy that must be understood as distinct from that of monolinguals (Bialystok, 2001; Dworin, 2003; Gort, 2006, 2008; Valdés, 1992). Biliteracy development is a dynamic, flexible process in which children's transactions with two written languages mediate their language and literacy learning for both languages (Dworin, 2003; Gort, 2006, 2008; Moll et al., 2001; Reyes & Costanzo, 2002). That is, bilinguals employ literacy behaviors and skills cross-linguistically and bi-directionally so that skills in one language bootstrap into the other language and vice versa. Successful bilingual writers employ a number of effective strategies (e.g., searching for cognates, translating and/or alternating between languages, using context and prior knowledge developed in one or the other language) to create text in either language, suggesting that bilinguals have a unique dual language reservoir of cross-language skills to draw on when engaged in literacy tasks (Genesee et al., 2005).

Bilinguals use two languages strategically in oral and written communication (Baker, 2001; Genesee, 2002; Kenner, 2004; Zentella, 1997). With respect to literacy learning, bilinguals frequently use both languages in flexible and innovative ways to accomplish literacy tasks (Gort, 2006, 2008; Gutiérrez et al., 1999b; Mor-Sommerfeld, 2002; Pérez, 2004). This practice of drawing upon multiple linguistic codes, semiotic modalities, or participation structures during literacy events is referred to as "hybridization." Research suggests that hybrid literacy practices "are not simply … the alternation between two language codes," but rather "a systematic, strategic, affiliative, and sense-making process" (Gutiérrez et al., 1999a, p. 88) and, as such, are typically principled, purposeful, and organized.

A qualitative study of the bilingual writing processes of first grade emergent bilinguals from Spanish and English backgrounds enrolled in a dual language program illuminates the connection between young bilinguals' languages (Gort, 2006). Young bilingual writers demonstrated evidence of cross-linguistic and language-specific literacy application; that is, participants drew upon skills/knowledge learned in either language when writing. Further, oral and written code-switching appeared to be an important composing strategy for both Spanish- and English-dominant writers, as children drew on their developing bilingual and biliteracy repertoires in the process of creating texts in two languages in order to capture and detail their lives in multiple worlds. Strategic code-switching facility depended on several factors, including language dominance, bilingual development, linguistic context, and language proficiency of interlocutors.

Relationship Between Metalinguistic Awareness and Writing

Metalinguistic awareness refers to the general ability to manipulate written and oral language as a formal system. This ability to attend to language patterns in a systematic and purposeful way is characteristic of bilingual children (Bauer, 2000; Francis, 1999; Gort, 2006, 2008; Kenner et al., 2004) as they tend to approach these tasks with higher initial levels of mastery of analysis and control of language processing than monolinguals (Bialystok, 1991; Bialystok & Hakuta, 1994). In bilingual situations, e.g., dual language classroom contexts where two languages are purposefully used for teaching and learning, access to two languages and the possibility of contrasting those languages are considered to be metalinguistic insights that can facilitate bi/literacy development.

Research has uncovered a particularly productive line of inquiry into the nature of and processes associated with metalinguistic reflections of bilingual children (e.g., Francis, 1999, 2002; Gort, 2008; Kenner, 2004; Kenner & Kress, 2003; Kenner et al., 2004). In a study of bilingual peer interactions in the context of parallel dual language Writing Workshops, Gort (2008) found that bilinguals demonstrated metalinguistic awareness in different ways, including using two languages strategically for explanation/clarification, discussing the language structures of English and Spanish, attending to written language patterns of each language in systematic and purposeful ways, and categorizing common Spanglish[1] colloquialisms as representing English or Spanish terms. In the process of translation, linguistic/literacy scaffolding, and negotiation, children became more aware of their own bilingualism.

Studies emerging from the "Signs of Difference" research project (e.g., Kenner, 2004; Kenner & Kress, 2003; Kenner et al., 2004) provide further insight into emergent bilingual children's ideas about the concepts involved in literacy learning, in general, and the act of writing two different scripts, in particular. For example, Kenner (2004) illustrates how six-year-old children who were learning to write in Chinese, Arabic, or Spanish while also learning to write in English demonstrated awareness of characteristics which differentiated their two writing systems (i.e., boundaries between writing in Chinese, Arabic, or Spanish and writing in English) as well as particular characters or written marks that appeared similar across writing systems but were in fact different (e.g., Arabic symbol that looks like the Roman letter "u"). These findings suggest that young children growing up in bilingual/biliterate environments develop an expanded range of semiotic resources from which they draw in order to represent and construct their identities as readers and writers.

What We Know About Bilinguals and Revising

Despite the importance of written communication in a global information economy (Brandt, 2005) and the critical role of evaluation and revision in the composing process, there is a scarcity of multilingual research on the revising practices of school-age bilingual writers.[2] Research on the relationship between languages in the context of the revising process of young bilinguals is especially limited. Of particular relevance to the study of young bilinguals' revising processes and language use are Francis' (2002, 2005) studies of the editing and correction strategies of 45 Spanish/Náhuatl[3] bilingual children across second, fourth, and sixth grades. Francis found that younger and older bilinguals demonstrated similar patterns of cross-linguistic correction and revision behaviors across languages despite minimal exposure to Náhuatl texts and the near absence of any literacy instruction in the language, as well as significant developmental differences in the effectiveness of their revising/correction attempts. That is, students who were more skillful in correcting and revising Spanish texts tended to carry these skills over to their Náhuatl texts, and older students appeared more likely to successfully attempt corrections or revisions at the higher levels of language processing. Based on these findings, Francis proposed a developmental sequence of editing/correction categories beginning with word level orthographic corrections and moving toward morphosyntactic/semantic revisions (i.e., corrections at the phrase or sentence level), discourse-level revisions (i.e., corrections beyond the sentence level), and punctuation/capitalization revisions and corrections. These studies lend support to the construct of "spontaneous biliteracy" (Reyes, 2001, p. 97), whereby bilinguals use both of their languages as tools for higher-order biliteracy development without formal instruction in both languages. However, with so few studies of young bilingual writers available, no composite picture of their revising processes can be claimed.

This chapter builds upon and extends the literature on early bilingual writing by analyzing the revising processes and strategies of six bilingual/biliterate first graders from English and Spanish backgrounds as they composed stories in Spanish and English in a WW context. In the sections that follow I describe the school and instructional context, including the teachers and the focal students, to provide an orientation to the research context.

Research Context

The School and TWBE Program

The larger study from which the current work emerged was situated in two parallel first grade classrooms in a Spanish/English Two-Way Bilingual Education (TWBE) program, in an urban, culturally and linguistically diverse, K-5 elementary school in the northeastern United States. The TWBE program is a controlled choice program that attracts English and Spanish speaking students throughout the district. While the main goals of the TWBE program reflect those documented in the literature,[4] the distribution of languages differs from commonly researched models. Initially, the language of instruction is approximately 75% native/dominant language (L1) to 25% second language (L2) for each group of students. This means that all students receive more instruction in their stronger language initially and increasing amounts of instruction in their L2 at each new grade level until reaching a 50/50 ratio by grade 4. There are two parallel classrooms per grade, a Spanish classroom and an English classroom. At times classes are scheduled to be composed of all L1 speakers, all L2 speakers, or integrated L1 and L2 language speakers.

The Teachers

The teachers in these two first grade classrooms were experienced elementary educators who held views about literacy learning reflective of emergent literacy and process writing perspectives. Both teachers had been implementing the WW approach for several years and attended numerous professional development workshops and seminars in the area of process writing each year. At the time of the study, the Spanish teacher had been teaching first grade within the TWBE program for a period of seven years. She held a Masters Degree in Bilingual Education, with teaching certification in the areas of elementary, bilingual, and English-as-a-Second-Language education. This teacher was a bilingual Spanish/English speaker from birth of Mexican and Anglo descent.

The English teacher was a native English speaker of European descent who had been teaching first grade for over ten years. Although she had worked with English-language learners in her previous classroom position, this was her first year in the TWBE program. She had a basic understanding and command of the Spanish language and was knowledgeable of second-language acquisition theory, processes, and teaching methodology. She held a Bachelor's degree and teaching certificate in the area of elementary education.

The Writing Workshop

Writing Workshop (WW) in each of the two classrooms was an integrated 45–60 minute period of the day in which students wrote in either L1 or L2. The process writing approach employed during WW promoted writing as a craft in which the writer engages in a number of individual and interactive stages as the child develops an idea and expresses it in writing (Graves, 1994; Calkins, 1994). The particular classroom in which the activity occurred (i.e., English or Spanish room), determined the language of instruction, and therefore the target language of children's texts. Bilingual writers participated in English and Spanish WW on alternate days, keeping separate writing folders in each of the classrooms. That meant, for example, that a story which originated in the English WW stayed in the child's English WW folder to be continued when the child returned to that class two days later.

The Children

Three English-dominant students and three Spanish-dominant students participated in the study. Participant selection was based on students' L1 literacy levels and L2 proficiency levels. Students' language dominance, or language of greater proficiency (Baker, 2000), and program placement were determined by performance on the Language Assessment Scales-Oral (Duncan & De Avila, 1990), a school-administered standardized language proficiency test. Native language literacy level (e.g., grade-level, above grade-level) was determined by classroom and school assessment measures and teachers' ratings of students' general literacy skills, and supported by student work to date. Participants' names, ages at beginning of data collection, and native and dominant languages are presented in Table 5.1.

Five of the six participants were born in the United States. Katherine was born in the Dominican Republic and came to the United States at the age of two. Lucy, Katherine, Brian, and Barbara are native Spanish speakers who speak Spanish at home. Steven and José are bilinguals from birth, who speak both Spanish and English at home. All participants are of Dominican descent.

Four of the six children had been enrolled in the TWBE program since kindergarten. Steven and Barbara attended kindergarten in an English-only program, subsequently enrolling in the TWBE program as English-dominant speakers at the beginning of the first grade. The dominant language and

TABLE 5.1 Participant information

Name	Age	Native language	Dominant language	L1 literacy skills
Lucy	6:03	Spanish	Spanish	Above grade-level
Katherine	6:08	Spanish	Spanish	Grade-level
Brian	7:00	Spanish	Spanish	Grade-level
Steven	7:01	Bilingual English/ Spanish	English	Grade-level
José	6:11	Bilingual English/ Spanish	English	Above grade-level
Barbara	6:05	Spanish	English	Grade-level

language of initial literacy instruction of five of the six participants was also their native language, with the exception of Barbara whose L1 is Spanish but who was English-dominant at the time of the study (as determined by TWBE program placement tests). José attended an English-only Head Start program prior to enrolling in the TWBE program in Kindergarten. Prior to the study, all children had been receiving literacy instruction and participating in the WW in their dominant language only.

Methodological Aspects of the Study

The study focused on children's revising behaviors and talk as they drafted personal narratives; that is, the study emphasized both students' revising processes as well as the products that resulted (including oral and written language) from their engagement with revision and evaluation. For six months, the Spanish–English bilingual researcher and two research assistants observed and interviewed the students and collected artifacts from all stages of the writing process. In any given week throughout the duration of the study, researchers collected data systematically on three occasions for each focal child: either twice in Spanish WW and once in English WW, or vice versa. As participant-observers, researchers watched and talked with the students as they went about their daily WW activities. At no time during this period, however, did the researchers engage in any direct instruction of the children. Researchers interviewed the focal children systematically once every two weeks at the end of a WW session in order to have the children further reflect on their writing and revision processes and behaviors. Interviews were conducted in the language of the corresponding WW session.

Data sources collected throughout the duration of the study included: student writing samples in Spanish and English from all stages of the writing process and accompanying illustrations; audio tapes of individual focal students in Spanish and English WWs; field notes of observations describing student writing and revising behaviors; audio tapes of formal and informal interviews with focal children; and field notes of observations during student interviews. This led to a corpus of data that included audiotapes and field notes from a total of 126 classroom observations (64 observations in the Spanish WW and 62 observations in the English WW), 327 student writing samples, and audiotapes and field notes from 73 student interviews. A subset of these data representing participants' writing products and processes across all stages of the writing process in both languages[5] was selected for in-depth analysis of bilingual learners' evaluation and revision practices.

A bilingual writing profile (Bear and Barone, 1998; Clay, 2001; Morris, 1993; Sulzby, 1985) was created for each child by teasing out from field notes, transcripts, interviews, and written artifacts any evidence of a child's cross-linguistic and language-specific revising processes, behaviors, and development. The profiles, as well as all transcripts and field notes, were shared with the classroom teachers for accuracy. The teachers often contributed additional information that supported the developing themes and helped to refine our collective understanding of the writing development of individual children.

I employed qualitative methods to analyze data for evidence of evaluative ability, revising strategies, and language use. I analyzed written products for amount and type of revision employed by each participant. Revisions and revising acts evident in WW and interview transcripts, accompanying field notes, and written pieces were coded using Sommers' (1980) revision operations: (1) additions, (2) deletions, (3) substitutions, and (4) reorderings. Further analysis of classroom observation and interview-related data sources was guided by Hilgers' (1984, 1986) classification scheme for evaluation statements. I analyzed data for evidence of behaviors that participants engaged in to meet their writing goals, the role of peers and teachers in evaluating text and promoting revision, and language use throughout the composing process. Coding categories included *crafting* (i.e., how well a text was developed), *retelling* (i.e., paraphrasing all or part of a text), *surface features* (i.e., the form of the text, such as spelling, length, or handwriting), *liking* (i.e., indicating personal liking of an element or an association with the text), *understanding* (i.e., efforts to process or make sense of the text), and *entertainment* (i.e., degree to which text prompted an emotional response).

Findings: A Window Into the Writing and Revision Process of Young Bilinguals

Throughout the study, and in both WW contexts, emergent bilingual/biliterate writers engaged in complex cognitive and linguistic revision tasks throughout all stages of the writing process. Participants were not reluctant to make changes to their stories in progress. They crossed out, erased, and wrote in the margins and between the lines of their papers. Revisions were made at different levels of discourse processing, to different degrees, and at all four categories of operations. Participants made a total of 199 changes in their Spanish and English stories.

Most changes involved additions (116); other changes included substitutions (47), deletions (18), and reorderings (18). These findings confirm and extend research on young monolingual English writers (Calkins, 1980; Graves, 1983) where additions were more frequent than deletions.

Emergent bilingual writers recognized the need to revise their stories on their own and were also prompted by peers and teachers to make changes. Students actively drew on their developing dual language and literacy skills, collaborated with their peers, and used classroom resources in order to evaluate and revise their drafts. As the following examples illustrate, emergent bilingual writers employed a variety of language and literacy strategies while revising, demonstrated critical reflective skills in the evaluation process, and applied a number of criteria for evaluating their writing.

Revising To Make Sense

Emergent bilingual writers recognized writing and revising as thinking and sense-making processes (Murray, 2004). That is, students were concerned with, among other things, the comprehensibility of their stories and thought extensively about the message they were trying to convey through their writing. An excerpt from an English WW session illustrates how young writers commonly employ the reading process as an effective means to detect incongruence in their work. In the beginning of May, Steven was working on a story in the English WW about a recent field trip to a roller skating rink. He sat by himself, hoping to push ahead on his story so that he could share it during an upcoming "author's chair." As he settled in his seat for the day's WW session, he pulled out his story in progress from his writing folder and began to read what he'd written so far. Rereading page one of his draft out loud, Steven said, "I went to Roller Palace on April vacation with the whole daycare in Beverly. The teachers … [pause] … Hmmm…" Steven erased the period at the end of the last phrase on this page ("The teachers.") and added "go there"; the sentence now read: "The teachers *go there*."[6] Steven reread his revised sentence silently, while pointing to the words on that page. He then inserted a caret after "The teachers" and wrote "wanted to"; the revised sentence now read: "The teachers *wanted to* go there." In the meantime, Steven's teacher came by to check in with him and asked why he'd erased the period and made those additions. Steven looked back at this writing and responded, "It didn't make sense before but … [it] makes sense now."

In this example, Steven made two revisions, both of which involved insertions. The first insertion, "go there," was intended to complete the original sentence. Although the resulting sentence, "The teachers *go there*," is grammatically acceptable, it did not seem to make sense in the context of the story. With the second insertion, "[The teachers] *wanted to* [go there.]," Steven fine-tuned his intended message and achieved his goal of making meaning through his writing.

Similarly, other young writers engaged in a recursive process of evaluation and revision which allowed them to reflect on whether their writing effectively conveyed the meaning they intended. The following excerpt, taken from an interview following a Spanish WW session, illustrates one of the ways in which emergent bilingual writers look for incongruence in their drafts and revise accordingly. Katherine, the focal student in this example, had been working on a recount about a recent trip she took with her family to Disney World. As I prompted her to reflect on her work that day in WW, Katherine described a critical reflection process that involved thinking, writing, rereading (her own writing), and reworking what she'd written based on her evaluation of her work:[7]

RESEARCHER: ¿Cómo te fué hoy en el taller de escritura? (How did it go today in writing workshop?)

KATHERINE: Alguno no tiene sentido ... lo leí ... y lo borré. (Some didn't make sense. I read it... and I erased it.)

RESEARCHER: ¿Me puedes enseñar alguna parte que tu cambiaste porque algo no tenía sentido? (Can you show me a place where you made changes because something didn't make sense?)

[Katherine flipped through pages in her story.]

KATHERINE: Esta página ... yo dije "nos dimos pan." ¡Eso no tiene sentido: "nos dimos pan!" Entonces yo lo borré y lo cambié. (This page ... I said, "we gave ourselves bread." That doesn't make sense: "we gave ourselves bread!" So I erased it and changed it.)

RESEARCHER: ¿Entonces como lo cambiaste para que tuviera sentido? (How did you change it so that it made sense?)

[Katherine reread the revised sentence in its entirety.]

KATHERINE: "Nos dió hambre y mi mama *me dió pan.*" (We got hungry and my mom *gave me bread.*)

In the example above, Katherine explained how she monitors whether her stories are "making sense" by reading and rereading throughout the writing process. Katherine's revision involved a substitution which more closely approximated standard usage and made more "sense" to her. It is interesting to note that her original production ("we gave ourselves bread") is grammatically acceptable, although it is not a common way to express the notion of giving something to oneself. With her revision and explanation, Katherine demonstrates an emerging sociolinguistic awareness and provides evidence that writing is an active thinking process. Although this particular revising event occurred while she was still in the process of drafting her story and not during an official revising session with a peer or the teacher, Katherine's account of her revision process illuminates how "making sense" was an important goal for these young writers.

Revising to Clarify and Expand Ideas

Emergent bilingual writers recognized the need to add details to their stories in order to clarify and expand their ideas on their own and with peer and teacher assistance. Peer and teacher interactions around a story in progress often provided writers opportunities to explore ideas, to find the right words to express these ideas, and to negotiate with their audience about these ideas – all of which are critical in second-language acquisition and cognitive growth (Mendonça & Johnson, 1994). In the following excerpt, Barbara and the English WW teacher negotiated what information would be added, deleted, and substituted to strengthen Barbara's draft:

BARBARA: [rereading page 2 out loud] First we went in the car with all the people that came.
TEACHER: Where were you going? Where were you driving to in the car?
BARBARA: mmmm ... the airport.
TEACHER: Alright, so ... What would be one way we could say it?
BARBARA: We went to the airplane in a car. I'm gonna cross out those [pointing to words "with all the people that came" on page] and put this one.
TEACHER: You want to cross out all of this?
BARBARA: [crossed out "with all the people that came."] [rereading out loud after deletion] First we went in the car ... [began to write, saying words out loud as she wrote them] to ... the ... airport. I wrote it on here.
TEACHER: Okay, good. So why don't you reread what you have now.
BARBARA: [rereading outloud] First we went in the car *to the airport.*

In this brief, scaffolded interaction, we see how Barbara was able to focus on the ideas and meaning conveyed by the text with the guiding support of her teacher. The teacher brought a genuine sense of audience by listening to Barbara's story in progress, asking questions about (missing) story content and providing Barbara an opportunity to work through new ideas and construct meaning. Hyland's (1990) research with adult writers suggests that such specific, idea-based, meaning-level feedback is more effective in promoting student revisions and more likely to positively affect their writing.

Considering the Audience

Emergent bilingual writers acknowledged that writing is a collaborative/social act between the writer and the reader and, thus, evaluated and revised their stories for real purposes and for real audiences. Students were conscientious about their audience as they drafted and encouraged their peers to be as well. As members of the writing communities of the parallel writing workshops who served the dual roles of authors and each other's audience, students regularly offered suggestions, posed questions, and provided explicit feedback to their peers from the perspective of a potential reader/listener. The following excerpt highlights students' awareness of an audience, not only for their stories but for their peers' stories as well. In this example, Lucy and Steven were sitting side by side at one of the Spanish classroom tables and working independently on their respective stories. As they wrote, both Lucy and Steven reread aloud their stories in progress and occasionally made comments to themselves, providing real-time accounts of their thoughts and next steps. Throughout this WW session, Steven had made a number of changes to his story which resulted in various erasures, cross-outs, insertions, and rewrites. At one point, Lucy looked over at Steven's draft and commented on what she perceived to be a potential problem for anyone who might try to read his story:

LUCY: [to Steven] Mira, vamo a ver. Mira, tu tiene mucho borre-borre. ¡Nadie va a entender tu cuento! ¡Mira yo ni se lo que puede decir ahi! Mira. ¿Que dice ahi? (Look, let's see. Look, you have too much erasing. No one will understand your story. Look, I don't even know what that could say. Look. What does that say?)

Lucy's concern that Steven's draft was too messy for anyone to decipher illustrates emergent writers' general awareness of a future audience for their stories. That is, these writers understood that they were writing not only for themselves but for others as well, and that their editing and revising practices could prevent others from getting access to their stories.

Revising to Entertain

Additionally, emergent bilingual writers often recrafted their work in order to prompt an emotional response from their audience. An excerpt from the Spanish WW illustrates this finding.

LUCY: [rereading page 9 of her draft out loud] La pasta es tan grande. (The toothpaste is so big.) [Lucy inserted a caret after "tan" and added text. The sentence now read: "La pasta es tan *tan tan tan* grande" (The toothpaste is so *so so so* big)].

LUCY: [rereading her revised sentence out loud] La pasta es tan *tan tan tan* grande (The toothpaste is so *so so so* big.)

LUCY: [laughing] Dice "tan tan tan tan tan tan grande." Se van a reir. (It says "so so so so so so big." They're going to laugh.)

Lucy's attempt to incorporate "humor" in her story about the movie *Stuart Little* suggests a sophisticated understanding about audience and the ways in which authors can play with words to engage and entertain others. In this case, Lucy experimented with repetition and exaggeration to make her audience laugh. Her prediction about the audience's reaction, revealed through her self-talk, provides a window into Lucy's expectations about the effects of her writing. These purposeful and explicit manipulations of text illuminate young writers' development beyond having a general awareness of audience toward the emergence of strategic efforts to please and entertain those who might read or listen to their work.

The Role of Students' Bilingualism in Revising

Bilingual writers used their developing dual language and literacy skills in the process of creating L1 and L2 texts. With few exceptions (e.g., loan words, common colloquialisms), the texts emergent bilingual children created were monolingual. In contrast, the writing processes of these emergent bilingual writers were bilingual to different degrees. Participants used both of their languages in the act of revising to express creativity, to add authenticity to their writing, to teach their audience, and to solve problems. Spanish-dominant and English-dominant children exhibited different patterns in their oral use of strategic code-switching, depending on several different factors. All Spanish-dominant children used both languages in the process of creating Spanish texts; some also used both languages in the process of creating English texts. Bilingual "conversations," including self-talk and with peers, demonstrate how students draw on their developing bilingualism, biliteracy, and sociolinguistic competence to negotiate meaning (Gort, 2006).

Like other young writers, emergent bilinguals expressed their writing intentions verbally. Self-talk during writing appeared to help children plan and monitor their own writing, as well as sustain their composing efforts. Unlike monolinguals, however, emergent bilingual writers sometimes alternated between their two languages in their writing-related self-talk. The following Spanish WW excerpt, in which Katherine continued to work on a story in progress about a field trip to the Museum of Science, illustrates this finding.[8]

KATHERINE: [rereading page 4 out loud] Llegué ...a Boston (Spanish pronunciation) ... Con con un un ... grupo ... grupo. (I arrived in Boston with a group.) [Katherine turned to the next page and reread aloud what she'd written the previous day "A bia unaescalera musical" ("There were musical stairs").]
KATHERINE: [talking to herself, out loud] *I think I wanna write something new ...*
KATHERINE: [paused, then began to add new details at end of page; said words out loud as she wrote them] Baaaaa ... jéeeee ... yyyyy ... su ... bíiiiiiiii [wrote "*baje y sudi*"] (I went down and up).

As Katherine wrote, read, and reread what she'd written thus far, she used code-switching as a way to problem-solve the events in the story. Through the recursive and interactive processes of writing and reading her ongoing text, Katherine identified an incomplete description of a story event. She expressed her intention to add a detail related to this event through the use of an intersentential code-switch, or a switch from one language to another that occurs between sentences. Katherine then returned to the target language, Spanish, immediately following this switch to English in order to write the new detail. Although the text of Katherine's Spanish story was monolingual, her self-talk, reading aloud, and oral encoding (i.e., sounding out of syllables and words as they are being written) provide a window into the bilingual nature of children's writing process.

Bilingual conversations among peers were also common in the two WW classrooms. The following excerpt depicts a typical bilingual exchange in which two Spanish-dominant writers (Lucy and Katherine) collaborate on a word-level revision involving a substitution. From a sociocultural perspective, the excerpt illuminates the ways in which peer interactions support writing participation and how students use discussion to create written language (Dyson, 2004):

KATHERINE: [rereading draft out loud] Compramos soda y *popcorn*. (We bought soda and popcorn.)

KATHERINE: [to herself, but speaking loud enough for Lucy to hear] ¿Cómo se escribe *popcorn*? (How do you write popcorn?)

LUCY: Escríbelo en español, palomitas de maíz. (Write it in Spanish, "palomitas de maíz.")

KATHERINE: A si, palomitas... (Oh yes, popcorn.)

KATHERINE: Palomitas... [pause] ¡No, en inglés! *I don't know how to write* palomitas. (No, in English! ...)

[Lucy helps Katherine "sound out" the target word at the syllable level]

LUCY: paaaaa ... loooo ... miiii ... taaaas

[Katherine writes "palomitas," as Lucy dictates.]

KATHERINE: ¡de maiz! (...of corn!)

Lucy and Katherine's exchange highlights how children's use of two languages to talk (and think) about writing might support the development of an enhanced awareness that positively influences their understanding of language structure and flexibility in manipulating languages (Bauer, 2000). Lucy's suggestion to use the Spanish term for "popcorn" in a Spanish-medium story implies that she distinguishes between her two languages and uses them in systematic ways. Katherine's initial evaluation and subsequent rejection of Lucy's suggestion, presumably due to a potential spelling challenge, suggests an awareness of the different language structures of English and Spanish and the strategic use of two languages. Such cross-linguistic interactions appear to provide bidirectional language and literacy learning opportunities for participants as, in the process of translation, linguistic/literacy scaffolding, and negotiation, each child becomes more aware of her own bilingualism (Gort, 2008).

In the English WW context, Spanish-dominant bilinguals also used both languages as resources while writing and thinking about writing. For example, Katherine often used both languages to express her understanding of the social nature of writing and her concern that her emerging, non-standard English spelling may hinder the audience's understanding of her story:

KATHERINE: I don't know how to write it ... I wrote it *mal* (wrong), I know I did! But I want to write it good so people can understand.

Katherine's code-switch from English to Spanish appears to be functional in that it signals a point of emphasis. Evidence in the corpus of data suggests that Katherine knows the equivalent term of "mal" in English; thus, her use of code-switching, in this case, demonstrates a strategic use of bilingual (self) talk to monitor, self-regulate, and sustain her composing efforts.

In contrast to Spanish-dominant children's flexible language use across both WW contexts, English-dominant children were predominantly observed to code-switch in the Spanish WW. This included oral and written code-switching. Findings related to English-dominant children's use of English in Spanish compositions and the Spanish WW context corroborate Francis' (2002, 2005) earlier findings which document an apparent sociolinguistic imbalance between bilingual students' written pieces. In Francis' research on the literacy development of Spanish/Náhuatl young bilinguals, all but one Náhuatl (minority language) composition contained Spanish (majority language) lexical items. On the contrary, no code-switching appeared in any Spanish sample.

Supporting Children's Bilingualism, Biliteracy Development, and Metalinguistic Awareness Through Writing: Implications for Practice

The purpose of this study was to provide insights into the relationships between bilingual development, biliteracy learning, and metalinguistic awareness through the processes of evaluation and revision. Findings show that emergent bilinguals can acquire second-language (L2) literacy skills during developmental stages of acquiring the L2 and expand our understanding of the processes and strategies young bilingual writers engage in when making decisions about their writing. Taken together, findings further support our growing understanding of the interrelated nature of first and second language and literacy development, and the role of metalinguistic awareness in the process.

Participants were able to revise their written work on their own and with assistance from peers and teachers. Revisions were made for a range of purposes including to convert written language into standard grammar, to more appropriately express ideas, and to entertain and better inform the audience. Emergent bilingual/biliterate writers used their developing bilingual repertoire and engaged in hybrid literacy practices in the process of creating and revising L1 and L2 texts. With few exceptions, the texts the children created were monolingual. Their writing and revising processes, however, were bilingual to different degrees. Viewed from a Vygotskian perspective, these findings support the notion of a "bilingual zone of proximal development," in which bilingual learners' acquisition of new knowledge and skills depends on their opportunity to draw upon their two languages to mediate their learning in interaction with others (Moll & Diaz, 1987).

A multilingual perspective provided a window into these students' composing and revising behaviors and the role of their developing bilingualism in the writing process. The findings have important implications for designing and implementing effective language and literacy learning environments for bilingual children from minority- and majority-language backgrounds. First, they illustrate that *emergent bilingual writers, like their monolingual English-speaking counterparts, have the ability to engage in critical evaluations and revision of their own and others' work. Yet, unlike their monolingual peers, bilingual writers can do this within and across two languages* within a bilingual zone of proximal development. That is, emergent writers use their developing bilingual repertoire and engage in hybrid literacy practices in the process of creating, evaluating, and revising L1 and L2 texts. In spite of a conscious effort by program staff to separate the two target languages for instruction, teachers in these classrooms created spaces for hybridized discourse in the social context of the WW. That is, teachers redefined what counted as legitimate writing and oral language practices by creating opportunities for mixed-language student interactions within the rich interactive space of the WW, and supported bilingual children's use of both languages in the process of evaluating and revising their writing. Thus, even in "monolingual" classroom contexts, teachers can support bilingual children's linguistic and literacy development and validate their bilingual/bicultural identities by encouraging children to draw on their dual language reservoir and bicultural experiences when engaged in literacy tasks. For example, by accepting emergent bilingual children's contributions and encouraging their participation in English and other languages, teachers can create supporting learning situations where children can use oral and written language based on their strengths, prior knowledge, interests, experience, and culture.

Findings also underscore the ways in which *writing (and talking about writing) in two languages supports dual language/literacy learning and metalinguistic awareness in bilingual children*. Findings appear to be compatible with the emphasis that second-language researchers have placed on the benefits of focusing bilingual learners' attention on the form of their written message through tasks that stimulate learners to engage in linguistic analysis (Swain & Lapkin, 1995). As Wenden (1998) suggests, opportunities to apply strategies that require reflection upon language learning will help students "become more autonomous in their approach to the learning of their new language" (p. 532). This means allowing flexibility in language use across the writing process and planning for flexible peer/grouping strategies to maximize opportunities for cross-linguistic talk and reflection in the writing classroom. Such opportunities to reflect on linguistic form–function relationships between bilinguals' languages set the stage for linguistic problem solving. In some respect, this ability to reflect upon and manipulate one's own discourse marks the highest level of literacy development.

A final implication of *bilingual writing/literacy development through a process approach* relates to its potential *as a resource for thinking and learning* through which students establish and mediate relationships between two linguistic and cultural systems to create knowledge and transform it for meaningful purposes. Emergent bilingual learners in this study used two languages strategically to engage in both private and collaborative speech when cognitively challenged. They also used code-switching to communicate their knowledge, developing understandings, questions, and observations about their own and their peers' writing while negotiating participation in ongoing conversations. Educators of bilingual learners, thus, should facilitate their transactions with two literate worlds through collaborative opportunities for writing, reading, evaluating, and revising in two languages in order to expand children's resources for thinking and learning and support their full potential as competent bilinguals and biliterates.

Notes

1. Spanglish is a hybrid language and literacy form, characterized by the interaction and blending of Spanish and English, that is common in bilingual contexts and communities. Spanglish represents a positive way of identifying the normal borrowing and code-switching events of stable bilingual communities that reflect the bicultural experiences of Latino bilinguals living in the U.S. (Morales, 2002; Zentella, 1997).
2. A small number of studies examine the second-language revising behaviors of older school-age and adult learners (e.g., Manchon et al., 2000; Paulus, 1999; Whalen & Menard, 1995; Williams, 2004). A few others have taken a bilingual approach to the study of revision processes of older learners (e.g., Hall, 1990; Stevenson et al., 2006). These L1 and L2 investigations suggest that revising processes are likely to look similar across languages (Hall, 1990).
3. Náhuatl is an indigenous language of central Mexico.
4. Two-way bilingual education (TWBE) offers opportunities for dual language/literacy and academic content learning for English learners and English speakers within a multicultural education framework that promotes the value of linguistic and cultural plurality and provides positive intergroup educational experiences for both groups of students (Howard et al., 2003; Potowski, 2007). For English learners, TWBE provides an additive bilingual environment where students' native languages are considered resources for learning, and maintenance of those native languages is as much a priority as the development of English. For English speakers, TWBE provides a unique immersion experience in which majority-language students learn a second language in integrated settings with native speakers of that language, many of whom are members of a different cultural group.

5. The data subset included two transcripts (and related data sources) in each language for each four week time period of the study (six periods total) for each participant, i.e., a total of 24 transcripts and related data sources per participant.
6. Revisions are italicized for emphasis.
7. Translations from Spanish to English are indicated in parentheses. Additional information is described in brackets.
8. Code-switches are italicized for emphasis. Student-produced text is presented exactly as written.

References

Baker, C. (2000). *A parents' and teachers' guide to bilingualism* (2nd ed.). Clevedon, UK: Multilingual Matters.

Baker, C. (2001). *Foundations of bilingual education and bilingualism*. Clevedon, UK: Multilingual Matters.

Bauer, E. B. (2000). Code-switching during shared and independent reading: Lessons learned from a preschooler. *Research in the Teaching of English, 35*(1), 101–130.

Bear, D., & Barone, D. (1998). *Developmental literacy: An integrated approach to assessment and instruction*. Boston, MA: Houghton Mifflin.

Bialystok, E. (1991). Metalinguistic dimensions of bilingual language proficiency. In E. Bialystok (Ed.), *Language processing in bilingual children* (pp. 113–140). New York: Cambridge University Press.

Bialystok, E. (2001). *Bilingualism in development: Language, literacy, and cognition*. Cambridge, UK: Cambridge University Press.

Bialystok, E., & Hakuta, K. (1994). *In other words: The science and psychology of second-language acquisition*. New York: Basic Books.

Brandt, D. (2005). Writing for a living: Literacy and the knowledge economy. *Written Communication, 22*(2), 166–197.

Calkins, L. M. (1980). Notes and comments: Children rewriting strategies. *Research in the Teaching of English, 14*(4), 41–44.

Calkins, L. M. (1994). *The art of teaching writing* (2nd ed.). Portsmouth, NH: Heinemann.

Clay, M. (2001). *Change over time in children's literacy development*. Portsmouth, NH: Heinemann.

Duncan, S. E., & De Avila, E. A. (1990). *Language assessment scales-oral*. Monterey, CA: CTB McGraw-Hill.

Dworin, J. E. (2003). Examining children's biliteracy in the classroom. In A. I. Willis, G. E. Garcia, R. B. Barrera, & V. J. Harris (Eds.), *Multicultural issues in literacy research and practice* (pp. 29–48). Mahwah, NJ: Lawrence Erlbaum.

Dyson, A. H. (2004). Writing in the sea of voices: Oral language in, around, and about writing. In R. B. Ruddell & N. J. Unrau (Eds.), *Theoretical models and processes of reading* (pp. 146–162). Newark, DE: International Reading Association.

Francis, N. (1999). Bilingualism, writing, and metalinguistic awareness: Oral-literate interactions between first and second languages. *Applied Psycholinguistics, 20*(4), 533–561.

Francis, N. (2002). Literacy, second language learning, and the development of metalinguistic awareness: A study of bilingual children's perceptions of focus on form. *Linguistics and Education, 13*(3), 373–404.

Francis, N. (2005). Bilingual children's writing: Self-correction and revision of written narratives in Spanish and Náhuatl. *Linguistics and Education, 16*(1), 74–92.

Genesee, F. (2002). Rethinking bilingual acquisition. In J. M. Dewarle, A. Husen, & L. Wei (Eds.), *Bilingualism: Beyond basic principles* (pp. 158–182). Clevedon, UK: Multilingual Matters.

Genesee, F., Lindholm-Leary, K., Saunders, W., & Christian, D. (2005). English language learners in U.S. schools: An overview of research findings. *Journal of Education for Students Placed At Risk, 10*(4), 363–385.

Gort, M. (2006). Strategic codeswitching, interliteracy, and other phenomena of emergent bilingual writing: Lessons from first-grade dual language classrooms. *Journal of Early Childhood Literacy, 6*(3), 327–358.

Gort, M. (2008). "You give me idea!" Collaborative strides toward bilingualism and biliteracy in a two-way partial immersion program. *Multicultural Perspectives, 10*(4), 192–200.

Graham, S., & Harris, K. R. (1996). Self-regulation and strategy instruction for students who find writing and learning challenging. In C. M. Levy & S. Ransdell (Eds.), *The science of writing: Theories, methods, individual differences, and applications* (pp. 347–360). Mahwah, NJ: Lawrence Erlbaum.

Graves, D. H. (1983). *Writing: Teachers and children at work.* Portsmouth, NH: Heinemann.

Graves, D. H. (1994). *A fresh look at writing.* Portsmouth, NH: Heinemann.

Gutierrez, K., Baquedano-Lopez, P., & Tejada, C. (1999a). Rethinking diversity: Hybridity and hybrid language practices in the third space. *Mind, Culture, and Activity, 6*(4), 286–303.

Gutiérrez, K., Baquedano-López, P., Alvarez, H., & Chiu, M. (1999b). Building a culture of collaboration through hybrid language practices. *Theory into Practice, 38*(2), 67–93.

Hall, C. (1990). Managing the complexity of revising across languages. *TESOL Quarterly, 24*(1), 43–60.

Hilgers, T. L. (1984). Toward a taxonomy of beginning writers' evaluative statements on written compositions. *Written Communication, 1*(3), 365–384.

Hilgers, T. L. (1986). How children change as critical evaluators of writing: Four three-year case studies. *Research in the Teaching of English, 20*(1), 36–55.

Howard, E. R., Sugarman, J., & Christian, D. (2003). *Trends in two-way immersion education: A review of the research.* Baltimore, MD: John Hopkins University, CRESPAR.

Hyland, K. (1990). Providing productive feedback. *ELT Journal, 44*(4), 279–285.

Kenner, C. (2004). Living in simultaneous worlds: Difference and integration in bilingual script-learning. *International Journal of Bilingual Education and Bilingualism, 7*(4), 43–61.

Kenner, C., & Kress, G. (2003). The multisemiotic resources of biliterate children. *Journal of Early Childhood Literacy, 3*(2), 179–202.

Kenner, C., Kress, G., Al-Khatib, H., Kam, R., & Tsai, K. (2004). Finding the keys to biliteracy: How young children interpret different writing systems. *Language and Education, 18*(2), 124–144.

Lindholm-Leary, K. (2001). *Dual language education.* Clevedon, UK: Multilingual Matters.

Manchon, R. M., de Larios, J. R., & Murphy, L. (2000). An approximation to the study of backtracking in L2 writing. *Learning and Instruction, 10*(1), 13–35.

Mendonça, C. O., & Johnson, K. E. (1994). Peer review negotiations: Revision activities in ESL writing instruction. *TESOL Quarterly, 28*(4), 745–768.

Moll, L., & Diaz, S. (1987). Change as the goal of educational research. *Anthropology and Education Quarterly, 18*(4), 300–311.

Moll, L., Saéz, R., & Dworin, J. E. (2001). Exploring biliteracy: Two student case examples of writing as a social practice. *Elementary School Journal, 101*(4), 435–449.

Mor-Sommerfeld, A. (2002). Language mosaic. Developing literacy in a second-new language: A new perspective. *Reading, Literacy and Language, 36*(3), 99–105.

Morales, E. (2002). *Living in Spanglish: The search for Latino identity in America.* New York: St. Martin's Press.

Morris, D. (1993). The relationship between children's concept of word in text and phoneme awareness in learning to read: A longitudinal study. *Research in the Teaching of English, 27*(2), 133–154.

Murray, D. (2004). *The craft of revision* (5th ed.). Boston, MA: Thomson-Wadsworth.

Ovando, C. J., Collier, V. P., & Combs, M. C. (2003). *Bilingual and ESL classrooms: Teaching in multicultural contexts* (3rd ed.). Boston, MA: McGraw Hill.

Paulus, T. M. (1999). The effect of peer and teacher feedback on student writing. *Journal of Second Language Writing, 8*(3), 265–289.

Pérez, B. (2004). *Becoming biliterate: A study of two way bilingual immersion education.* Mahwah, NJ: Lawrence Erlbaum.

Potowski, K. (2007). *Language and identity in a dual immersion school.* Clevedon, UK: Multilingual Matters.

Raimes, A. (1985). What unskilled ESL students do as they write: A classroom study of composing. *TESOL Quarterly, 19*(2), 229–258.

Reyes, M. L. (2001). Unleashing possibilities: Biliteracy in the primary grades. In M. L. Reyes & J. J. Halcón (Eds.), *The best for our children: Critical perspectives on literacy for Latino students* (pp. 96–121). New York: Teachers College Press.

Reyes, M. L., & Costanzo, L. (2002). On the threshold of biliteracy: A first grader's personal journey. In L. Díaz Soto (Ed.), *Making a difference in the lives of bilingual/bicultural children* (pp. 145–156). New York: Peter Lang.

Samway, K. D. (1993). "This is hard, isn't it?" Children evaluating writing. *TESOL Quarterly, 27*(2), 233–258.

Sommers, N. (1980). Revision strategies of student writers and experienced adult writers. *College Composition and Communication, 31*(4), 378–388.

Stevenson, M., Schoonen, R., & de Glopper, K. (2006). Revising in two languages: A multi-dimensional comparison of online writing revisions in L1 and FL. *Journal of Second Language Writing, 15*(3), 201–233.

Sulzby, E. (1985). Children's emergent reading of favorite storybooks: A developmental study. *Reading Research Quarterly, 20*(4), 458–481.

Swain, M., & Lapkin, S. (1995). Problems in output and the cognitive processes they generate: A step towards second language learning. *Applied Linguistics, 16*(3), 371–391.

Urzua, C. (1987). "You stopped too soon": Second language children composing and revising. *TESOL Quarterly, 21*(2), 279–304.

Valdés, G. (1992). Bilingual minorities and language issues in writing: Toward profession-wide responses to a new challenge. *Written Communication, 9*(1), 85–136.

Wenden, A. (1998). Metacognitive knowledge and language learning. *Applied Linguistics, 19*(4), 515–537.

Whalen, K., & Menard, N. (1995). L1 and L2 writers' strategic and linguistic knowledge: A model of multiple-level discourse processing. *Language Learning, 45*(3), 381–418.

Williams, J. (2004). Tutoring and revision: Second language writers in the writing center. *Journal of Second Language Writing, 13*(3), 173–201.

Zamel, V. (1982). Writing: The process of discovering meaning. *TESOL Quarterly, 16*(2), 195–209.

Zamel, V. (1983). The composing processes of advanced ESL students: Six case studies. *TESOL Quarterly, 17*(2), 165–187.

Zentella, A. (1997). *Growing up bilingual: Puerto Rican children in New York*. Boston, MA: Blackwell Publishers.

6

ZEHRA'S STORY

Becoming Biliterate in Turkish and English

Zeynep Çamlibel and Georgia Garcia

Much still needs to be discovered about young bilingual children's language and literacy development. Key questions include how these children make sense of new academic environments, acquire a second language (L2) as they further their development of their first (L1) or home language, and learn to read and write in two languages. The language and literacy experiences at home and school of Zehra (a pseudonym), a young Turkish sojourner in the United States, provide some answers to the above questions.

Related Literature

Adjusting to a New Academic Environment and Acquiring a New Language

Several researchers have described the anxiety that L2 learners feel when school personnel do not provide them with a safe and caring environment (Commins & Miramontes, 2005; Igoa, 1995) and comprehensible instruction (i.e., structured instruction they can understand) (Krashen, 1985). Although the parents of immigrant children often decide to leave their home country for a new country, young children seldom are partners in this decision. Immigrant children face enormous stress as they accommodate to a new culture, learn new schooling practices, and acquire a new language. Krashen (1985), in particular, has emphasized the importance of reducing the affective filter (adverse emotional and motivational responses) for effective L2 acquisition.

Many school personnel and parents do not understand the stages of language acquisition that characterize L2 language development. Often, when children are exposed to instruction in a new language, they undergo a silent period for up to six months, in which they say very little in the L2 (Krashen, 1981). During the silent period, they pay attention to the use of the L2, but are not ready to use it.

Similarly, school personnel and parents do not always realize how long it takes children to acquire an L2. Cummins (1981) observed that L2 learners who live in the country where the L2 commonly is used typically acquire social use of an L2 in two to three years, whereas to acquire the L2 academic language needed to participate at grade level takes at least four to seven years. Individuals' speed of language acquisition is affected by a range of factors: personality, motivation to learn the L2, age of arrival in the L2 country, previous schooling in the L1, type of L2 instruction, and socio-political factors, such as the status of the L1 in the L2 country (Cummins, 1989; Thomas & Collier, 2001).

Many parents, anxious for their children to become fluent L2 speakers, ignore the continued development of their children's L1. They often are unaware of the benefits of cross-linguistic transfer (i.e., bilinguals' ability to use knowledge and skills acquired in one language in another language) and do not understand the optimal conditions for transfer. Cummins (1989) theorized that cross-linguistic transfer occurs when students already have developed a high level of cognitive development in one language, usually the L1, and have been adequately exposed to the other language, usually the L2.

Parents may not understand that their children need to continue to learn in their L1, the language they know best, so that they do not delay their learning of new academic content or skills until they have sufficient L2 proficiency to learn new material through the L2 (Echevarria et al., 2008). If parents plan to return to their home country when their children are school age, then their children should continue to learn in their L1 so that they can later perform at grade level in their L1.

L1 and L2 Literacy Development and Instruction

Our understanding of bilingual children's literacy development and instruction still is limited (August & Shanahan, 2006; García, 2000). The roles of L2 oral proficiency and Ll literacy in children's L2 literacy development are two areas that merit investigation. Some researchers consider L2 oral proficiency to be a prerequisite for L2 literacy development (Bialystok, 2002; Snow, 2006). Others report that L2 learners are able and willing to engage in L2 literacy activities before they have complete L2 oral proficiency (Barrera, 1984; Hudelson, 1984). In a review of bilingual reading, García (2000) noted that L1 reading is a stronger predictor of young bilingual children's L2 reading than their oral L2 proficiency, whereas for older bilingual children, oral L2 proficiency is a stronger predictor than L1 reading. One explanation for the predictive role of L1 reading is that many bilinguals can transfer early literacy skills acquired in their L1 to their L2 without much formal instruction (Lesaux & Geva, 2006).

Another reason why young bilingual children may do well on L2 measures of early reading, such as measures of word recognition (identification), decoding, and spelling, without high levels of L2 oral proficiency is that the former skills lend themselves to explicit modeling, instruction, and repeated practice, and do not require much L2 comprehension. In fact, the National Literacy Panel on Language-Minority Children and Youth reported that L2 learners performed as well as native speakers on L2 measures of word recognition, decoding, and spelling, regardless of whether they were instructed in both languages or just in L2 (Snow, 2006).

On measures that require L2 learners to understand the L2 words and texts they are reading, and the L2 texts they are writing, bilingual children's levels of L2 proficiency do seem to play an influential role (García, 2000; Snow, 2006). L2 readers frequently know less of the L2 vocabulary and background knowledge emphasized in L2 texts and reading assessments than native speakers (García, 2000; Lesaux et al. 2006).

The importance of providing students with reading instruction in the language they know best, their L1, while they are learning to read in their L2, was highlighted in a recent meta-analysis (Francis et al., 2006). Francis et al. compared the English (L2) standardized reading test performance of Spanish-speaking children instructed in Spanish *and* English to those who had only received instruction in English, and concluded that the children who received reading instruction in both languages significantly outperformed those children who only received English reading instruction.

Whether the above findings characterize the literacy development and instruction of children from non-related languages, such as Turkish and English, is not well known. By sharing Zehra's story below, we hope to contribute to what is known about the biliteracy development of young immigrant children.

Getting To Know Zehra

Constructing the Case Study

Zehra's story was constructed from qualitative data that the first author (henceforth known as the researcher) collected from Zehra's home and school over a six-month period (March to August). When the study began, Zehra was 6:5 years old, and had been in the U.S. and at Kent Elementary School (a pseudonym) for six months. Per state law, Kent School provided English learners with a transitional program of instruction. Zehra received 30 minutes of daily instruction in Turkish, 110 minutes of daily instruction in a content-based ESL classroom, and 185 minutes of daily instruction in an all-English mainstream classroom.

The researcher, a Turkish–English bilingual, was Zehra's Turkish instructor. She used fieldnotes, audio recordings, and video recordings to document classroom observations in the ESL and all-English classrooms and retrospective fieldnotes, audio recordings, and video recordings to document observations in the Turkish classroom. The researcher also conducted open-ended, semi-structured (audio-recorded) interviews with Zehra, her parents, and the ESL and (all-English) mainstream classroom teacher. Classroom assignments, essays, notebooks, work samples, report cards, and language test scores also were collected. During the summer, the researcher conducted two (audio-recorded) performance-assessment literacy tasks in Turkish and English with Zehra.

The researcher transcribed the field notes, audio and video recordings, and interviews, and entered the English data into a qualitative research data analysis program. The program aided in the organization of data, creation of themes, grouping of data in related categories, and retrieval of coded data for further examination. Initially, there were 107 codes, which included specific topics related to Zehra's English language and literacy use, development, and instruction, such as *student questions the teacher, English writing strategies, English verb missing or incorrect, student self-corrects,* and *link between Turkish and English.* Some of the codes were later combined or eliminated depending on their importance and relevance to the study. The researcher then read the Turkish classroom data, performance task data, and writing samples as well as the home interview data, and identified codes similar to those found in the English data, as well as codes that emerged only in the Turkish contexts.

We used the constant-comparison method and analytic induction processes (Strauss & Corbin, 1994) to analyze the data and construct Zehra's case study. Analytic induction involves finding commonalities in the data which lead first to a description and then to an explanation of the regularity (Krathwohl, 1998). It also includes checking the proposed explanation against already collected data to see how well it fits. In constructing the case, we pursued grounded theory (Glaser & Strauss, 1967) by developing an understanding of how the data characterized Zehra's language and literacy development.

Zehra's Family and Home Language and Literacy Experiences

Zehra was an only child and lived with her father and mother. Her family had come to the U.S. from Turkey for two years so that her father could obtain a Master's degree in International Business from the local university. Zehra and her family were supposed to return to Turkey after her father graduated. The family lived in a two-bedroom apartment in the university housing complex, where Zehra frequently met and played with Turkish and international friends.

Immediately before coming to the U.S., Zehra had attended kindergarten for one year in Turkey. However, she had not received any formal literacy instruction in Turkish since literacy instruction in Turkish public schools is not provided before first grade.

Turkish was the native language of both parents, and they used it at home to communicate with each other. Zehra's father was proficient in English, but her mother, who was a housewife, spoke very little English and attended an English-language class offered in the community. On the school Language Information Survey that Zehra's parents completed at the beginning of the school year, they indicated that they only used Turkish with Zehra.

At the beginning of the school year, Zehra was a fluent speaker of Turkish, but did not know any English. Her oral language development in Turkish appeared normal for her age and developmentally was similar to that of the other 12 Turkish students at Kent School. As Zehra learned English at school, she contentedly helped her mother understand some basic English used in TV programs or in interactions with native English speakers. Her father said that Zehra generally did not use English with them although she spoke English with her friends outside of the home.

It was not until the first parent–teacher conference that Zehra's parents realized that first graders were given homework at Kent School. At this conference, her ESL teacher told them that they needed to help her with her homework. According to the ESL teacher, "They didn't know she was bringing homework home." The mainstream teacher also asked Zehra's father to help with mathematics instruction because she could not convey the concepts to Zehra in English: "Zehra took a couple of sheets home so her dad could explain to her place values – ones, tens, hundreds, thousands. I just could not get that across at all." Although her father helped her with her English schoolwork and homework, her parents did not monitor or help her with her Turkish schoolwork or homework. Her parents explained that her ESL development was the most important skill she could gain while they lived in the U.S., and that they wanted her to maintain her English when they returned to Turkey.

Zehra's parents were genuinely surprised at her motivation for learning in Turkish, and were amazed when she tried to read and write in Turkish "on her own." They knew that Zehra was receiving Turkish literacy instruction at school, but did not expect her to become literate in Turkish so quickly. Her mother reported:

> Ama kendi kendine, belki de İngilizce'nin zorluklarını görünce, odasına çekilip Türkçe kitaplar okumaya çalışıyordu. Bir baktım, kendi okuyor kitabı, inanamadım. [But on her own, maybe after seeing the difficulties of English, she would go to her room and try to read Turkish books. All at once, she was reading the book by herself. I couldn't believe it.]

Zehra's Varied Experiences at Kent School

Zehra was placed in Ms. H.'s mainstream classroom with two other Turkish students, Alp and Dilara (pseudonyms). There were 25 students in this classroom, with half of them native English speakers and the other half English learners. All three Turkish first graders also were enrolled in Ms. M.'s first grade

ESL classroom, along with 14 other English learners. Dilara was more proficient in English than Zehra or Alp, so the mainstream and ESL teachers used Dilara as a translator between themselves and Zehra. When Dilara left the school during the school year, Alp, who was more verbally proficient in English than Zehra, took over Dilara's role and started helping Zehra.

At the beginning of the fall semester, Zehra preferred to use Turkish in school and was reluctant to use English. Her ESL teacher said that Zehra did not want to try English and over-relied on translators. When asked to recall what had happened when she first arrived at Kent School, Zehra remembered getting bored when she could not understand what was happening in school. According to her father, she became frustrated when she could not understand the English instruction, did not want to go to school, and often cried when she was forced to go to school:

> Birkaç defa tepkisi oldu, okula gitmek istemedi. Sebebi okuldaki soruları, problemi anlayamamış, yapamamış. Zorladık gönderdik ama ağlayarak gitti…. [She reacted a few times; she didn't want to go to school. The reason was that she couldn't understand and do the questions, the problems at school. We forced her to go to school, sent her to school, but she went crying….]

At the beginning of the school year, there were three kindergarten and three first grade Turkish speakers in the Turkish classroom. In the second semester, the first graders and kindergartners were split into two separate classes. Zehra was independent and self-confident in the Turkish class across both semesters. In contrast to her behavior in the ESL and (all-English) mainstream classrooms, where she initially depended on Turkish speaking students and was the seeker and receiver of help, she provided help to other students in the Turkish classroom.

Toward the middle of the second semester, Zehra became more self-confident in the ESL classroom. Her ESL teacher realized that she was a talkative and outgoing child, describing her as a "social butterfly."

Zehra's Literacy Instruction

Due to scheduling issues, native language instruction at the school did not begin until a month into the school year. Therefore, Zehra received initial reading instruction in English, her L2, a little earlier than she received reading instruction in Turkish, her L1.

Formal Literacy Instruction in the ESL Classroom

The ESL teacher primarily was responsible for the English literacy instruction of the English learners. Information on the type of reading instruction that students received in ESL during the first semester of the school year is based on the ESL teacher's interview. According to the teacher, the students were taught the English alphabet, common sound–symbol correspondences in English, and how to decode. During the second semester, when the classroom observations occurred, teacher read-alouds, choral reading, and small group instruction, in which individual students took turns reading text aloud and answering short comprehension questions, characterized the teacher's formal reading instruction.

It also is important to note that much of the children's instruction in the ESL classroom took the form of content-based ESL instruction. Accordingly, reading and writing activities often occurred as part of thematic instruction, which typically focused on science. ESL techniques – e.g., demonstrating and modeling instruction or verbal explanations; using illustrations, photographs, and realia to define unfamiliar English vocabulary; acting out words with physical demonstrations or gestures – accompanied verbal explanations and teacher read-alouds. The teacher also integrated reading, writing, listening, and speaking, so that when she introduced a new word in English, she said the word, wrote it on the board, had the students say it, write it, and read it.

Lack of Formal Literacy Instruction in the Mainstream Classroom

English learners who received ESL instruction left the mainstream classrooms during formal (planned) literacy instruction. Accordingly, Ms. H., the mainstream teacher, said that she did not provide any formal literacy instruction for Zehra, and that formal instruction in English reading and writing was the responsibility of the ESL teacher. When the ESL students were in attendance in the English mainstream classroom, literacy activities were short and mainly involved completing math or science tasks. Although students wrote in journals, Ms. H. did not expect the English learners to participate. It was not until Zehra and Alp volunteered to write at the end of the school year that Ms. H. allowed them to do journal writing in English, as she explains below:

> So now, ... they've been asking me, can they write things in the morning on the journal sheets? ... Suddenly, both of them said they would like to write something.... Because I never required them to write anything for me because that's more or less the language arts part of the program, and they get that [in ESL].

Turkish Literacy Instruction: Instruction and Curriculum from Turkey

Instruction in the Turkish first grade classroom focused on learning to read and write in Turkish according to a literacy curriculum, textbooks, and materials used in Turkey. Students were first introduced to the Turkish alphabet and the sounds of the Turkish letters. They also initiated beginning writing practice by tracing the Turkish letters. Then, they were introduced to words, which they learned and practiced to read and write (copying) with the help of flashcards and pictures. The same procedure was followed with simple sentences. As new sentences were introduced and learned, the students practiced reading and writing the previous words. Through exercises such as fill in the blanks, they used the words in new sentences. Throughout the year, the students also participated in other types of literacy activities, such as teacher read-alouds of stories in class, word/sentence recognition and identification, and dictations. The last two months of the spring semester were allocated to syllable practice and student reading of short texts. Syllables in Turkish consist of consonant and vowel combinations. The students practiced reading and writing different combinations to show that they knew how to use sound–symbol correspondence in Turkish.

Zehra's Literacy Development in English

Initial Problems with the English Alphabet

According to the ESL teacher, Zehra, like other Turkish-speaking students, had problems learning the English alphabet, and "struggled with it longer than other students in the classroom, who were from other language groups." Zehra could say the sounds of the English letters but did not know their names, and could not differentiate between the sounds and names of the letters. Zehra's father thought that simultaneously learning the two alphabets had confused her, as he explains belows:

> İlk başlarda karıştırdı harfleri. Hem Türkçe alfabeyi öğreniyordu hem İngilizce. Mesela *a* harfini *e* ile yani telaffuzu karıştırdı. [At first she mixed up the letters. She was learning the Turkish and English alphabets at the same time. For example, she mixed up the pronunciation of the letter *a* with *e*].

Zehra might have been using what she was learning in Turkish to approach English. In Turkish, the sound is usually the name of the letter, and there is much higher one-to-one correspondence between the sounds and names of the letters. To be successful in English, Zehra had to learn that an English letter can have more sounds than its name.

A Limited and Hesitant English Reader

Ms. M. reported that by the end of the first semester, Zehra had learned the English letter names and sounds. She sounded out new words based on phonological knowledge of English but still had not developed much sight vocabulary. When tested in November, she read five of ten words at the pre-primer level on a basic reading test for native-English speakers. On the *Directed Reading Assessment* (DRA), Zehra misread three out of ten words on Level A, indicating that the text was too difficult for her.

At the beginning of the second semester, during ESL whole-class reading instruction, Zehra was quiet and not very involved. When she did interact, which was rare, she replied with a "yes" or "no" to repetitive questions in the story, laughed at the content and pictures, or repeated words.

Becoming a Risk Taker and Participant

Despite what her ESL teacher considered to be slow oral language development in English, over the course of the second semester, Zehra showed more interest and enthusiasm for reading. When the class chorally read a story or was engaged in activities such as finding words in the story, she participated. She began to take risks, without stopping much or getting frustrated. For instance, in March, when the teacher in her music class asked for the next reader, Zehra volunteered to read aloud, even though she made mistakes, and the teacher corrected her:

ZEHRA: [reads] Color the three sam
TEACHER: Smallest
ZEHRA: [reads] /Bans/
TEACHER: Bones

In April, Zehra was eager to read aloud, even though the ESL teacher was not ready for her to read and asked her to stop several times:

TEACHER: We're gonna read together guys. Ready?
ZEHRA: Oh. [reads] In [pause] the
TEACHER: Wait a minute. Ready, Zehra?
ZEHRA: Yes. [reads] Sp-ring, a small baby.
TEACHER: Ok, ready? Zehra.
...
ZEHRA: [reads] The mother raccoon looks like.
TEACHER: Zehra. I wasn't ready. Ready?

A Strong Decoder with Limited Comprehension of Written and Oral English

In April, Zehra's ESL teacher described her as a fluent reader, and rated her reading high. On a scale of 11, she gave Zehra a 9 indicating that Zehra used "context clues, sentence structure, structural analysis, and phonic analysis to read new passages in a functional, effective, and strategic manner."

Zehra's standardized test scores at the end of first grade were promising as well. She accurately read most of the words for Level 2 (first grade equivalent) on a basic reading test for native-English speakers. On the DRA, she read Level 16 text with 94% accuracy (or at the instructional level), indicating that her decoding skills had substantially improved. The tester reported that her miscues (variation from the text) sometimes interfered with meaning, and that she read slowly, word by word or in short phrases. She mainly used letters or sounds to solve reading problems, and did not appeal for any help.

Despite her strengths as a developing reader, Zehra still experienced some difficulties in English reading. Due to her limited oral English proficiency, she had difficulty understanding long instructions in her workbook or in her teacher's literacy instruction. For instance in May, she insistently asked the first author for explanations of the instructions, even though her teacher told Zehra that she could do it on her own. Zehra was able to decode the instructions, but could not comprehend them; therefore, she was not sure what was required. As shown in the transcript below, it was not until after she confirmed her understanding of the instructions in Turkish that she was able to complete the exercises:

ZEHRA: [to the researcher, showing instructions in the workbook] Burda ne oluyor? [What is happening here?]

RESEARCHER: [makes Zehra read the instructions, then explains them in English]

ZEHRA: Resim yapacakmışız, yanlarına isimlerini yazacakmışız. [We are supposed to draw pictures and write their names next to them.]

RESEARCHER: İsimlerin başharfini. [The initial letters of the names.]

...

ZEHRA: Böyle mi? Oldu mu? [Like this? Is this correct?]

RESEARCHER: Başka ne yapmak gerekiyor? [What else is to be done?] [Reads the sentence for Zehra]

ZEHRA: [writes *d* on *dog* and *v* on *van*] Bitti mi? [Is it done?]

Zehra also focused more on decoding texts than on comprehending them. She did not want to stop and discuss a story, and seemed disinterested in any text discussion. As shown in the transcript below, she did not want to discuss the story even when the teacher directed her to answer the questions by looking at the illustrations:

TEACHER: Zehra, what season is it?

ZEHRA: I don't know.

TEACHER: In that picture, what season is it?

ZEHRA: [turns the page]

...

TEACHER: This. Is it summer outside?

ZEHRA: Yes. No.
TEACHER: No. It's what?
ZEHRA: Aaaaaaa.
STUDENTS: Cold.
TEACHER: Winter.

Her standardized test scores support the finding that Zehra mainly focused on form. According to the tester's comments, even though she did well with reading aloud, Zehra's retelling indicated that she "missed the point of the story and misunderstood some parts." She did not provide complete information on the characters, and "couldn't determine the ending of the story," although she included special words from the story and told the events in sequence. The tester concluded that Zehra needed to "work on comprehension."

Understanding Zehra's Reading Processes

During the summer following her first year in the U.S., Zehra read an English narrative text and an English expository text for the performance assessments that the researcher conducted. She read each text only once, and chose to answer the researcher's questions in English even though the researcher told her she could use Turkish or English.

Narrative Text: Issues Related to L2 Development

While reading the narrative text, Zehra did not ask any questions or make any comments. She was interested in looking at the pictures only after finishing the text. She completed reading the text in two-and-a-half minutes, did not need any decoding assistance, and was not corrected. She decoded 92% of the text accurately, making only 15 miscues out of 186 words. Almost half of her miscues (47%) were substitutions, and the other half (53%) omissions and nonsense words.

Many of Zehra's miscues reflected her linguistic development in English. Just as she made tense mistakes while speaking, she also made tense mistakes while reading. In both speaking and reading, she used present tense verbs for irregular past tense verbs, as shown in her reading below:

ZEHRA: [reads] She throw [sic: threw] a penny into the well and made a wish. / Ouch/ [sic: ouch] said the well. The next day [sic: the] mouse come [sic: came] back again. She throw [sic: threw] a penny into the well ... The mouse run [sic: ran] home.

Most of the tense miscues did not adversely affect her comprehension. However, one word that she claimed not to know was *threw*, which she later acknowledged understanding when she heard the researcher use the present tense in the example shown below:

ZEHRA: [scans the text] I don't know this one.
RESEARCHER: This one? Threw.
ZEHRA: Threw.
RESEARCHER: She throws the money.
ZEHRA: Oh, yeah.

All of her omissions were with the article *the*, the lack of which did not drastically affect the story's meaning. Zehra also omitted articles in her speech and writing, which probably reflects the non-existence of articles in Turkish.

Zehra's retelling of the story was rather short; she mentioned the characters, part of the main theme, and the resolution, but did not provide the main problem or the recurrence of plot episodes. She also added some items that were not written in the text (see italics), apparently drawn from her background knowledge: "The mouse was, going to the well and and saying, 'I wish,' something like, '*I wanna be better. I wanna be get big,*' like that. *But is won't getting true...*" Her omission of the main problem (i.e., that the well says *ouch* when a penny is thrown into it) was linked to her difficulty with the word *ouch*. Zehra did not include the word or its role in the story in her retelling, and it was not until the researcher elicited the word that she indicated she understood it, as shown in the following transcript:

RESEARCHER: What does it [the well] say?
ZEHRA: Your ticket doesn't get true [through].
RESEARCHER: Does it say that?
ZEHRA: Yes.
RESEARCHER: Ok. I think the well also says something like, *ouch!*
...
RESEARCHER: What does that mean?
ZEHRA: I don't know.
RESEARCHER: When ... when you hit something and you hurt yourself?
ZEHRA: Yeah, I know that. You say "ouch."

After hearing the researcher's clarification, Zehra was able to verbalize her comprehension of the main problem in the story:

RESEARCHER: Mmh. So why did the well say "ouch?"
ZEHRA: Because the penny – I think the penny hurts.
RESEARCHER: Aha. I think so. So, what does the mouse do?
ZEHRA: The mouse say, say "why you are saying ouch?"
RESEARCHER: What does she do then? What does the mouse do? Run home and do what?
ZEHRA: ... Oh, I understand. It's when you throw it, it's hurting, ... so the well – doesn't take it true [through] because its, she's hurted him.

RESEARCHER: Yes.

ZEHRA: Then she takes the pillow, put in there, then when she put the penny, that doesn't hurt her.

Expository Text: Difficulties with Vocabulary and Comprehension

Zehra's reading speed for the expository text was two minutes. The text consisted of 73 words, and Zehra made six miscues, decoding with 92% accuracy. All of her miscues were word substitutions, most of which (83%) changed the meaning of the text, such as saying *wool* instead of *whale*, as shown below:

ZEHRA: [reads] The biggest animal does not live on land. It is a wool [*sic*: whale], and it lives in the sea.

Because it was important for Zehra to understand that the passage was about a whale, the researcher corrected her miscue. However, Zehra's responses to the comprehension questions as well as her retelling indicated that she still did not comprehend the expository passage. In the transcript below, she tried to answer the researcher's question based on the pictures, her background knowledge, and imagination:

RESEARCHER: Why does the whale go up on the sea?

ZEHRA: Because, she's going to look at the, the water, jump at the water, she was running, I think.

Zehra seemed to be aware of her miscomprehension. In the following transcript after reading part of the passage, she asked a question to confirm her understanding:

ZEHRA: [reads] In the sea. You can ride on a boat and watch. [asks] Are they in the boat?

Zehra's difficulty in comprehending the last paragraph of the text probably resulted from her limited knowledge of the words in it, since three of the four words that she previously had reported as unknown were from this part of the text (*wide*, *perhaps*, *flat*, and *sink*). Although her ESL teacher had extensively covered the concept of *sink* and practiced the word in an experiment in her ESL class, Zehra did not remember what it meant in a different context.

English Writing Development

Writing observations and samples were from the ESL classroom and the performance task session. Zehra wrote in English by first sounding out words. She correctly spelled commonly used English words and showed steady improvement with the spelling of more complex words. Sometimes, she asked for help with the spelling of words. Other times, she volunteered spelling help for other students in the class. She liked spelling and often created a game by asking for help and providing help, as shown in the transcript below:

ZEHRA: How you spell *are*?
RESEARCHER: *Are*?
ZEHRA: Oh, yeah, I know.
ALP: [to the teacher] This?
ZEHRA: I know, t–h.

When problems with meaning occurred in her writing, they usually were due to her developing English (omission of key words or use of incorrect syntax or grammar), rather than spelling, as demonstrated in the following writing sample: "The child play The mom and are hot."

The length and quality of Zehra's written products also paralleled her English-language development. For instance, her ESL journal entries at the beginning of the spring semester consisted of formulaic phrases and simple, short sentences, such as: "This is the sun. This is a cat. This is water." Toward the end of the semester, her sentences not only were longer and more complex, but they also included invented spelling (italics), as demonstrated in the following writing: "Today is Tuesday April 15 2003 I go to the zoo. I see *manke*. And I see a horse." "I do not like boys *becoze* boys play cars I do not like play cars I like *barbiz*."

Zehra sometimes used an L2 strategy to cope with the challenges of writing in English, which we have labeled avoidance. For instance, when her ESL teacher gave her a word to write about in her ESL journal, she exchanged it (usually with Alp) if she was not sure what it meant or if she did not like it. Similarly, on the performance task, when she thought her use of a particular word (*language*) might be problematic, she chose a different word (*talk*).

At the end of the spring semester, Zehra's ESL teacher ranked her English writing skills six out of 11 (i.e., *invents spellings, story is a single factual statement, message is understandable [decipherable]*). According to the ESL report card, Zehra's vocabulary use, summaries, and effort in writing had improved from *average* to *excellent*, while her spelling, grammar, and punctuation remained *average*. In her ESL work, she frequently omitted periods and commas, and sometimes used upper- and lower-case letters inappropriately, as demonstrated in the following example: "I like Martians. because she is flying. I have one bird shie is very cute"

In many ways, Zehra's writing on the performance task in the summer after first grade paralleled what she did in the ESL class toward the end of first grade. For example, in the letter below, which she wrote for the performance task, she wrote all the words in lower-case, did not use any punctuation marks, and used invented spelling (italics) for several words: "*dir* pavla in turkey the homes are so *beg* its fun to play *wite* you *youl lav* to play at turkey in turkey my *frands* are talk so difficult *dane* you bye" In contrast, her free writing almost always was accompanied by a drawing and included dialog between characters, suggesting that she viewed writing as a way for people to express themselves. She typically did not ask how to spell words when she wrote on her own. For example, while waiting for the English performance task session, she voluntarily drew pictures and wrote formulaic sentences on the board in English, using some invented spelling (indicated by italics): "No, I can't do it, you do it *plece. Okeye.* I *wil halp* her *tanks* you *welkim.*"

Zehra's Literacy Development in Turkish

The Influence of English on Turkish Reading

Because English classes started first, Zehra was introduced to the English alphabet before the Turkish alphabet. For a short period of time at the beginning of the year, Zehra insisted on saying the Turkish alphabet in English. However, by February, she only had minor problems with the sounds and letters of the Turkish alphabet, and her Turkish reading only occasionally was influenced by her English knowledge. For example, she had difficulty differentiating between *e* in English and *i* in Turkish because they sound the same, and mixed them up for a while (e.g., read and wrote *zel* instead of the correct form *zil*). Another example occurred at the end of the school year when she read the word *canımı* as *kanımı*. In Turkish, *c* is never pronounced as a /k/, so this is an obvious transfer from her L2. She did not self-correct, most probably because *kanımı* is also a meaningful word in Turkish.

Developmental Trend in Turkish Reading

Similar to other beginning readers in Turkish, Zehra did have problems sounding out the letter for soft g (ğ). This sound is a slightly difficult one for beginning readers in Turkish because it is a silent sound that mainly elongates the vowel before it. Therefore, during the early phases of her Turkish reading development, Zehra needed support and confirmation while decoding words with the soft g. In April, she even verbalized this struggle by commenting on her own abilities: "Yumuşak g olunca yanlış söylüyorum, çünkü yumuşak g'yi zor okuyorum. [When it is a soft g, I say it the wrong way, because I can hardly read soft g.]"

Dual Focus on Decoding and Comprehension during Turkish Reading

Early in the fall semester, Zehra was able to decode basic Turkish words. In fact, she was the first of the three first graders to read in Turkish. By the end of the first semester, she was able to decode and read new words and sentences by herself. She also monitored and self-corrected (in italics in the translation) her own reading: "Benim kedim miyav diyor, der. [My cat is *saying*, says meow.]"

In contrast to her overemphasis on decoding in English, Zehra did attend to meaning in her Turkish reading. Her attention to meaning was inferred from the comments she made about the content of texts, as illustrated in the following example, which occurred toward the end of her second semester at school. In this example, she is commenting on the treatment of a character in the story: "Bu çok iyi ama ona kötülük yapıyorlar. [He is very good, but they're being bad to him.]" Another indication of her attention to meaning was that she first read by slowly sounding out the letters, then she repeated the whole sentence to herself, sometimes questioning the meaning of what she read: "Koş okul. [Run school.]" [asks] "Koş okul mu? [Run school?]"

A Self-Confident Turkish Reader and Writer

Zehra enjoyed literacy activities and often volunteered to read and write in the Turkish class. In addition, her competency in literacy gave her a sense of efficacy, as can be seen in the following comments, in which she credits herself as a learner: "Okuma yazmayı tek başıma öğrendim. Kitabımdaki harflerden okudum. Herşeyi biliyorum. [I learned reading and writing by myself. I read from the letters in my book. I know everything.]"

Occasionally she rated some texts as "too easy" or as "baby work" and refused to read basic sentences. As shown in the following two examples, Zehra also complained about the reading of her peers: "Ben okumayı biliyorum, onlar okusunlar. [I know how to read, they should read.]" "Çok yavaş okudukları için ben sıkılıyorum. [I get bored, because they read too slowly.]" Her confidence led her to read extensively, and she sometimes bragged about her ability to read difficult books: "Alp baksana, ne kadar zor yeri okuyorum. [Alp look, I am reading a really difficult part.]"

During the Turkish task session in the summer, she read both narrative and expository texts in a fast and fluent way. She read the texts by sounding out the letters and had very few miscues. Although her retellings were short, her answers to the comprehension and discussion questions revealed that she understood all parts of the texts. However, just as in her English task performance, she was disinclined to talk about the expository text and said that it was boring, indicating that she did not enjoy informational pieces as much as stories.

Metalinguistic Awareness

It was in the Turkish class that Zehra often commented on the similarities and differences between the Turkish and English-language systems. During alphabet practice, for example, she reflected on the differences between the two alphabets and what Americans would not know: "Amerikalılar *ö'yü* bilmiyorlar. [Americans don't know *ö*.]" She also was able to verbalize her thinking during the second semester about the difference between *e* in English and *i* in Turkish: "*e* İngilizce'de *i*, *i* Türkçe'de *i*. [e is i in English, i is i in Turkish.]"

When Zehra made metalinguistic connections between English and Turkish, she seemed to focus on the sounds and orthographic differences. For instance, while studying the syllable *gu* in May, she said "*Gum*, İngilizce'de sakız demek. [Gum, means chewing-gum in English.]" She said *fun* when she read and heard the Turkish syllable *fa*, and *food* when she read and heard the Turkish syllable *fu*.

She also demonstrated metalinguistic awareness by drawing attention to how changing letters in Turkish words could result in different English or Turkish meanings. For example, after reading the word *Leman* in Turkish, a proper name, she pointed out that changing the "a" to an "o" would result in the English word "lemon": "*o* olsaydı *limon* olurdu. [If that was an o it would be lemon.]" Similarly, during reading practice, when she saw the Turkish word *pencere* [window], she said "Türkçe'de *pen* kalem değil, başka kalem, tükenmez kalem. [Pen in Turkish is not pencil, it's another pencil, it's an ink pen.]"

Characteristics of her Turkish Writing

When Zehra wrote in Turkish, she sounded out the letters in the words. She managed to write basic words correctly without any difficulty. Although there is a great amount of one-to-one sound–letter correspondence in Turkish, the spoken language involves the collapsing of some sounds; hence it is slightly different from the written language. Therefore, Zehra usually wrote new or complex words as she heard herself saying them, creating certain misspellings, such as writing *bissürü* or *büsürü* instead of *bir sürü*, *datdı* instead of *dağıttı*, *onla* instead of *onunla*, and *gelecene* instead of *geleceğine*. When writing in the Turkish class, she did not demonstrate her habit of consulting others for spelling as frequently as she did in English, most probably because of her comfort level with the Turkish language and its spelling regularities.

Zehra was not very meticulous about copying words or sentences. She frequently was instructed and corrected, yet these kinds of mistakes continued in Turkish even after she finished first grade. For example, she rewrote the same words (e.g., *Zehra diledi diledi*), then self-corrected as she read them (*Zehra özür diledi*).

As in her English writing, Zehra's main problem in Turkish writing was mechanics. She interchangeably used upper and lower case characters and omitted commas and periods. This disinterest toward using writing mechanics lasted throughout the school year.

In the second semester, Zehra was able to express herself freely through writing, and became more motivated to write in Turkish. In her spare time in class, she independently and voluntarily wrote sentences and stories in her notebook. A drawing almost always preceded her writing. Similar to what she did prior to the English performance task, she wrote in Turkish on the board (invented spelling is italicized): "Bir adam ateş eder. Sonra *dier* adamda kendisini *kurtarıor*. [*sic*: Bir adam ateş eder. Sonra diğer adam da kendisini kurtarıyor.] [A man shoots a gun. Then the other man is saving himself.]

Zehra's writing in Turkish was more sophisticated than her writing in English. For example, in the writing sample below (which was part of the Turkish performance task), she used a range of vocabulary and moved beyond formulaic phrases to communicate with a friend in Turkey. She was more confident in her Turkish writing, and did not ask for help or confirmation of the spelling. For nine of the 30 words, she used invented spelling. However, similar to her English writing, she did not use any punctuation or capitalization except for the first word of the paragraph:

> Sevg]ili başak *buruya gelecene* çok sevindim *burdaki okular* çok güzel *öret-menler* çok iyi *deşik otobisler* var okulda çok yazı *yazıoruz dışarda* çok arkadaşlarım var *burda ingilijle* sınıfı var görüşürüz zehra [*sic*: Sevgili Başak, buraya geleceğine çok sevindim. Buradaki okullar çok güzel, öğretmenler çok iyi, değişik otobüsler var. Okulda çok yazı yazıyoruz. Dışarıda çok arkadaşlarım var. Burada İngilizce sınıfı var. Görüşürüz, Zehra]
> [Dear başak I am so happy that you will be coming here the schools here are very nice the teachers are very good there are different buses we write a lot at school I have many friends outside there is an english class here see you zehra]

Pedagogical Implications

Zehra's story illustrates key issues that educational personnel and parents need to understand about beginning English learners. We have organized the issues according to the three questions posed at the beginning of the chapter.

Adjusting to a New Academic Environment

Similar to other L2 learners who enter school without knowing the school language, Zehra had problems understanding English instruction (Igoa, 1995; Krashen, 1985). Her quiet and shy behavior in the ESL and English mainstream classrooms was in marked contrast to her confident behavior in the Turkish classroom, and later social behavior in her ESL classroom. In fact, her initial behavior suggested she was undergoing the L2 silent period described by Krashen (1981).

Acquiring a New Language

Although Zehra's ESL teacher characterized her L2 development as slower than other L2 learners, according to the literature, she was quite normal (Cummins,

1981; Thomas & Collier, 2001). Emergent bilingual children vary considerably in the amount of time that it takes them to develop social and academic proficiency in their L2. Also, it is clear that she was undergoing a lot of emotional stress, which adversely influenced the affective filter (Krashen, 1985).

Developing Literacy in Two Languages

Given Zehra's lack of L1 literacy development and beginning L2 status, we should not be surprised that introducing her to the English alphabet before she was introduced to the Turkish alphabet initially confused her about how to say either alphabet. However, it is important to note that she resolved this fairly quickly. As a bilingual, she demonstrated heightened metalinguistic awareness, which seemed to facilitate her ability to sort out the similarities and differences in the two languages (García, 2000).

The fact that Zehra developed strong decoding and reading comprehension skills in Turkish, but only developed strong decoding skills in English, suggests that her ability to comprehend English text was limited by her oral English proficiency and the type of reading instruction she received (Snow, 2006). She probably would have benefited from English reading instruction that explicitly emphasized text comprehension and taught her the meanings of key vocabulary words in the texts she was decoding. She illustrated García and Bauer's (1994) finding that many L2 learners will not automatically understand all the English words they can decode because the words are not in their oral English vocabulary, as they are for many English-speaking students.

When we compare Zehra's literacy development in Turkish to her literacy development in English, it is clear that receiving literacy instruction in a language she understood was important for Zehra (Francis et al., 2006). Although she only received 30 minutes of daily Turkish instruction, her excellent progress in becoming literate in Turkish showed the key role that learning in Turkish, the language she knew best, played for her. Her ESL status seemed to hide her academic and literacy potential.

When school personnel design, implement, and evaluate different types of bilingual and ESL programs, they need to examine the amount and type of instruction L2 learners receive in each of the instructional language settings and the instructional coordination that occurs across the settings. We question how useful the 185 minutes Zehra spent in the all-English mainstream classroom were for her English acquisition and literacy development, especially when for much of the school year, the mainstream teacher prevented her from participating in informal literacy activities and did not attempt to use ESL techniques or provide L1 resources. In Zehra's case, providing more classroom time for instruction in Turkish and ESL, and coordinating literacy and content-area instruction across the three classrooms (Turkish, ESL, and all English) might have been beneficial. For example, a coordinated focus on the same content-area topics in the Turkish and ESL classrooms – in which the Turkish instructor introduced new vocabulary and content, and the ESL teacher taught the English labels for the vocabulary and used ESL techniques to expand on the content previously taught in Turkish – might have enhanced Zehra's comprehension of content-area instruction in English and provided her with the necessary background knowledge to improve her decoding and comprehension of English expository text.

Zehra's story also illustrates the importance of meeting with parents of new English learners at the very beginning of the school year to explain how the school wants them to support their children's learning. School personnel need to remember that immigrant/foreign parents often do not understand how they can help support their children's academic learning in English when they do not speak the language well. They need to be told about cross-linguistic transfer, the importance of further developing their child's L1 academic and literacy development, and how to work with the school to support their child's development in both languages.

Concluding Remarks

Zehra's story shows that simply providing young English learners, who are not already literate, with L1 and L2 literacy instruction is not enough to ensure their effective L2 literacy or biliterate development. Important considerations include the sequencing and coordination of instruction in the two languages and the provision of high quality literacy instruction designed to address the specific needs of bilinguals. Finally, educational personnel and parents need to understand the long-term benefits of providing children with the continued opportunity to develop their bilingualism and biliteracy. Given Zehra's strong comprehension and writing skills in Turkish, and what we know about cross-linguistic transfer, providing her with continued literacy instruction in Turkish, along with high quality ESL and English literacy instruction, should aid her later development of strong reading comprehension and writing skills in English.

References

August, D., & Shanahan, T. (Eds.). (2006). *Developing literacy in second-language learners: Report of the National Literacy Panel on language-minority children and youth.* Mahwah, NJ: Lawrence Erlbaum.

Barrera, R. (1984). Bilingual reading in the primary grades: Some questions about questionable views and practices. In T. H. Escobedo (Ed.), *Early childhood bilingual education: A Hispanic perspective* (pp. 164–184). New York: Teachers College Press.

Bialystok, E. (2002). Acquisition of literacy in bilingual children: A framework for research. *Language Learning, 52*(1), 159–199.

Commins, N. L., & Miramontes, O. B. (2005). *Linguistic diversity and teaching.* Mahwah, NJ: Lawrence Erlbaum.

Cummins, J. (1981). The role of primary language development in promoting educational success for language minority students. In California State Department of Education (Ed.), *Schooling and language minority students: A theoretical framework* (pp. 3–49). Los Angeles: Evaluation, Dissemination, and Assessment Center.

Cummins, J. (1989). *Empowering minority children.* Sacramento CA: California Association for Bilingual Education.

Echevarría, J., Vogt, M., & Short, D. J. (2008). *Making content comprehensible for English Learners: The SIOP model* (3rd ed.). Boston, MA: Pearson/Allyn & Bacon.

Francis, D. J., Lesaux, N. K., & August, D. (2006). Language of instruction. In D. August & T. Shanahan (Eds.), *Developing literacy in second-language learners: Report of the National Literacy Panel on Language-Minority Children and Youth* (pp. 365–414). Mahwah, NJ: Lawrence Erlbaum.

García, G. (2000). Bilingual children's reading. In M. L. Kamil, P. B. Mosenthal, P. D. Pearson, & R. Barr (Eds.), *Handbook of reading research, volume III* (pp. 813–834). Mahwah, NJ: Lawrence Erlbaum.

García, G. E., & Bauer, E. B. (1994). The selection and use of English text with young English language learners. In J. V. Hoffman & D. L. Schallert (Eds.), *The texts in elementary classrooms* (pp. 177–194). Mahwah, NJ: Lawrence Erlbaum.

Glaser, B. G., & Strauss, A. (1967). *The discovery of grounded theory: Strategies for qualitative research.* New York: Aldine.

Hudelson, S. (1984). Kan yu ret an rayt en ingles: Children become literate in English as a second language. *TESOL Quarterly, 18*(2), 221–238.

Igoa, C. (1995). *The inner world of the immigrant child.* Mahwah, NJ: Lawrence Erlbaum.

Krashen, S. D. (1981). *Second language acquisition and second language learning.* Oxford: Pergamon Press.

Krashen, S. D. (1985). *Inquiries and insights.* Hayward, CA: Alemany Press.

Krathwohl, D. R. (1998). *Methods of educational and social science research: An integrated approach* (2nd ed.). New York: Addison-Wesley Educational Publishers.

Lesaux, N. K., & Geva, E. (2006). Synthesis: Development of literacy in language-minority students. In D. August & T. Shanahan (Eds.), *Developing literacy in second-language learners: Report of the National Literacy Panel on language-minority children and youth* (pp. 53–74). Mahwah, NJ: Lawrence Erlbaum.

Lesaux, N. K., with Koda, K., Siegel, L. S., & Shanahan, T. (2006). Development of literacy. In D. August & T. Shanahan (Eds.), *Developing literacy in second-language learners: Report of the National Literacy Panel on language-minority children and youth* (pp. 75–122). Mahwah, NJ: Lawrence Erlbaum.

Snow, C. (2006). Cross-cutting themes and future research directions. In D. August & T. Shanahan (Eds.), *Developing literacy in second-language learners: Report of the National Literacy Panel on language-minority children and youth* (pp. 631–651). Mahwah, NJ: Lawrence Erlbaum.

Strauss, A., and Corbin, J. (1994). Grounded theory methodology: An overview. In N. K. Denzin & Y. S. Lincoln (Eds.), *Handbook of qualitative research* (pp. 273–285). London: Sage.

Thomas, W., & Collier, V. (2001). *A national study of school effectiveness for language minority students' long-term achievement.* Berkeley, CA: Center for Research on Education, Diversity, and Excellence (CREDE).

7

TRAVELING THE BILITERACY HIGHWAY

Framing Biliteracy from Students' Writings[1]

María Fránquiz

Across the United States of America the prevailing climate of hostility toward the use of non-English languages influences the social construction of literacy in schools. The ways that young Latina/o children attending a rural school mediate messages from the wider community will be made visible in the research reported in this chapter.

I am not the first to argue that young children learn about language and literacy in the same way they learn about other experiences – by imitating, exploring, trying out new ideas, and participating in their in- and out-of-school cultures. These language and literacy experiences provide the foundation on which children's learning, identity formation, and socialization is based (Garcia, 1991). With many young children from Latina/o communities, particularly those who live along the U.S./Mexico borders, there is exposure to two languages within the context of their daily lives. The ways that these language and literacy experiences can be effective resources for children in classroom literacy events is often misunderstood. The intent of this chapter is to show how these resources can be useful for communicating, making meaning, and constructing one's identity as a bilingual person. New understanding is needed in an era of shifting demographics.

Shifting Demographics and Early Childhood Participation Rates

It is a fact that Latina/os are becoming an increasing presence across the country (U.S. Census Bureau, 2004). According to Calderón et al., (2004) Latina/os make up one in five children under the age of five. It is estimated that by 2050, the number of Latina/o children under five will increase by 146 percent.

Historically, Latina/os have concentrated in nine states (CA, TX, NY, FL, IL, AZ, NJ, CO, and NM); however, they are now a presence in every state in the U.S. (Hernandez, 2006). The result of this demographic trend for early childhood educators is that more Latina/o students are entering programs earlier nationwide.

While attending some form of preschool prior to formal schooling has now become normative in the United States (Takanishi, 2004), Latina/o children have been reported as having the lowest preschool participation rates (Brandon, 2004). In 1999, the White House released a report, *Latinos in America*, which found Latina/os under the age of five were less likely to be enrolled in early childhood programs than other groups: 20 percent as compared to 42 percent of non-Latino whites. The reasons for these reduced participation rates have not been found to reflect any negative attitudes by Latino families toward preschool education. A survey of 1,000 Latino families across the country found that 75 percent considered it "very important" that children attend prekindergarten, and 95 percent believed that attending prekindergarten was an advantage for school success (Pérez & Zarate, 2006). Thus, as focus has shifted to Latina/os in early childhood education, more is being done to address the disparity in preschool participation rates among Latina/os (Valdez & Fránquiz, 2009). In the research reported in this chapter, a rural community along the U.S./Mexico border with a majority Mexican heritage population was selected for study because it exhibits an extremely high participation rate of children attending preschool.

Persistent Problem Leads to Research Project

In early childhood settings the maintenance of the Spanish heritage language has typically been seen as a problem (Escamilla, 2006) to be expunged from Latina/o students rather than as a resource for their learning or as a fundamental human right (Ruiz, 1984; Skutnabb-Kangas, 2000). Consequently, children from Spanish speaking households are often misidentified as English-language learners (ELLs) and placed in special language programs when they are often native speakers of an ethnic dialect such as Chicano or Puerto Rican English (Zentella, 2005). The educational needs of such youngsters are very different from the needs of monolingual Spanish-speaking children who are recently arrived in the United States. The former are bilingual. They are accustomed to English borrowings and frequent language alternations that are labeled Spanglish, Tex-Mex, or *pocho*. However, these bilingual-bidialectical youngsters do function to some degree in both English and Spanish (Valdés, 2000). On the other hand, the monolingual (im)migrant students are unfamiliar with the language alternations of their ethnic peers, and typically are immersed in language programs that strongly encourage them to lose their fluency in Spanish as they acquire English proficiency (Portes & Hao, 1998; Wong-Filmore, 2000). While most research does not account for the unique language and literacy needs of Latina/o bilingual-bidialectical children from the needs of (im)migrant students, there is even less attention given to the language and literacy needs of Latina/o children attending schools in rural settings.

This chapter specifically addresses the limited access of Mexican-American children living in rural Texas to biliteracy development. Although much is written concerning the need to "honor student voices" (Oldfather, 1993, p. 672), there is little research that locates young bilingual students' voices in their writing as they demonstrate potential for becoming biliterate. To address this gap, the objective of the chapter is to provide samples of student work and discourse that clearly reflect how opportunities provided in a small rural school impacted students' orientation toward their heritage language. Thus, the research question considered is: In what ways do children in a borderlands rural community demonstrate biliterate potential through their writing in prekindergarten to second grade?

Overview of Research Literature on Biliteracy

Unleashing Languages on a Biliteracy Highway

In 1989, Hornberger published a comprehensive review of the literature on biliteracy development. She asserted that the most productive settings for developing biliteracy exemplify a balance between attention to receptive and productive skills, between oral and written languages, and between the use of native language and second language. Accordingly, the goal of biliteracy is for students to have the type of literacy encounters where they can arrive at a proficient level of English language and subject area literacy without detriment to their home language and literacy development. Since thousands of young students attend schools located near the U.S./Mexican border and daily bring to school their language and their culture, I will use a metaphor of children taking a successful trip on a biliteracy highway. This metaphor will be used in this chapter to show how students in a rural community in the U.S./Mexico borderlands took up opportunities to "unleash" their biliteracy potential when English and Spanish were "promoted, modeled, valued, nurtured, legitimized and utilized" (De La Luz Reyes, 2001, p. 119) during their journey in a planned unit of study.

Research in contexts with significant Latina/o student population has focused on better understanding how the presence of two languages impacts learning, teaching, and academic outcomes for young children. This research for the most part concludes that language input and support for literacy in the early years are predictive of later success in school (Tabors & Snow, 2001). Such research suggests that bilingualism and biliteracy are interrelated language processes that develop in a parallel fashion with one enriching the other (Grosjean, 1982; Moll

& Dworin, 1996; Pérez & Torres-Guzman, 1996; Reyes, 2006). However, these parallel paths of development in two languages intersect at many points along a bilingual/biliteracy continuum (Hornberger, 1989, 2003) or, in metaphorical terms, a biliteracy highway. For example, Moll and Dworin (1996) described case studies of elementary Latina/o students where multiple and intersecting pathways to biliteracy were impacted by students' histories, the social contexts they have for learning, and their opportunities to use each language in language and literacy events. I agree with the premise undergirding these research projects that assumes an emerging bilingual person is not a "double-monolingual" person. Rather, an emerging bilingual person has linguistic resources beyond those of a monolingual person in either of her languages. Becoming bilingual, then, requires the ability to employ language resources from two codes strategically and with great sensitivity to contextual factors (Martínez-Roldán & Fránquiz, 2009).

Research on biliteracy also suggests that literacy development for someone who is exposed to two languages presents itself in some unique ways and must be studied from a bilingual perspective (Berzins & López, 2001; De La Luz Reyes, 2001; Dworin, 2003; Gort, 2006; Hornberger, 2003; Moll & Dworin, 1996; Moll et al., 2001; Reyes, 2006). As a result, recent studies have sought to document this uniqueness. Among the characteristics documented are: (a) tracing the use of *strategic code-switching* (Gort, 2006), or *strategic translation* (Fránquiz, 2008), where the alternating of languages is used purposefully for instructional and learning purposes, (b) identifying the practice of *code-switching* and the use of a dialect such as Spanglish as a routine language practice (Poplack, 1980; Gumperz, 1972; Zentella, 1997, Martínez-Roldán & Sayer, 2006; Reyes, 2006), (c) the phenomenon of *spontaneous biliteracy* where the development of literacy in one language occurs despite not receiving literacy instruction in both languages (De La Luz Reyes, 2001; Gort, 2006), (d) the occurrence of *interliteracy* where in the process of developing a two language system, linguistic elements of one language are used in the other language (Gort, 2006), and (e) the *bidirectional* nature of bilingualism and biliteracy development between parents and their children and children with their peers (Reyes, 2006). Unfortunately, such characteristics documented in the language development of young children too often goes untapped, is discredited, and remains a hidden fund of knowledge (Martínez-Roldán & Fránquiz, 2009).

In many of the cases documented in the research on biliteracy, there were key factors that facilitated the presence of these phenomena in the classrooms. For example, De La Luz Reyes (2001) found that as she followed four bilingual girls from K-2 grade, it was the teacher's ability to set up an environment that respected the use of both languages without any negative stigma that promoted the strong foundation for the development of biliteracy. Another key factor is that literacy experiences be connected to the local context in order to assist students in gaining meaningful understanding of their multiple realities (Harris,

1997; Jiménez & Gomez, 1996; Moll et al., 1992). Laliberty (2001) used this premise in her classrooms and found that inviting bilingual students to tap into lived experiences in the official space of the classroom improved the quality of their writing development. These factors of unmarked languages in the classroom and connecting language to children's lived experiences were important features of the literacy events documented in the rural setting selected for study.

Setting and Methods

The Setting: Life in Encinal, Texas

Texas provides a rich context for studying issues surrounding bilingualism and education. Unlike other U.S. states that have passed ballot initiatives dismantling bilingual education (i.e., California, Arizona, and Massachusetts), it is a state that has strong legislative support for bilingual education. On the other hand, Texas in the twentieth century has not always favored bilingualism among its residents and school children and the Spanish language has often been a target for erasure (Blanton, 2007, González, 1999; San Miguel, 1999). These subtractive orientations many times impact parental decisions about the preschool and bilingual education participation of their children.

The rural community central to this study is Encinal, Texas. It is located 37 miles from the Texas/Mexico border with a total population at the time of the study of 620. In the past, Encinal was an agricultural community but more current employment is related to ranching. There is one elementary school serving a majority Mexican-origin population (97 percent). The school is part of the Cotulla Independent School District (ISD). Once students reach middle and high school, they travel 30 miles to and from Cotulla. In contrast to urban districts such as nearby Laredo ISD, the rural schools that comprise Cotulla ISD are isolated from many cultural and educational resources. Consequently, there is limited availability of enrichment programs for school-age children.

At the time of the study (2003–2005) Spanish was spoken by 57 percent of the families of the children attending Encinal Elementary School. Enrollment at the school during the time of the study did not exceed a total of 100 students from prekindergarten to fifth grade. There was one class at each grade level and two preschool classes. The building has all classes facing the library that is located at the center of the school. The school is part of a unified school district that encompasses various other rural communities and at the time of the study there were no bilingual services delivered at these rural school sites. In order to participate in bilingual education it was necessary for children to ride the school bus to the larger neighboring city of Cotulla where bilingual classes were offered. This was the same school bus that transported secondary students to their middle and high school classes. Most families opted not to send their young children on the long school bus ride to receive bilingual literacy services.

Ethnographic Stance for the Study of Biliteracy in a Rural Community

In order to learn how these isolated ranching communities addressed the lack of cultural and educational resources, the two-year long ethnographic study was not restricted to study in the elementary school. Accordingly, data were collected in community spaces such as the local café, park, veteran hall, and homes of artists, teachers, and students as well as in the school. During the first year of the study the researchers focused on documenting opportunities for children's development and maintenance of bilingualism, biculturalism, and biliteracy through visual literacy events conducted in a community arts center (*Hecho en Encinal*/Made in Encinal) adjacent to the school. These activities included the use of Spanish and English for interpreting, using, appreciating, and creating images using both conventional and twenty-first century media in ways that advance thinking, decision making, communicating, and learning (see Fránquiz & Brochin, 2006). During the second year the focus was on documenting students' potential for biliteracy in a majority English-only environment at the school.

Several community members were key informants if not collaborators in the ethnographic study. Janet Krueger, a local visual artist living on a ranch near the city of Encinal, facilitated entry into sites during our research project. She was instrumental in helping the researchers understand the wide range of Spanish and English ideologies within the school community and in providing solutions to address the disparities between visual arts opportunities in urban places and those available in the rural community where she chose to live. She and Donna Lednicky, an author and writer, shared the same vision. Together, in 1999 they opened the doors of *Hecho en Encinal* and offered a variety of after-school programs and community workshops. The programs brought visual and performing arts including dance, music, creative writing, and art to the students and families. As stated earlier, the trailer that is home to the community arts center is located on the same grounds as Encinal Elementary School. Because my research assistant and I were centered in an ethnographic perspective, we spent time in the trailer, at the school, and in all the community spaces previously mentioned.

One of our earliest observations in the small rural community related to language use. Although adults and children tended to use English when speaking with us, we noticed that the grandparents typically used Spanish with their grandchildren and us. The children sometimes also used Spanish or Spanglish when talking to each other in the playground, stores, and park. For the purposes of this chapter, student-produced artifacts from preschool to second grade are analyzed to show evidence of emergent bilingual and biliterate identities in a community that in the past had experienced strong doses of linguicism. Linguicism arises when "ideologies and structures ... are used to legitimate, effectuate, and reproduce an unequal division of power and resources between groups that are defined on the basis of language" (Skutnabb-Kangas, 1988, p. 46).

Theoretical Perspective: Sociocultural Contexts and Identity Constructions

Sociocultural theorists argue that language and literacy are not only socially, culturally, and historically situated tools but are also used by participants in social settings such as homes and classrooms in order to mediate thoughts and experiences (Vygotsky, 1978). In turn, the social uses of language and literacy have implications for personal and collective identity constructions (Gee, 1996) in school (Campano, 2007; Finders, 1996; Myers, 1992) and outside of school (Fránquiz, 2001; Fránquiz & Brochin, 2006; Heath, 1983; Hull & Schultz, 2002; Moll & Greenberg, 1990). Thus, a view of literacy from a sociocultural theory of learning values the cultural context within which young children grow and develop their multiple identities (Pérez, 2004).

Ivanic (1994, p. 4) made an important distinction in the way literacy theorists conceptualize identity construction. She states,

> The word "identity" is useful because it is the everyday word for people's sense of who they are. However, it is a misleading singular word. The plural word "identities" is better because it captures the idea of people identifying simultaneously with a variety of social groups; for example, a person may simultaneously identify herself as a student, a feminist, black, and experienced worker, and more. One or more of these may be foregrounded at different times; they are sometimes contradictory, sometimes interrelated. A person's diverse identities constitute the richness and the dilemmas of her sense of self.

Other scholars theorize the highly textured and multiplicitous condition of foregrounding and/or backgrounding identities (Anzaldúa, 1987; Zentella, 1998). Their work suggests that living between and across the borderlands or interstices of multiple identities (Anzaldúa, 1997) is a location with tremendous transformational potential. This body of scholarship integrates perspectives from cultural studies and feminist studies with educational studies in literacy and language in ways that can help educators understand how students' identities develop and whether and when school-based literacies are material resources in the learning process.

From a sociocultural perspective, the development of literacy for Latina/o students can be viewed as the struggle of living in a state of *in-betweenness*. Scholars have described the powerful influence of living between ideas (Cintrón, 1997). In particular, Anzaldúa (1993) and Mora (1993) refer to *in-betweenness* using the concept of *nepantla*.

References to *nepantla* refer to being positioned or positioning oneself somewhere "in the middle" ground between available positions (points of view). From this perspective, *in-betweenness* is an uncertain process an individual or group experiences as each moves from one state of cultural understanding to another. In such a process there are shifting stages a child or adult encounters. The challenge for the researcher inspired by the theory of *nepantla* is well stated by González (2001) who acknowledged that her study of interactions between mothers and children in the borderlands between Arizona and Mexico was complex. She explained her research as "a multivocal process, involving contexts that cannot be examined only in the household, but must encompass regional, national, and transborder zones" (p. 19).

Documenting Writing in a Cycle of Activity

In this study, I explored how oral and written texts provided an avenue for learning about the complexity of living between languages and cultures. Specifically, the potential for biliteracy among young learners who do not have access to an official bilingual education curriculum was traced through a unit of instruction. The unit was viewed as a cycle of activity (Green & Meyer, 1991), a series of connected events around the topic of quilting. In the cycle, a range of activities provided students with opportunities to interact with texts about important people and places in their community. To understand the potential for biliteracy in classrooms I drew on the construct of *nepantla* because it provides a way of conceptualizing what students experience when the official English-only curriculum is made permeable during the study of the cultural practice of quilting.

Data collected included audio and video records, field notes, formal and informal interviews, collaborative lesson plans, student-produced artifacts, copies of school communications, and photographs of school and classroom activities. The cycle selected for analysis in this chapter included seven months that began in mid-October 2004 and ended in mid-April 2005.

Findings

Why the Theme of Quilting?

Because of limited availability to art and the heritage language in the curriculum, two art educators agreed to work with me and a doctoral student in using a set of culturally relevant literature books that would immerse the entire elementary school in an integrated thematic study of quilting. The objective was to create six to eight quilts that would capture images, historical traditions, communal memories, important people and places from their rural town. At the end of the school year the quilts would be donated to the city's museum.

Initially teachers were unaware that the craft of quilting had been part of Mexican-American women's domestic arts from the arrival of the first *mestizo* settlers in the area in the late 1700s and early 1800s. These traditions were explored in a workshop provided by the artists of *Hecho en Encinal* and the researchers. It was critical for the school personnel to understand quilting as an authentic as well as symbolic property of many Mexican-American families (The Handbook of Texas Online). The workshop included literature (fiction, poetry, and nonfiction) on topics associated with the quilting theme. The cycle of activity that ensued yielded a total of 56 quilt lessons involving students, their teachers, and parents in the study of patterns, designs, textures, drawing, writing, and sewing. Although it was atypical to use Spanish in school, the artists-in-residence, the teacher, and the researchers deliberately encouraged students to use all their linguistic, academic, and cultural resources for responding to selected literature. These textual responses were to be incorporated in quilt squares.

Across the academic year several books were used to elicit students' written responses. One of the books was *Sweet Clara and the Freedom Quilt* by Deborah Hopkinson (1995). It was used to show the historical uses of and messages embedded in quilts. *Going Home* by Eve Bunting (1998) was used to elicit writing describing home and community. *Family Pictures/Cuadros de mi Familia* by Carmen Lomas Garza (1990) was used to elicit children's stories of family traditions. Finally, *Recordando Mis Raíces y Viviendo Mis Tradiciones/Remembering my Roots and Living my Traditions* by the group, Transnational Latinas (TNL) (2005), was used in the upper grades for the same purpose of eliciting stories of family and community traditions. Various pieces of poetry were also used across the prekindergarten through fifth grade classes. The teachers were impressed with and supportive of the ways that the two "guest" art educators assisted teachers in using quilt patterns for reinforcing mathematical concepts, teaching new vocabulary in English as well as Spanish, capturing patterns from everyday life, and eliciting individual children's stories and family traditions. In the analysis that follows, the responses to *Going Home* by Eve Bunting are highlighted.

Before moving to analysis it is important to note that just like scholars who speak to the value of students seeing themselves in literature, the teachers at Encinal Elementary were interested in using literature as a way for their students to learn about themselves, to develop a positive sense of self, and to author their own texts (Barrera & Garza de Cortes, 1997; Nieto, 1997; Jiménez et al., 1999). They agreed that even when race, class, and other social categories were the same, culturally relevant literature served at least two purposes – it was beneficial for all students and allowed students to learn about situated realities different from their own (Harris, 1997) as well as validating their own realities. In the following sections I provide five examples to show how individual students (Yesenia, Osvaldo, Marisa, Olivia, Eddie) and a class of kindergarteners took up opportunities to learn and work in the in-between space between the official English-only curriculum and the unofficial biliterate curriculum.

Literature Responses of Simultaneous Bilingual Learners in Preschool

The theme for one of the quilts was *Places in Encinal*. In the prekindergarten class the teacher used the story, *Going Home* (Bunting, 1998), as a read aloud to elicit short stories about what an outsider would see if they visited the students' community. Parts of these short stories would then be used to create a square for a paper quilt; some squares were subsequently transferred to cloth. In the prekindergarten classes the teacher or an assistant scribed for the children once they had drawn their literature response to the read aloud. Some of the stories produced by the four year olds were in English; others were in Spanish. Interestingly, many included code-switching. For example, when her teacher asked what visitors to Encinal would see Yesenia replied,

TEACHER: What do you think visitors would see in Encinal?
YESENIA: My grandma's house.
TEACHER: Oh, tell me about grandma's house.
YESENIA: *Tiene una puerta* (pointing to it and teacher writes *puerta*/door) *ventanas* (pointing to two areas and teacher writes *ventanas*/window) *espejo* (pointing to it and teacher writes *espejo*/mirror) *tiene cuna*, hmm, (pointing and correcting herself) *cunita del*, hmm, *la bebé* (baby's crib).

In Figure 7.1 each part of Yesenia's story is labeled. When her teacher asked her about what visitors would see in her community she answered in English. However, when she was asked to give details about her drawing she switched her "reading" of the drawing to Spanish. This may be an indication of the type of language choice available to the four year olds in the class when they were invited to share their stories. Nonetheless, Yesenia's switch from English to Spanish positioned her "in the middle" ground between available language positions in her prekindergarten class. Thus, Yesenia provided in English the fact that her grandmother's house was critical for a visitor to experience in Encinal. Her choice to dictate her story in the language of her home – Spanish – and not the language of school and visitors – English – aligns with the view of using specific language codes for specific sociocultural contexts. The literacy event also provided an informal context to assess her understanding of appropriate language structures to use for her story. In her self-correction to use the diminutive *cunita*, or little crib, to refer to her baby sister's bed instead of *cuna*, or crib, shows understanding of changing the root of a word to convey degree of meaning – in this case the smallness of her sibling's bed. Yesenia was also aware of the appropriate article to reflect the gender of her baby sister by correcting a detail of her story from *del bebé* to *la bebé*. However, even though her teacher as the scribe for the story corrected *cuna* to *cunita*, she did not change *del bebé* to *la bebé* and instead wrote down both of Yesenia's responses referencing the gender of her baby sister; the teacher wrote *del la bebé*. When Yesenia pointed to two windows in her drawing and referred to them as *ventanas* she further demonstrated in illustration and discourse an understanding of how plural nouns work in a sentence. The teacher indicated this plural form by scribing *ventanas* and drawing arrows between Yesenia's representations of windows. Per researcher observations and teacher informal assessments, Yesenia showed a consistent growth in emerging biliteracy readiness skills as a simultaneous bilingual learner.

Baker (2001) has defined simultaneous bilingual learners such as Yesenia as those who, from the ages of zero to five, have been exposed to and are acquiring two languages. In contrast, sequential bilinguals are persons who begin the process of second-language acquisition after the age of six with a well-established first language base (Baker, 2001). This latter theory of sequential bilingualism typically informs bilingual education policy and ignores the specific capacities and language and literacy potential of children like Yesenia who are simultaneous bilingual learners. Given that literacy strategies found to be effective for monolingual English learners have not had the same results for learners like Yesenia who speak two or more languages (August & Shanahan, 2006) this brief example embedded in a meaningful literacy context for eliciting the perspectives of four year olds regarding important places in their borderlands community constituted a key speech event (Gumperz, 1986) of the ethnographic study.

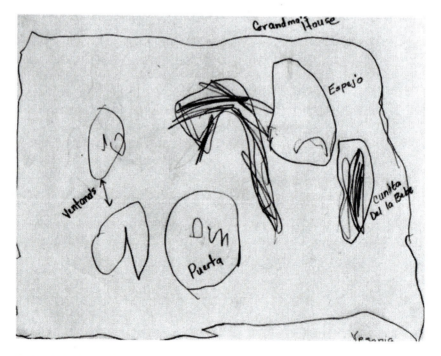

FIGURE 7.1 Yesenia's literature response.

The drawing in Figure 7.1 was relocated from Yesenia's desk to a *Places in Encinal* paper quilt completed on the classroom rug at the end of the lesson. Among the pieces included on the paper quilt was Osvaldo's. While Yesenia was "reading" her story to her teacher, Osvaldo was dictating his story in English to an aide assisting in the classroom. He pointed to four round figures he had drawn; each figure had what looked like a sail on top. Osvaldo "read" his story softly, "These are boats on my *güelos* ranch. He takes me there. We see fish." Directly above Osvaldo's representations of boats (see Figure 7.2) are images that, unfortunately, were not discussed with him. These images could be illustrations of the sky or a lake on his grandfather's ranch. Notably, in Yesenia's story she referred to her grandmother as grandma but Osvaldo referred to his grandfather as *güelo*, a shortened regionalism in Spanish for *abuelo* or grandfather. The sentence structure also includes a correct form of the English possessive for grandfather's ranch. Since an apostrophe is missing it is assumed that the scribe only wrote what was dictated. Given that assumption, it can be inferred that Osvaldo was thinking and "reading" his story in English; if he had been thinking in Spanish he would have said, "the ranch of my *güelo*" as occurs in the discourse of many dominant speakers of Spanish. Nonetheless, cross-linguistic

FIGURE 7.2 Osvaldo's literature response.

borrowing was used by these two young children when referencing a grandparent as they shared with their teachers about the important places of their hometown – in the case of Yesenia, her grandmother's house and in the case of Osvaldo, his grandfather's ranch.

Integrating Language Arts with Mathematics in Kindergarten

In the kindergarten class the teacher also read *Going Home* (Bunting, 1988). The story prompted a discussion of names for places in Mexico and in the United States. Some of the students were not aware of the fact that cities often had meanings based on names of famous persons or in reference to geographical characteristics. The researchers and teacher realized the students did not know the name of their community was a Spanish name or the reason for the name. This realization prompted us to collaborate on the creation of a lesson that could bring the meaning of the word Encinal to the foreground as well as reinforce content area skills. Together with the artists in residence we decided to conduct a lesson that would accomplish three objectives: (1) reinforce numeracy skills through the creation of patterns (big/small; big/small/big, small/small/big; big/big/small, etc.), (2) provide opportunity for use of fine motor skills (cutting and gluing), and (3) provide tactile experience with different types of cloths that would eventually be incorporated in a quilt. The kindergarteners were so proud to learn that *Encinal* meant a grove of oak trees and that *Encino* was the singular form of oak tree. Along with the numeracy skills they wrote down the two words whose meanings were so intimately tied to the history of their community. Although the kindergarteners were not able to understand that the Spaniards named the rural community Encinal when the land was part of Mexico, they were very enthusiastic about learning to make oak groves with patterns and writing words in English and in their heritage language. They labeled their patterns to indicate the singular unit (*encino*, oak tree) and the plural forms (*encinal*, oak grove) that together created a particular pattern. See Figure 7.3 for a representative sample of a square that was integrated into the paper quilt; each square encapsulated the newfound understandings about Encinal in the kindergarten class. The new knowledge was shared with family and friends and undoubtedly would be shared with any future visitors to Encinal.

Code-switching and Cross-Linguistic Borrowings in Writing

After reading the story *Going Home* in the second grade classroom the children were also invited to tap into their lived experiences in relation to what visitors would see in Encinal. Children wrote brief responses and then chose one sentence, or golden line, from their short narrative to include on their paper quilt. One student named Marisa wrote, "When I drive through

FIGURE 7.3 Reinforcing mathematical concepts bilingually.

Encinal I see the train, and a cat, dog, trees and I see *jente caminando pare sus casas.*" In her complex sentence Marisa gives the reader an idea of what a seven year old sees in her community if she were the one in the driver's seat. Although there are orthographic errors in Spanish such as "jente" for "gente," the code-switch from English to Spanish occurs when the student refers to people from her ethnic group walking to their homes. Despite these spelling errors, Marisa has knowledge of the way intransitive verb conjugation (*caminando*) and possessives (*sus*) work in the Spanish language. While walking to their homes is typically written *caminando a sus casas* or *caminando hacia sus casas,* her sentence conveys the action and the meaning of the message. Given that Marisa has not had formal instruction in Spanish, her sentence shows many grammatical understandings of both languages that indicate she is developing simultaneous bilingualism and biliteracy. Marisa's language approximations in written Spanish were not initially corrected until the final transfer of her sentence to a cloth square. The intention of corrections to spelling conventions was to help her develop more accurate approximations in Spanish orthography. This written sample raises some important questions/tensions regarding the influence of language choice on young learner's biliterate identity development. As a simultaneous bilingual, is Marisa negotiating her personal and group identity in and through her written language choices? Should code-switching be valued or discouraged in classroom written assignments? What does the code-switch accomplish for the individual and the classroom as a group?

In the first grade classroom, Marisa's sibling, Olivia, also produced a sentence as a response to what visitors would see in Encinal. Olivia's sentence showed cross-linguistic borrowing (overt use of words from the other language) as opposed to a complete code-switch from English to Spanish. She wrote, "In Encinal you'll see *burros* and cattle horses and cows and oak trees." Olivia's reference to *burros* instead of donkeys is an indication of common linguistic borrowings in a borderlands community (see González, 2001, for more examples of linguistic borrowings in the borderlands of Arizona and Mexico). Such borrowing happens naturally in a community where more than one language is in contact. Although some researchers argue that code-switching and borrowing are distinct phenomena (Poplack, 1980; Sankoff et al., p. 97) others argue a continuum of relationships exists between all forms of code-switching including cross-linguistic borrowing (Myers-Scotton, 1992) as long as there are "lexicon driven congruencies" (p. 31). Such congruency is shown in Olivia's sentence. I also argue that *burro,* instead of donkey, has a high probability of being a discourse marker of the community – similar to the borrowing of Spanish regionalisms such as *güelo* or *güela* for grandfather and grandmother in students' English texts, as shown in Figure 7.2.

Cultural Referents in Students' Writing

Students at Encinal Elementary School took up opportunities to display bilingual skills during the quilting cycle of activities; they also shared cultural referents to family life and experiences in their rural community. For example, Eddie wrote an acrostic poem describing his community, and the description was portrayed with several code-switches (see Figure 7.4).

The cultural references in the acrostic poem include linguistic code-switches regarding knowledge of a ranching community. For example, "*novios*" for the Spanish word *novillos* or "calves," is not a common word in urban bilingual Spanish/English programs. Eddie let the reader know that "calves are for roping." He makes a common error of Spanish native speakers in confusing "s" for "z" in "*lazar*" and "b" for "p" in "*pa'[para]*". He also makes a common error of English native speakers in confusing "-el" for "-le" in "pickle." Unless you had visited this particular rural community you would not know that Iris is the name of the local grocery store. Even more puzzling to an outsider is the sentence, "*Nachos son wanos*," because this sentence shows how Texans use Spanish uniquely. For example, *bueno* bye, is a common way to bid farewell to friends. However, in the local pronunciation the "b" in *bueno* is silent. Because

FIGURE 7.4 Bilingual acrostic poem.

Eddie had receptive and productive knowledge of this local linguistic marker, he approximated that the English phonology for "wa" could reproduce the sound of the Spanish blend "ue" in order to explain to the reader, "Nachos are good." Overall, it is clear that this child dances with phonologies of two languages even though he has received formal schooling in English only. This is remarkable given that language shift to English from the heritage language is reported to occur faster in the United States than anywhere else in the world (Crawford, 1992; Grosjean, 1982; Veltman, 1988), and Texas is a big part of those phenomena. One substitute teacher that we interviewed presented a hypothesis as to why the young children at Encinal Elementary School could demonstrate skills in Spanish when given the opportunity. She stated, "I sub at the school and what I find is they [the students] don't speak Spanish. They speak mostly English, but the *abuelita* [grandmother] speaks Spanish, so they speak Spanish with her" (interview, December 2004).

Toward the final phase of the research project, the second grade teacher, Ms. Ovando, made a decision. She had become more interested in building on students' cultural resources from home and commented,

> A lot of the kids have animals, and they know about the ranches ... so I did like that idea of the paper quilt, and I thought, "well, I think I'll just keep that and use it next year," and I know it'll fit different subjects that you could actually do a quilt on, like even in science. We could do an animal quilt or quilts on other topics in science.
>
> (interview, May 2005)

Based on the positive and enthusiastic engagement of her students as well as students in other classrooms, Ms. Ovando rethought her curriculum and came up with ways to better nurture the life world of emerging and evolving identities in her classroom along the U.S./Mexico border.

Lessons Learned

In the face of rising Latino demographics and evolving notions of childhood, what can the field of early childhood education learn from the cases presented in this chapter? Foremost is the construct of multiple identities that are in flux depending on age, gender, class, ethnicity, language, time in the U.S., and status of citizenship. In schools that attempt to subtract any one of students' identities (Valenzuela, 1999), even young children must decide to resist or give in to subtractive assimilation (Gibson, 1995). In schools such as Encinal Elementary School, students are provided opportunities to develop positive orientations toward their heritage language and culture. Students are also able to write as they naturally speak in the borderlands between the U.S. and Mexico. This means they are sometimes invited to participate in activities in the in-between place between languages. Examples are Osvaldo's use of "güelo" or Eddie's use of "wano bye." Focusing on what young Latina/o students can do and achieve with the linguistic and cultural resources brought into the classroom from outside of school has been the principle that guides the literacy practices of teachers such as Ms. Ovando in Texas. The idea is to bring in and discuss all possible selves in the in-between location of *nepantla*, a state where ambiguity between identities and languages is the norm.

Conclusion

In rural areas such as Encinal, where enrichment and bilingual programs are not as accessible, teachers can expand the repertoire of possible selves available to not only Latina/o students, but to all students, by involving them in project-based literacy such as quilt making. In the case of Encinal Elementary School two guest artists, two researchers, parents, and community members were receptive to working together to help young students use their linguistic and cultural resources to create quilts that would eventually be housed in the town museum. As Yesenia, Marisa, and Eddie respectively wrote pieces about grandma's house, the animals and *gente* (people) of Encinal, and the joys of roping calves and eating pickles at the local Iris Store, they asserted the phenomenon of spontaneous biliteracy where the development of literacy in one language occurred despite not receiving literacy instruction in both languages (De La Luz Reyes, 2001; Gort, 2006). When languages in contact are seen from an asset perspective they can be tremendous resources for the construction of possible selves (Ginorio & Huston, 2001). More specifically, if a biliteracy continuum can be imagined as an authentic journey on a biliteracy highway then the Spanish lane and the English lane share the same road simultaneously. Since sequential biliteracy instruction has been named a central characteristic of many bilingual programs (Lindholm-Leary, 2001), the writings of the students in Encinal provide much food for reflection. Sequential bilingual assumptions are informed in large part by Cummins' (1981) theory of "common underlying proficiency." According to this theory, literacy gained in one language serves as a foundation and facilitates the development of literacy in the other, often as a result of formal instruction. However, the study at Encinal Elementary School demonstrates that without formal instruction young students were able to show robust potential for biliteracy development in a spontaneous (De La Luz Reyes, 2001) or authentic way.

Rivera and Huerta-Macias (2008) provide a more comprehensive description of biliteracy as "more than reading and writing; it includes the ability to construct and communicate meaning in two languages across diverse social contexts and in socioculturally appropriate ways" (p. 5). The five young students presented in this chapter read their world in socioculturally appropriate ways and were able to communicate to the reader visiting their community an accurate portrayal of their way of life – a life where two languages are intergenerationally bound, where ranching and animals are central to community cultural events, and where elders such as *güelos* and *güelas* are cherished.

One of the critical strategies that assisted the young children in this study to demonstrate their biliterate potential in prekindergarten through second grade was code-switching, or moving easily between one linguistic code and another within a sentence or an utterance. Using such a linguistic strategy was a natural part of being bilingual (Hornberger, 2005; De La Luz Reyes, 2001; Zentella, 1997). Children drew on both (or all) of the codes available to them in grammatically structured ways in order to express their meanings (Clyne, 2000; Myers-Scotton, 1995; Poplack, 1980). Yet at the level of pragmatics, code-switching in some environments is considered inappropriate. Despite over half a century of study in the field of linguistics looking at the complexity of code-switching and demonstrating the richness of the practice (Clyne, 2000), many multilingual speakers believe that code-switching is a sign of linguistic weakness or inadequacy and many bilingual teachers work hard to discourage code-switching when it occurs in their classrooms. This was not the case at Encinal Elementary School.

Pedagogical Implications

Even though the extent to which the interpretations from this study are transferable to other youngsters within the same population is limited, future research regarding effective literacy for Latina/o students can benefit by considering ways that biliteracy can be fostered in rural as well as urban classroom educational settings, be they designated as bilingual or monolingual. As we look toward the future with an increasing diversity in school enrollment, it is important for teachers and researchers to identify areas that require our attention if we are to maximize Latina/o children's opportunities for developing positive social and academic identities. Following are some specific theory to practice recommendations to keep in mind in order to promote biliteracy in the early years of schooling.

- Use of locally situated, culturally relevant literature provides young students with multiple opportunities to explore societal issues and to understand diverse perspectives. Therefore, teachers should select bilingual literature that reflects students' lived experiences.
- A variety of reading selections in the classroom should include literature that reflects the bilingual varieties of students in the classroom, because when provided the opportunity, students take up strategic use of the Spanish language, including Spanglish, even when there is no formal bilingual instruction.

- Adaptation of instructional practices to fit the linguistic and cultural environment of the classroom community mandates the nurturance of linguistic border crossings in oral and written classroom activities. That is to say, all teachers and students, even those bound to honor the language of the day, ought to be able to strategically code-switch for purposes such as clarification, poetic expression, and affiliation.
- Classroom anthologies with multicultural content should be supplemented with materials and activities for deeper student exploration, discussion, and production of writing related to their emerging identities. Activities can include the production of student-authored texts – such as a bilingual class quilt.
- Collaborative partnerships between schools and community arts organizations enrich the literate lives of students. Schools should facilitate these partnerships by prioritizing stronger community engagement initiatives that do not inadvertently communicate English-only practices.

Future Research Directions

For future studies in bilingual classrooms, teachers and researchers are urged to go beyond the teaching and researching of stand-alone teaching methods. This was the same conclusion reached by Bartolomé (1996) in her work with bilingual teachers more than 15 years ago. While I unequivocally agree that educators must go beyond the typical requirements of teaching, I find it useful to consider the theoretical concept of living *nepantla* as young bilingual students travel the highway toward biliteracy. The experience of how young bilinguals use their linguistic resources is rarely captured in ethnographic studies and is the innovative contribution of this book. If teachers and researchers purposely plan for learning opportunities where young students can utilize all their developing linguistic and cultural resources, then future research will document the many ways reading and writing at school can be fluid and flexible in moving learners along on the biliteracy continuum.

As future research captures more images of teachers cultivating linguistic and cultural hybridity in early childhood, then new images will likely emerge that position teachers and their collaborations with researchers and other caring adults as strong bridges between home/community knowledge and school knowledge, and between experiential and academic knowledge. Longitudinal studies would be complementary if they can capture early childhood bilingual use and its effects on later abstract learning. The types of questions that may be considered in order to continue learning about the linguistic resources used by young bilinguals are: What are the literacy strategies that can engage young Latina/o students in healthy constructions of possible selves? What are the resources Latina/o students draw on to construct positive dispositions toward heritage language and culture across years of schooling?

Note

1. Research for the study was partially funded by the Academy for Teacher Excellence at the University of Texas at San Antonio. My utmost thanks go to Carol Brochin-Ceballos who collected data with me for this project during her doctoral program and the teachers, students, and community members who let us become part of their daily lives.

References

Anzaldúa, G. (1987). *Borderlands/la frontera: The new mestiza.* San Francisco, CA: Aunt Lute Books.

Anzaldúa, G. (1993). *Border arte: Nepantla, el lugar de la frontera.* San Diego, CA: Centro Cultural de la Raza, 107–114.

Anzaldúa, G. (1997). Movimientos de rebeldía y las culturas que traicionan. In A. Darder, R. D. Torres, & Henry Gutiérrez (Eds.), *Latinos and education* (pp. 259–265). New York: Routledge.

August, D., & Shanahan, T. (Eds.) (2006). *Developing literacy in second-language learners: Report of the national literacy panel on language-minority children and youth.* Mahwah, NJ: Lawrence Erlbaum Associates.

Baker, C. (2001). *Foundations of bilingual education and bilingualism* (3rd ed.). Clevedon, UK: Multilingual Matters.

Barrera, R. B., & Garza de Cortes, O. (1997). Mexican American children's literature in the 1990's: Toward authenticity. In V. J. Harris (Ed.), *Using multiethnic literature in the K-8 classroom* (pp. 129–153). Norwood, MA: Christopher-Gordon Publishers, Inc.

Bartolomé, L. (1996). Beyond the methods fetish: Toward a humanizing pedagogy. *Harvard Educational Review, 64*(2), 173–194.

Berzins, M. E., & López, A. E. (2001). Starting off right: Planting the seeds of biliteracy. In M. de la Luz Reyes & J. J. Halcon (Eds.), *The best for our children: Critical perspectives on literacy for Latino students* (pp. 96–121). New York: Teachers College Press.

Brandon, P. (2004). The child care arrangements of preschool age children in immigrant families in the United States. *International Migration Review, 42*(1), 65–88.

Calderón, M., González, R., & Lazarín, M. (2004). *State of Hispanic America 2004: Latino perspectives on the American agenda.* Washington, DC: National Council of La Raza.

Campano, G. (2007). *Immigrant students and literacy: Reading, writing, and remembering.* New York: Teachers College Press.

Cintrón, R. (1997). *Angel's town: Chero ways, gang life, and rhetorics of the everyday.* Boston, MA: Beacon Press.

Clyne, M. (2000). Constraints on code-switching: How universal are they? In L.Wei (Ed.), *The bilingualism reader* (pp. 257–280). New York: Routledge.

Crawford, J. (1992). *Hold your tongue: Bilingualism and the politics of "English Only."* Reading, MA: Addison-Wesley.

Cummins, J. (1981). Age on arrival and immigrant second language learning in Canada: A reassessment. *Applied Linguistics, 11*(2), 132–149.

De La Luz Reyes, M. (2001). Unleashing possibilities: Biliteracy in the primary grades. In M. De La Luz Reyes & J. J. Halcon (Eds.), *The best for our children: Critical perspectives on literacy for Latino students* (pp. 96–121). New York: Teachers College Press.

Dworin, J. E. (2003). Insights into biliteracy development: Theory of bilingual pedagogy. *Journal of Hispanic Higher Education, 2*(2), 171–186.

Escamilla, K. (2006). Monolingual assessment and emerging bilinguals: A case study in the U.S. In O. García, T. Skutnabb-Kangas, & M. Torres-Guzman (Eds.), *Imagining multilingual schools* (pp. 184–199). Clevedon, UK: Multilingual Matters.

Finders, M. (1996). "Just girls": Literacy and allegiance in junior high school. *Written Communication, 13*(1), 93–129.

Fránquiz, M. (2001). It's about YOUth! Chicano high school students revisioning their academic identity. In M. de la luz Reyes & J. J. Halcón (Eds.), *The best for our children: Latina/o voices on literacy* (pp. 213–228). New York: Teachers College Press.

Fránquiz, M. E. (2008). Learning English with high interest, low vocabulary literature: Immigrant students in a high school new arrival center. *English Leadership Quarterly, 30*(3), 5–8.

Fránquiz, M. E., & Brochin, C. (2006). Cultural citizenship and visual literacy: U.S.-Mexican children constructing cultural identities along the U.S./Mexico border. *Multicultural Perspectives, 8*(1), 5–12.

Garcia, E. E. (1991). Caring for infants in a bilingual child care setting. *Journal of Educational Issues of Language Minority Students, 9*, 1–10.

Gee, J. P. (1996). *Social linguistics and literacies: Ideology in discourses.* Bristol, PA: Taylor and Francis.

Gibson, M. (1995). Additive acculturation as a strategy for school improvement. In R. Rumbaut & W. Cornelius (Eds.), *California's immigrant children: Theory, research, and implications for educational policy.* La Jolla, CA: Center for U.S.–Mexican Studies, University of California, San Diego.

Ginorio, A., & Huston, M. (2001). *¡Sí, se puede! Yes, we can: Latinas in school.* Washington, DC: American Association of University Women.

González, G. G. (1999). Segregation and the education of Mexican children, 1900–1940. In J. F. Moreno (Ed.), *The elusive quest for equality: 150 years of Chicano/Chicana education.* Cambridge, MA: Harvard Education Press.

González, N. (2001). *I am my language: Discourses of women and children in the borderlands.* Tucson, AZ: University of Arizona Press.

Gort, M. (2006). Strategic codeswitching, interliteracy, and other phenomena of emergent bilingual writing: Lessons from first grade dual language classrooms. *Journal of Early Childhood Literacy, 6*(3), 323–354.

Green, J. L., & Meyer, L. (1991). The embeddedness of reading in classroom life: Reading as a situated process. In C. Baker and A. Luke (Eds.), *Toward a critical sociology of reading pedagogy* (pp. 141–160). Amsterdam: Benjamins Publishing Company.

Grosjean, F. (1982). *Life with two languages: An introduction to bilingualism.* Cambridge, MA: Harvard University Press.

Gumperz, J. J. (1972). The communicative competence of bilinguals: Some hypotheses and suggestions for research. *Language in Society, 2*(1), 143–154.

Gumperz, J. J. (1982). *Discourse strategies.* Cambridge: Cambridge University Press.

Gumperz, J. J. (1986). Interactional sociolinguistics in the study of schooling. In Jenny Cook-Gumperz (Ed.), *The social construction of literacy* (pp. 45–68). Cambridge: Cambridge University Press.

Harris, V. J. (1997). Children's literature depicting blacks. In V. Harris (Ed.), *Using multiethnic literature in the K-8 classroom* (pp. 21–58). Norwood, MA: Christopher-Gordon Publishers, Inc.

Heath, S. B. (1983). *Ways with words.* Cambridge: Cambridge University Press.

Hernandez, D. (2006). *Young Hispanic children in the U.S.: A demographic portrait based on Census 2000.* Report to the National Task Force on Early Childhood Education for Hispanics. Tempe, AZ: Arizona State University.

Hornberger, N. H. (1989). Continua of biliteracy. *Review of Educational Research, 59*(3), 271–296.

Hornberger, N. H. (Ed.) (2003). *Continua of biliteracy: An ecological framework for educational policy, research, and practice in multilingual settings.* Clevedon, UK: Multilingual Matters.

Hornberger, N. H. (2005). Student voice and the media of bi(multi)lingual/muticultural classrooms. In T. McCarty (Ed.), *Language, literacy, and power in schooling* (pp. 151–167). Mahwah, NJ: Lawrence Erlbaum Associates.

Hull, G., & Schultz, K. (2002). *School's out! Bridging out-of-school literacies with classroom practice.* New York: Teachers College Press.

Ivanic, R. (1994). I is for interpersonal: Discoursal construction of writer identities and the teaching of writing. *Linguistics and Education, 6*(1), 3–15.

Jiménez, R., & Gomez, A. (1996). Literature-based cognitive strategy instruction for middle school Latina/o students. *Journal of Adolescent and Adult Literacy, 40*(2), 84–91.

Jiménez, R. T., Moll, L. C., Rodríguez-Brown, F. V., & Barrera, R. B. (1999). Latina and Latino researchers interact on issues related to literacy learning. *Reading Research Quarterly, 34*(2), 217–230.

Laliberty, E. A. (2001). Hooked on writing: Linking literacy to student's lived experiences. In M. de la luz Reyes & J. J. Halcón (Eds.), *The best for our children: Critical perspectives on literacy for Latino students* (pp. 142–150). New York: Teachers College Press.

Lindholm-Leary, K. J. (2001). *Dual language education.* Clevedon, UK: Multilingual Matters, Ltd.

Martínez-Roldán, C., & Fránquiz, M. E. (2009). Latina/o youth literacy: Hidden funds of knowledge. In L. Christenbury, R. Bomer, & P. Smagorinsky (Eds.), *Handbook of adolescent literacy research* (pp. 323–342). New York: Guilford Press.

Martínez-Roldán, C., & Sayer, P. (2006). Reading through linguistic borderlands: Latino students' transactions with narrative texts. *Journal of Early Childhood Literacy, 6*(3), 293–322.

Moll, L. C., & Dworin, J. (1996). Biliteracy in classrooms: Social dynamics and cultural possibilities. In D. Hicks (Ed.), *Child discourse and social learning* (pp. 221–246). New York: Cambridge University Press.

Moll, L. C., & Greenberg, J. (1990). Creating zones of possibilities: Combining social contexts for instruction. In L. C. Moll (Ed.), *Vygotsky and education* (pp. 319–348). New York: Cambridge University Press.

Moll, L. C., Saez, R., & Dworin, J. (2001). Exploring biliteracy: Two student case examples of writing as a social practice. *Elementary School Journal, 101*(4), 435–449.

Moll, L. C., Amanti, C., Neff, D., & González, N. (1992). Funds of knowledge for teaching: Using a qualitative approach to connect homes and classrooms. *Theory into Practice, 31*(2), 132–141.

Mora, P. (1993). *Nepantla: Essays from the land in the middle.* New Mexico: University of New Mexico Press.

Myers, J. (1992). The social contexts of school and personal literacy. *Reading Research Quarterly, 27*(4), 296–333.

Myers-Scotton, C. (1992). Comparing codeswitching and borrowing. In C. Eastman (Ed.), *Codeswitching* (pp. 19–40). Clevedon, UK: Multilingual Matters.

Myers-Scotton, C. (1995). *Social motivations for code switching: Evidence from Africa.* Oxford: Oxford University Press.

Nieto, S. (1997). We have stories to tell: Puerto Ricans in children's books. In V. J. Harris (Ed.), *Using multiethnic literature in the K-8 classroom* (pp. 59–93). Norwood, MA: Christopher-Gordon Publishers, Inc.

Oldfather, P. (1993). What students say about motivating experiences in a whole language classroom. *Reading Teacher, 46*(8), 672–681.

Pérez, B. (2004). *Becoming biliterate: A study of two-way bilingual immersion education.* Mahwah, NJ: Lawrence Erlbaum.

Pérez, B., & Torres-Guzmán, M. (2002). *Learning in two worlds: An integrated Spanish/English biliteracy approach.* Boston, MA: Allyn and Bacon.

Pérez, P., & Zarate, M. E. (2006). *Latino public opinion survey of pre-kindergarten programs: Knowledge, preferences, and public support.* Los Angeles, CA: Tomás Rivera Public Policy Institute, University of Southern California.

Poplack, S. (1980, 2000). Sometimes I'll start a sentence in Spanish y termino en español: Toward a typology of code-switching. In L. Wei (Ed.), *The bilingualism reader* (pp. 221–256). London: Routledge.

Portes, A., & Hao, L. (1998). E. pluribus unum: Bilingualism and loss of language in the second generation. *Sociology of Education, 71*(10), 269–294.

Reyes, I. (2006). Exploring connections between emergent biliteracy and bilingualism. *Journal of Early Childhood Literacy, 6*(3), 267–292.

Rivera, K. M., & Huerta-Macias, A. (2008). Adult bilingualism and biliteracy in the United States: Theoretical perspectives. In K. M. Rivera & A. Huerta-Macias (Eds.), *Adult biliteracy: Sociocultural and programmatic responses* (pp. 3–28). New York: Lawrence Erlbaum.

Ruiz, R. (1984). Orientations in language planning. *Journal for the National Association of Bilingual Education, 8*(2), 15–34.

San Miguel, Jr., G. (1999). The schooling of Mexicanos in the Southwest, 1848–1891. In J. F. Moreno (Ed.), *The elusive quest for equality: 150 years of Chicano/Chicana education.* Cambridge, MA: Harvard Education Press.

Sankoff, D., Poplack, S., & Vanniarajan, S. (1990). The case of the nonce loan in Tamil. *Language Variation and Change 2*(1), 71–101.

Skutnabb-Kangas, T. (1988). Multilingualism and the education of minority children. In O. Garcia & C. Baker (Eds.), *Policy and practice in bilingual education: A reader extending the foundations* (pp. 40–59). Philadelphia, PA: Multilingual Matters.

Skutnabb-Kangas, T. (2000). *Linguistic genocide in education: Or worldwide diversity and human rights?* Mahwah, NJ: Lawrence Erlbaum.

Tabors, P., & Snow, C. (2001). Young bilingual children and early literacy development. In S. Neumann & D. Dickinson (Eds.), *Handbook of early literacy research* (pp. 159–178). New York: Guilford Press.

Takanishi, R. (2004). Leveling the playing field: Supporting immigrant children from birth to eight. *Future of Children, 14*(2), 61–80.

The Handbook of Texas Online. *Mexican-American folk arts and crafts.* Retrieved May 15, 2010, from www.tshaonline.org/handbook/online/articles/MM/lim1.html.

U.S. Census Bureau, Washington, DC. (2004). Roberto R. Ramirez, *We the people: His-panics in the United States,* Census 2000 Special Reports, CENSR-18. Retrieved June 2, 2011 from: www.census.gov/prod/2004pubs/censr-18.pdf.

Valdés, G. (2000). Bilingualism and language use among Mexican Americans. In S. L. McKay & S. C. Wong (Eds.), *New immigrants in the United States: Readings for second language educators* (pp. 99–136). Cambridge: Cambridge University Press.

Valdez, V. E., & Fránquiz, M. E. (2009). Latin@s in early childhood education: Issues, practices, and future directions. In S. A. Villenas, R. T. Galván, J. S. Muñoz, C. Martínez, & M. Machado-Casas (Eds.), *Handbook of Latinos and Education* (pp. 474–487). New York: Routledge.

Valenzuela, A. (1999). *Subtractive schooling: U.S. Mexican youth and the politics of caring.* New York: State University of New York Press

Veltman, C. (1988). *The future of the Spanish language in the United States.* Washington, DC: Hispanic Policy Development Project.

Vygotsky, L. S. (1978). *Mind in society: The development of higher psychological processes.* Cambridge, MA: Harvard University Press.

Wong-Filmore, L. (2000). Loss of family languages: Should educators be concerned? *Theory into Practice, 39*(4), 203–210.

Zentella, A. C. (1997). *Growing up bilingual: Puerto Rican children in New York.* Walden, MA: Blackwell.

Zentella, A. C. (1998). Multiple codes, multiple identities: Puerto Rican children in New York City. In S. M. Hoyle & C. T. Adger (Eds.), *Kids talk: Strategic language use in later childhood* (pp. 95–112). New York: Oxford University Press.

Zentella, A. C. (Ed.) (2005). *Building on strength: Language and literacy in Latino families and communities.* New York: Teachers College Press.

Children's Literature Cited

Bunting, E. (1998). *Going home.* New York: Harper Trophy.

Garza, C. L. (1990). *Cuadros de mi familia/Family pictures.* San Francisco, CA: Children's Book Press.

Hopkinson, D. (1995). *Sweet Clara and the freedom quilt.* NewYork: Dragonfly Books.

TransNational Latinas (2005). *Recuerdo mis raices y vivo mis tradiciones/Remembering my roots and living my traditions.* New York: Scholastic.

8

THE EVOLUTION OF BILITERATE WRITING DEVELOPMENT THROUGH SIMULTANEOUS BILINGUAL LITERACY INSTRUCTION

Wendy Sparrow, Sandra Butvilofsky, and Kathy Escamilla

Introduction

"I like dat book picas Jellinourbredman rons awei from en old lairi and en old man." Teachers often pose the following questions about this writing: "What is the child trying to say?" "Is she writing in English?" "This sentence is not readable." A child in one of our research classrooms wrote: "I like that book because Gingerbread man runs away from an old lady and an old man."

This chapter posits that this type of text is, in fact, readable, for if we are to understand emerging biliterate behavior, we must look at emerging bilingual children's writing development over time and from a bilingual perspective. Oftentimes, emerging bilingual children are judged on their weaknesses instead of their strengths. For this reason, we use the term *emerging bilingual children*, as it acknowledges the dynamic process of acquiring two languages, rather than focusing solely on English-language acquisition. Similarly, *emerging biliterate development* accounts for the process through which children progress as they learn how to think, speak, read, and write simultaneously in two languages. As was the case of 2,000 other children involved in this study, this child used multiple rule-governed strategies to express herself in writing. The chapter details the writing development of emerging biliterate children and urges teachers to look at emerging bilingual students' writing from a bilingual perspective.

We explored emerging bilingual children's simultaneous development of Spanish and English writing as they received literacy instruction in both languages beginning in first grade. Providing students with *paired literacy instruction*, or literacy instruction in two languages, allows students the opportunity to develop biliteracy. We agree with others positing that biliterate development does not merely entail one language influencing or transferring to another, but instead, it is an interplay between both languages (Dworin, 2003; Moll et al., 2001; Valdés, 1992).

We examined the longitudinal writing behaviors of emerging bilingual children receiving paired literacy instruction. To do so, we explored the cross-language transfer of writing behaviors and examined how students' linguistic complexity developed in Spanish and English writing by measuring the relative growth of student idea production over three years from first through third grade. This chapter adds a new dimension to the research in that it focuses on the longitudinal development of biliterate writing, and it examines children's cross-language writing strategies using both quantitative and qualitative methods. Throughout this chapter, we discuss the positive cross-language transfer between Spanish and English, and we examine the longitudinal development of students' ideas in writing by looking at the progression of linguistic complexity. Within this chapter, we also provide pedagogical implications that corroborate earlier findings that demonstrate that literacy instruction in two languages does not adversely affect children's academic development (Carlisle & Beeman, 2000; Collier, 1992; Slavin & Cheung, 2003), but rather it supports their biliterate development.

Literature Review

Much of the research on biliterate development has been focused on how first-language reading skills transfer to the second language (Rodriguez, 1988; Slavin & Cheung, 2003). While a dearth of research exists on writing, growing evidence shows that writing skills also transfer across languages, particularly in Spanish and English. In fact, some researchers have argued that writing instruction, perhaps even more than reading instruction, provides a powerful vehicle for cross-language transfer (Carlisle & Beeman, 2000; Carlo & Royer, 1999; Dworin, 2003; Escamilla et al., 2005). Furthermore, in the U.S. context, research has demonstrated a relationship between writing in Spanish and writing in English (Carlisle, 1989; Escamilla et al., 2005; Moll, et al., 2001). This research showed that students who learned to write simultaneously in both languages wrote just as effectively, if not more so, in their second language as students who learned to write only in their second language. Finally, research by Gort (2006) and Hernández (2001) demonstrated that cross-language transfer was bidirectional (Spanish to English as well as English to Spanish).

Traditionally, research examining the literacy development of emerging bilingual children has been viewed from a monolingual perspective where students were instructed in one language and their writing in that language was often compared to monolingual students' work, leading to notions that cross-language transfer is unidirectional (Edelsky, 1982; Carlisle, 1989; Carlisle & Beeman, 2000). However, we believe the relationship between the two languages is reciprocal. That is, one language does not always dominate or influence the other, but both languages are capable of influencing one another for different purposes and in different situations.

Edelsky (1982) studied the relationship between first- and second-language writing in classrooms where Spanish-speaking students only received instruction in Spanish. She analyzed the Spanish and English writing samples of elementary students in a bilingual program (though they were not yet receiving second-language literacy instruction) to determine how students' language of instruction influenced the application of skills from one language to the other. Edelsky argues that literacy development in the first language does not interfere with literacy development in the second language, but rather that knowledge from the first language is applied to the second. In addition, she found that although varying levels of second-language proficiency do not deter children from writing, they do influence the complexity of second-language writing. While Edelsky acknowledges the transfer, rather than the interference, of first-language knowledge of writing to the second language, it is important to note that her study included a program with only one language of instruction. Thus, the opportunity to investigate students' simultaneous literacy development in two languages, and the idea that both languages can influence or mediate one another, was not explored.

Carlisle and Beeman (2000) examined the writing of native Spanish-speaking children instructed in only one language (Spanish or English). The students receiving Spanish literacy instruction performed just as well on the English literacy tasks as those instructed in English and outperformed them in the Spanish literacy tasks. While Carlisle and Beeman did not find that students transferred their knowledge of English literacy skills to Spanish, it is important to note that these students did not receive any instruction in Spanish. However, Carlisle and Beeman believe that if students were to receive literacy instruction in two languages, they would likely exhibit literacy improvement in both languages. We believe that students receiving literacy instruction in two languages would not only show growth in both languages, but that they would also be able to transfer knowledge bidirectionally between the two languages.

Davis et al. (1999) explored the development of first through third grade Spanish/English bilingual students' writing when receiving instruction in English. They found that while students could transfer writing skills from English to Spanish, they were not provided with literacy instruction in Spanish to support their development of English literacy skills. Although their research was a snapshot analysis rather than a longitudinal study, they were able to explore the developmental transfer of students' writing skills from English to Spanish at different grade levels. Acknowledging this idea of literacy skills transferring from students' second to first language, as well as using the prior knowledge of transfer from students' first to second language, illustrates the potential of exploring bidirectional transfer of literacy skills when providing students with paired literacy instruction.

Dworin's (2003) work further supports the bidirectionality of biliteracy development. From his research on biliterate development, Dworin concluded that language transfer is not linear, transferring from the first language (L1) to the second language (L2), but that it is bidirectional in that transfer occurs from L1 to L2 and from L2 to L1. Dworin also emphasizes that bilingual students develop biliteracy differently from one another, as multiple paths to biliteracy are mediated by individual experiences and classroom contexts. As children are learning literacy simultaneously in two languages, Dworin questions the "relevance of the concepts of first and second language" (2003, p. 180), because such concepts support the existence of a set sequence in which students acquire language and literacy, and such is not always the case. These theoretical understandings have led Dworin to call for a change in the perspective of how we view children's bilingual and biliterate development.

As illustrated in the literature reviewed above, emerging bilingual children's literacy development is generally viewed through a monolingual paradigm, and monolingual research and instructional practices are often applied to bilingual situations with no regard for the unique circumstances of bilingual learners (Dworin, 2003; Moll & Dworin, 1996; Valdés, 1992). However, to deepen our understanding of emerging bilingual children, we must begin to view their literacy development from a bilingual perspective (Dworin, 2003; Grosjean, 1989; Valdés, 1992). Grosjean explains that rather than examining bilinguals by looking at one language without looking at the other, we must "study how the bilingual structures and uses the two languages, separately or together, to meet his or her everyday communicative needs" (p. 13), and in this case, writing needs.

Using the research base as a foundation, we conducted a study of the biliterate development of emerging bilingual children's writing. We theorized that emerging bilingual children could develop Spanish and English literacy simultaneously, but not at equivalent rates, if they received paired literacy instruction. In other words, if students were progressing along a *trajectory toward biliteracy*, their Spanish literacy would be slightly more advanced than their English literacy, but a large discrepancy would not appear between the two, and students would be considered to be on a positive trajectory toward biliteracy. Utilizing a bilingual perspective, we analyzed students' Spanish and English writing samples simultaneously, rather than independently from one another. The remainder of this chapter reports the results of this study and its pedagogical implications.

Methods

Both quantitative and qualitative methods were used in this study. Data were collected as part of a larger study on biliteracy development entitled Literacy Squared® (Escamilla et al., 2005), which was a five-year longitudinal study that examined the biliteracy development of emerging bilingual children in 15 schools across two states. The Literacy Squared research team worked closely with teachers to implement the project that consisted of teaching *Spanish literacy, literacy-based ESL,* and *cross-language connections,* where teachers were encouraged to help students make connections between languages. Spanish literacy broadens literacy teaching by placing equal emphasis on the productive skills of writing and speaking, as well as the receptive skills of listening and reading. Literacy-based ESL is a book-based approach to English literacy instruction that also promotes the development of productive and receptive skills to ensure emerging bilingual children's biliteracy development. Some of the key components of literacy-based ESL include the use of appropriately leveled and culturally relevant texts, explicit and direct instruction of literacy skills and strategies that utilize explicit cross-language connections, and a focus on *oracy,* which is intended to help children develop the productive language necessary for success in reading and writing. Language time allocations were specified at each grade level, with more time dedicated to Spanish literacy in the primary grades and a gradual increase in time dedicated to literacy-based ESL in the intermediate grades.

Data Sources

Data sources included 25 students' writing samples from five schools where the majority of students were Latino and qualified for free or reduced priced lunch. All students in this study were Latino and English-language learners (ELLs), and for each of the 25 students, a Spanish and an English sample were available from first, second, and third grade.

Annually, students had 30 minutes to write to a prompt that varied by grade level. Spanish writing samples were collected first, and two weeks later, English samples were collected. Within a grade level, Spanish and English writing prompts were similar to elicit cross-language transfer, though sameness was avoided so as to not encourage translation.

Writing prompts were as follows:

Grade 1: Spanish: *Draw your favorite animal and write about why it is your favorite.*
English: Write about your favorite toy.

Grade 2: Spanish: *What is your favorite book? Why is it your favorite?*
English: What is your favorite TV program? Why is it your favorite?

Grade 3: Spanish: *What is the best thing that has happened to you in school this year? Why do you think it was the best?*
English: What is the best thing that has happened to you in your life? Why do you think it was the best?

Data Analysis

Samples were analyzed by counting the number of words per *T-unit* (Hunt, 1965). A T-unit, as defined by Miller (1995), is "any independent clause with all of its subordinate clauses and modifiers" (p. 425). Comparing the number of words per T-unit in students' writing is considered an objective measure of student growth in writing over a period of time, as it illustrates students' "ability to produce longer and more complex written sentences" (Lanauze & Snow, 1989, p. 327). Thus, the use of such a measure provides insight into the development of students' linguistic complexity in their Spanish and English writing. After reviewing arguments for and against the use of T-units, Gaies (1980, p. 54) concluded that the benefit of

> an index like mean T-unit length is twofold: first, it would be a global measure of linguistic development external to any particular set of data and second, it would allow for meaningful numerical comparisons between first and second language acquisition.

Critics of T-unit analysis claim that such analysis might not be useful as a tool for ELLs in the beginning stages of language development (Gaies, 1980). However, because students in this study received paired literacy instruction, the program encouraged English-language and literacy development starting in first grade. Further, the majority of students in this study (over 80%) are classified as limited English proficient (LEP), rather than non-English proficient (NEP), suggesting that the majority of students have some (albeit limited) level of English-language proficiency.

In analyzing students' writing samples for the number of words per T-unit, two of us (Butvilofsky & Sparrow) scored each sample independently from one another, first counting the total number of words and T-units in the sample, and then dividing the total number of words by the total number of T-units. We then compared our total counts of T-units and words for each sample. For any sample in which a discrepancy existed in the number of words per T-unit, we discussed the inconsistency until we reached a consensus. In the instance that an agreement could not be reached, we consulted two other researchers and reached a final decision. In counting T-units, some issues arose for which we needed to create standards to count or exclude certain words and T-units. Specifically, when words could not be deciphered within a student's sample, we excluded the entire T-unit. We felt as though this would not harm our analysis because we were computing the average number of words per T-unit, and, therefore, the omission of a T-unit would not affect the average number of words per T-unit. Furthermore, we counted proper nouns as one word because we found that it was not fair to compare a student who wrote about *The Suite Life of Zack and Cody* (a children's television show) with a student who wrote about *Clifford* (another television show), as the title or other proper noun added to the number of words in a T-unit but did not increase the complexity of that T-unit. The final issue that arose was that some samples contained lengthy lists of nouns. For example, a student wrote about a field trip and listed each student that was in the group. Because a long list does not contribute to the linguistic complexity of the writing, we counted each list as one word within the T-unit. For a more detailed description of these considerations and additional definitions pertaining to T-units, see Table 8.1.

When analyzing the data, first we compared students' Spanish writing complexity to their English complexity. Then, we began to quantitatively and qualitatively compare each individual student's writing samples (six per child) to determine longitudinal writing development from first through third grade in Spanish and English. Our final analysis examined the relationship of Spanish and English writing complexity in each grade.

Findings

Overall results of this study illustrated that to gain insight into emerging bilingual children's ability to develop and express their ideas in writing, their Spanish

TABLE 8.1 Counting number of words and T-units

Term	Definition
T-unit	"Any independent clause with all of its subordinate clauses and modifiers" (Miller, 1995, p. 425)
Independent clause	Stands alone as a complete thought/ sentence with a main subject and verb
Subordinate/dependent clause	Cannot stand alone – must be connected to an independent clause
Modifiers	Words, phrases, or clauses that provide description
Formula for average words per T-unit	Total number of words in sample ÷ Total number of T-units in sample
Special considerations	
Instance	Count
Indecipherable words and phrases	Exclude entire T-unit
Proper nouns/titles (*The Suite Life of Zack and Cody*)	One word
List of three or more words (Carlos, Michael, Joe, and Alicia)	One word

and English writing samples need to be read and rated together rather than as two independent writing samples in two different languages. Using a bilingual perspective to view students' writing development illustrated that the majority of students made gains in the complexity of their written expression in both Spanish and English as measured by T-units over a three-year period. In the first grade, students expressed themselves with greater linguistic complexity in Spanish, though by second grade, students' ideas had a comparable level of complexity in both languages. By third grade, students' English writing was slightly more complex in terms of T-units, thus illustrating their evolution toward becoming biliterate writers. While T-units provided a numeric understanding of student growth, a qualitative analysis was necessary to uncover the idiosyncrasies and nuances involved in each child's developmental trajectory toward biliteracy. Such improvement over time demonstrated that providing students with paired literacy instruction does not cause interference in their writing development in either language. Therefore, the best way to understand emerging bilingual children's biliterate development is to examine what they can do in both languages, as when looking at each language independently, one risks underestimating their full capabilities.

Comparison of Writing Complexity by Language

In examining how writing samples compared across languages and grade levels, mean words per T-unit were calculated for Spanish and English and compared across languages and grade levels. Results are presented in Table 8.2. In all grades, children appeared to be developing as biliterate writers, as most students grew in writing complexity in Spanish and English from first through third grade. Students in first grade expressed their ideas in a more complex manner in Spanish than in English, as the mean words per T-unit was higher in Spanish. In second grade, students wrote with the same complexity in both languages. By third grade, students' ideas appeared to be somewhat more developed in their English writing, as demonstrated by the negative difference in mean scores in Table 8.2. This change could be attributed to the increase in time allocated to literacy-based ESL in school, as well as to students' daily experiences living in an English dominant society. Thus, when looking across grade levels, in first grade, students were better able to express their ideas in Spanish than in English, as the difference between their means was significant. However, as students advanced in their schooling and were instructed in two languages, their linguistic complexity in English writing became equivalent to that of their Spanish writing and no significant difference emerged between languages. By third grade, a significant difference appeared between the two, with English writing surpassing Spanish writing in complexity, though on average, it was only one more word per T-unit.

TABLE 8.2 Literacy squared writing sample descriptives in words/T-unit and paired samples test

Grade	Number of samples/language	Mean Spanish (SD)	Mean English (SD)	Mean score difference	Std. error mean
1	25	7.56 (2.8)	5.81 (2.2)	1.74★	0.74
2	25	7.84 (2.5)	8.13 (2.4)	−0.29	0.49
3	25	9.60 (2.3)	10.74 (2.9)	−1.14★	0.56

Note
★ Mean differences are significant at the 0.05 level (two-tailed).

One important consideration in looking at words per T-unit is the grammatical differences between languages. One might be inclined to think that it takes more words to express ideas in Spanish than in English because of the grammatical structures of language. For example, the phrase, *my uncle's horse* is three words in English. However, the Spanish translation, *el caballo de mi tío*, is five words in Spanish. While this example illustrates that more words are needed to use the possessive in Spanish, more words are often used in identifying the subject of a verb in English, as in Spanish, the subject is often implied within the conjugation of the verb. For example, in English, two words are necessary to say *we play*. However, in Spanish, the same phrase can be stated using both the subject and the verb, *nosotros jugamos*, or only the verb, *jugamos*, which is more common because the pronoun is identified in the conjugation of the verb. Because each language has different instances in which expressing some ideas can use more words, it is believed that at this level of writing development, the number of words per T-unit can be compared across languages (Gaies, 1980).

Longitudinal Comparison of Writing Development

As students progressed in the biliteracy program, both their Spanish and English writing increased in complexity. Because the majority of students showed continued growth in both languages each year, paired literacy instruction did not seem to delay the acquisition of English writing skills. Further, learning to write in English beginning in first grade did not negatively affect writing in Spanish. When examining the average words per T-unit for each language, it appeared that student writing matured each year in both languages. Students showed the most growth in linguistic complexity between first and second grade English writing. As students in this project continued through school, they developed literacy skills simultaneously in both Spanish and English, as illustrated in Table 8.2, where the mean words per T-unit increased in each progressive grade in both languages. A qualitative analysis also showed students' improvement in writing as they advanced from first to third grade.

Although T-units have been shown to be a good measure of linguistic complexity (Gaies, 1980; Lanauze & Snow, 1989), they do not provide a complete understanding of the intricacies involved in bilingual students' writing. Because the emerging bilingual children in this study received paired literacy instruction, it was important to examine their work from a bilingual perspective, as students' English writing mirrored some of the skills and strategies that they utilized in Spanish writing. Recognizing these similarities can help teachers focus instruction on highlighting those concepts that do and do not transfer.

Diego's writing samples illustrated the importance of examining student work from a bilingual perspective. As Table 8.3 shows, Diego fell within one word per T-unit of the average in terms of linguistic complexity, with the exception of third grade English, in which he scored over four words per T-unit above the mean. His samples (Figures 8.1–8.6) showed the progress he has made in writing from first through third grade in Spanish and English. However, what was most insightful when examining Diego's biliterate development was not the number of words per T-unit that he produced, but rather the intricacies that arose throughout his work.

In first grade, it was apparent that Diego could clearly communicate his ideas in both languages (Figures 8.1–8.2). However, while his Spanish sample illustrated his ability to accurately hear and record sounds, his English sample showed that he was encoding dominant consonants, approximating some vowels, and omitting muted sounds. While Diego demonstrated some common native English grade-level errors, he also transferred his graphophonemic knowledge from Spanish to encode words in English. For example, he wrote *favorite* as *fabret*. In Spanish, the *b* and *v* sounds are hard to differentiate, and it is common for students to replace one for the other in their writing.

Diego showed growth in his writing from first to second grade in both languages (Figures 8.3–8.4). Again, he was able to communicate his ideas in both Spanish and English. In contrast to his first grade English writing, in second grade, Diego represented all consonant sounds, but still omitted some vowels, and his transfer of Spanish sounds to English was still apparent. Where Diego

TABLE 8.3 Diego's words per T-unit grades 1–3

Grade	Language	Average	Diego
1	Spanish	7.56 (2.8)	7.3
	English	5.81 (2.2)	6.5
2	Spanish	7.84 (2.5)	7
	English	8.13 (2.4)	9
3	Spanish	9.60 (2.3)	8.9
	English	10.74 (2.9)	14.5

wrote *sestr* in first grade to represent the word *sister*, in second grade he wrote it correctly. Furthermore, to write *came*, Diego wrote *caym*, illustrating his knowledge that the Spanish vowel *a* cannot make such a sound alone, but instead must be combined with another letter, thus leading him to approximate the long /a/ sound in *came* using the letters *ay*. In his English sample, he demonstrated the knowledge he was gaining from his exposure to English print. Not only did he retell the plot of his favorite English story, but he was also acquiring vocabulary in his writing, as he wrote about a character taking a sleeping bag and fishing gear on a camping trip. Diego's second grade English writing sample

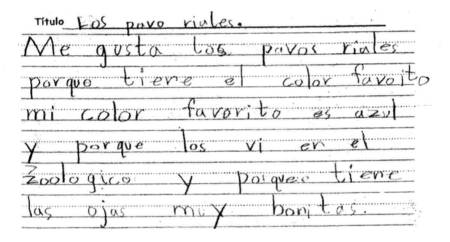

FIGURE 8.1 Diego's first grade Spanish writing sample. "I like peacocks because they are my favorite color. Blue is my favorite color. I also like peacocks because I saw them at the zoo and because they have very pretty eyes."

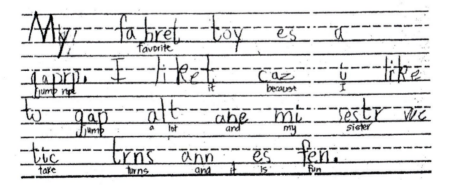

FIGURE 8.2 Diego's first grade English writing sample. "My favorite toy is a jump rope. I like it because I like to jump a lot and [so does] my sister. We take turns and [it] is fun."

also illustrated the importance of looking at his writing from a bilingual perspective. A second grade teacher with no knowledge of biliteracy development might overlook Diego's idea development and his ability to communicate, and instead be overly concerned with his inability to use conventional spelling. Yet, we would argue that he was able to provide a detailed summary of the story in a coherent and organized way. Viewing Diego through a bilingual perspective, we acknowledge that he had an understanding of the way story structures function, in that he could produce a composition with a beginning, middle, and end in both languages. He also used some punctuation in both languages. Perhaps he was more proficient in conventional spelling in Spanish, but, overall, he could produce quality work in both languages. As bilingual teachers, we would not be worried about his ability to develop and communicate ideas in his writing, but rather we would recognize his need for more direct instruction in certain aspects of English writing. To support Diego in his writing, we would recommend that his teacher use an explicit cross-language method such as *The Dictado* that teaches language structures, vocabulary, and spelling in a meaningful way (Escamilla et al., 2009).

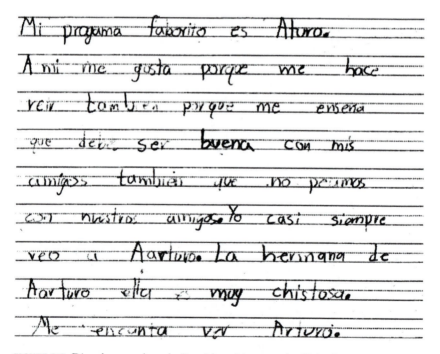

FIGURE 8.3 Diego's second grade Spanish writing sample. "My favorite program is Arthur. I like it because it makes me laugh. I also like it because it teaches me that I should be nice to my friends and that we shouldn't fight with our friends. I almost always watch Arthur. Arthur's sister is very funny. I love to watch Arthur."

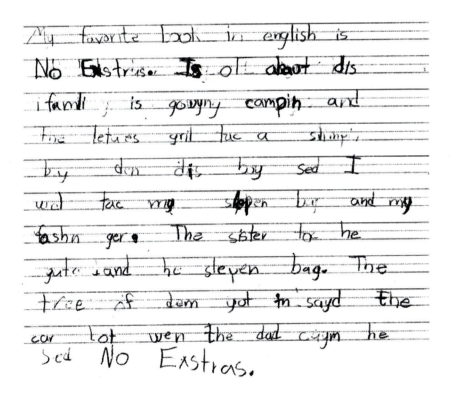

FIGURE 8.4 Diego's second grade English writing sample. "My favorite book in English is No Extras. It's all about this family that is going camping and the littlest girl takes a sleeping bag. Then this boy said, 'I will take my sleeping bag and my fishing gear.' The sister took her cat and her sleeping bag. The three of them got inside the car, but when the dad came he said, 'NO Extras.'"

Diego's third grade writing samples (Figures 8.5–8.6) illustrated that he was maturing as a writer in both Spanish and English, and when given the proper support, he could improve even more. Diego's writing showed his ability to describe a personal experience with detailed descriptions and voice. In his English sample, he made analogies to communicate his experiences to the audience, as he described the wind as "geding hardr and hardr like if a tornadr came [sic]" and the snow as "stiky [sic] as glue and cold as ice cubes." While Diego's English writing did contain some errors, it was apparent that his knowledge of how words are written was becoming more sophisticated, as he moved from the phonetic phase of spelling into the transitional phase where vowels are almost always used, but letters are sometimes transposed (Hernández, 2001). Diego attempted to produce more complex language by experimenting with the use of similes. It is only by taking such risks and making errors that he will eventually

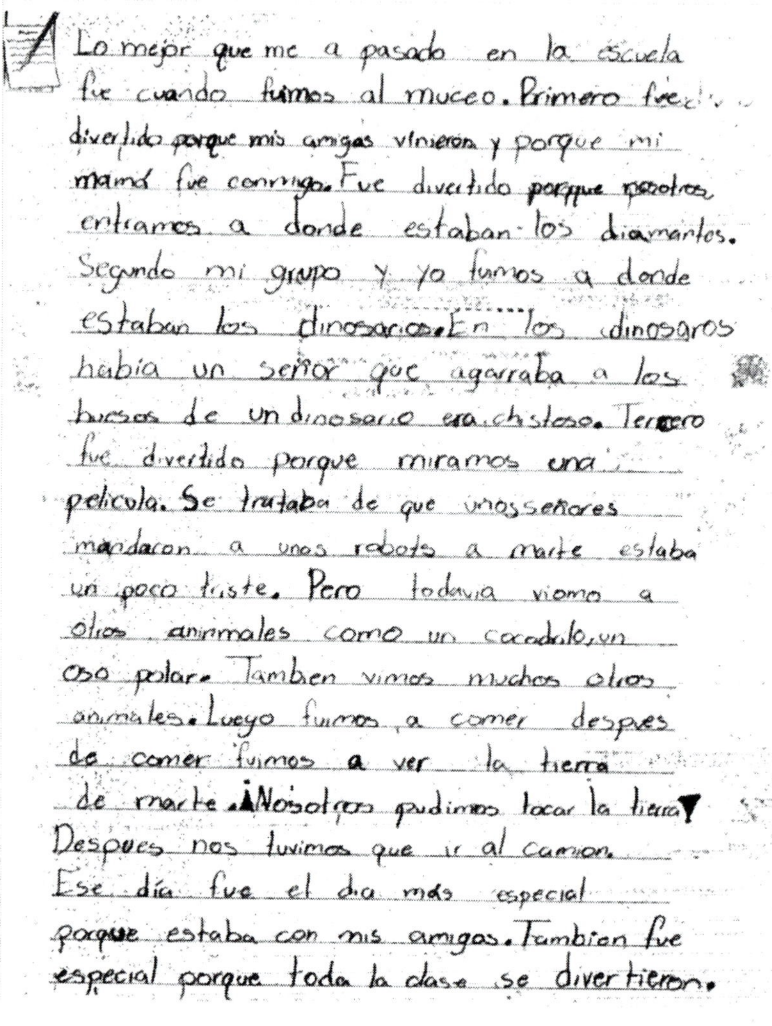

Lo mejor que me a pasado en la escuela
fue cuando fuimos al museo. Primero fue
divertido porque mis amigas vinieron y porque mi
mamá fue conmigo. Fue divertido porque nosotros
entramos a donde estaban los diamantes.
Segundo mi grupo y yo fuimos a donde
estaban los dinosarios. En los dinosaros
había un señor que agarraba a los
huesos de un dinosario era chistoso. Tercero
fue divertido porque miramos una
película. Se trataba de que unos señores
mandaron a unos robots a marte estaba
un poco taste. Pero todavía viomo a
otros animales como un cocodrilo, un
oso polar. Tambien vimos muchos otros
animales. Luego fuimos a comer despues
de comer fuimos a ver la tierra
de marte. Nosotros pudimos tocar la tierra.
Despues nos tuvimos que ir al camion.
Ese día fue el dia mas especial
porque estaba con mis amigas. Tambien fue
especial porque toda la clase se divertieron.

FIGURE 8.5 Diego's third grade Spanish writing sample. "The best thing that happened to me in school was when we went to the museum. First, it was fun because my friends and my mom went with me. It was fun because we went to where the diamonds were. Second, my group and I went to where there were dinosaurs. In the dinosaur [area] there was a man that was handling the dinosaur bones. It was funny. Third, it was fun because we saw a movie. It was about some men that sent robots to Mars and it was a little sad. But we still saw some other animals like a crocodile and a polar bear. We also saw many other animals. Then we went to eat. After eating we went to see dirt from Mars. We were able to touch the dirt! After that, we had to go to the bus. That was the best day because I was with my friends. It was also special because the whole class had fun."

acquire accuracy, for "accuracy is the outcome, not the process of learning" (Clay, 2007, p. 70). His samples also showed his application of the same rhetorical structure to sequence events in both languages. An interesting, though unusual, example of transfer was Diego's use of accents in English, as in writing the word reason(s), he wrote, "rezón(s)". His English writing development from second grade to third grade illustrated his growth in conventional spelling of high frequency words and linguistic complexity.

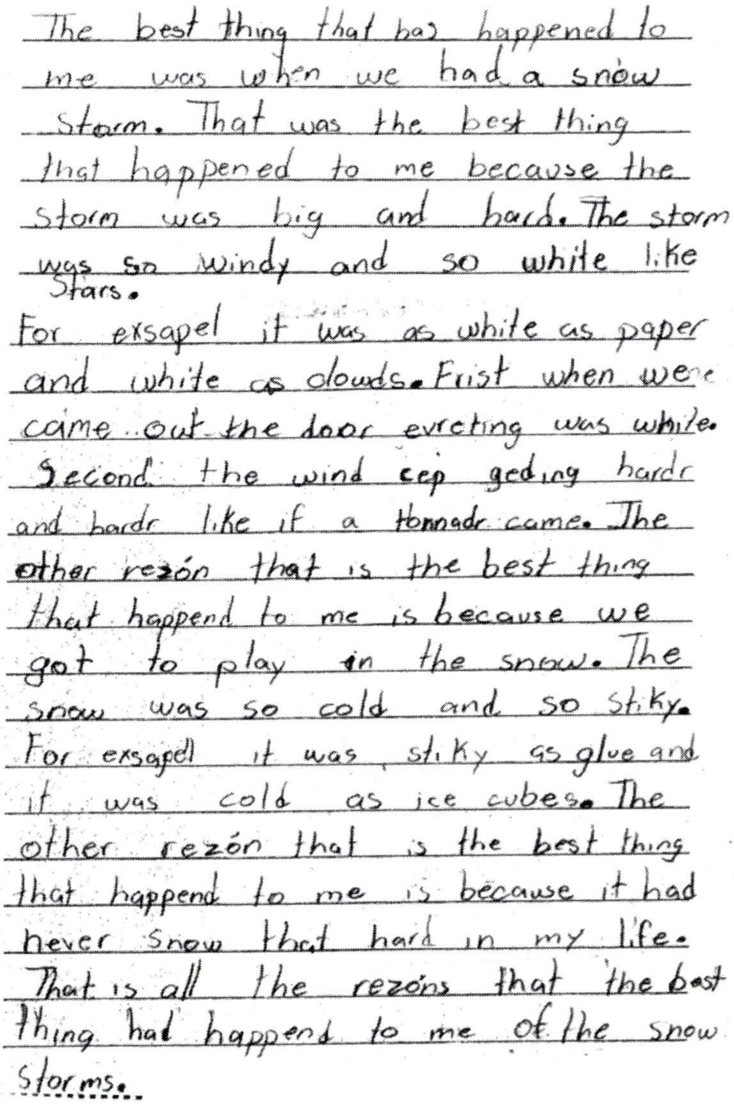

The best thing that has happened to me was when we had a snow storm. That was the best thing that happened to me because the storm was big and hard. The storm was so windy and so white like stars.

For exsapel it was as white as paper and white as clouds. Frist when we came out the door evreting was white. Second the wind cep geding hardr and hardr like if a tonnadr came. The other rezón that is the best thing that happend to me is because we got to play in the snow. The snow was so cold and so stiky. For exsapel it was stiky as glue and it was cold as ice cubes. The other rezón that is the best thing that happend to me is because it had never snow that hard in my life. That is all the rezóns that the best thing had happend to me of the snow storms.

FIGURE 8.6 Diego's third grade English writing sample.

Relationship Between Spanish and English

The relationships between words per T-unit in Spanish and English at each grade level were determined by calculating the correlation coefficients between Spanish and English. In second and third grade, the relationships between Spanish and English words per T-unit showed significant correlations that were both moderate and positive ($r = 0.49$ and $r = 0.45$, respectively). That is, as students developed a more complex way of expressing their ideas in Spanish writing, they were becoming more adept at transferring such expression of ideas to their English writing.

As students advanced in their writing, the relationship between Spanish and English became more apparent. Although correlations between students' expression of ideas in Spanish and English were not significant in first grade, students appeared to be using their knowledge of Spanish writing as a foundation for their English writing, especially in phonetic representation. As their ability to communicate and express ideas increased in complexity, the relationship between such expressions became significant in second and third grade. The amount of time dedicated to each language equalized and students' ability to use both languages became more productive, thereby making the distinctions between which skills and strategies transferred difficult to determine. As students progressed in both languages, distinctions between the two became insignificant and the implication that L1 was their dominant language is not necessarily accurate (Dworin, 2003) because students' fluency levels depend on their individual needs and experiences in each language (Grosjean, 1989).

Complexity Verses Quality

Similarly to Carlisle (1989), we discovered that when using T-units to analyze writing, the quality of student work might be overlooked. For example, a student might have a high number of words per T-unit, but under closer inspection, one discovers the complexity of the student's knowledge of acquiring two languages. In contrast, a sample might contain fewer words per T-unit while demonstrating good organization, rich description, and voice. Thus, although T-units may illustrate student growth, it is important to examine students' writing beyond such a measurement.

While the number of words per T-unit seems to be a good measure of growth over time, instances in which T-units do not always indicate quality writing were apparent. For example, as illustrated in Table 8.4, in third grade, Lucinda wrote below average words per T-unit in her Spanish sample about her Valentine's Day celebration at school and in her English sample about her trip to Sea World. Yet, when examining her samples (Figures 8.7–8.8), it became evident that she demonstrated the capacity to develop her ideas in a well-organized and descriptive manner. In both her Spanish and English samples,

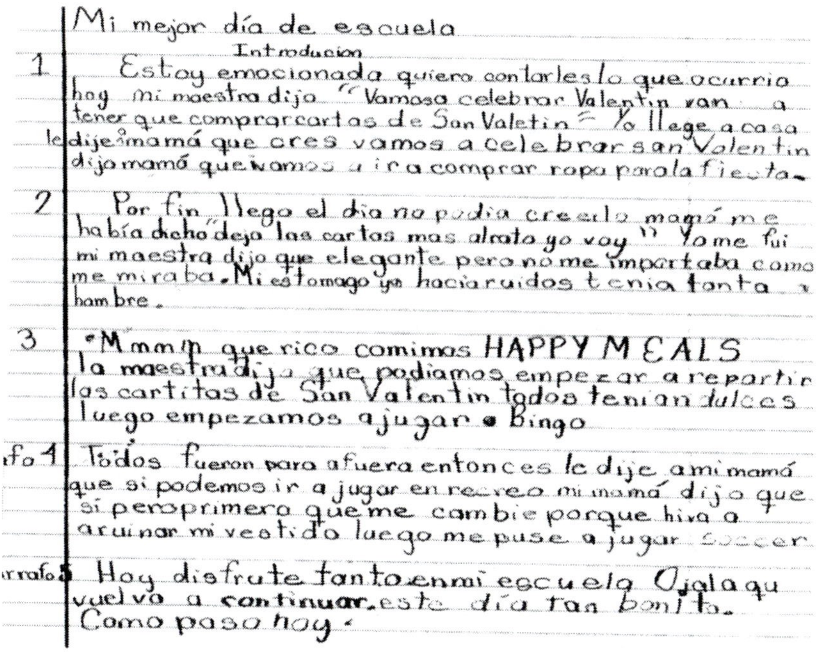

Mi mejor día de escuela

Introducion

1. Estoy emocionada quiero contarles lo que ocurrio hoy mi maestra dijo "Vamos a celebrar Valentin van a tener que comprar cartas de San Valetin" Yo llege a casa le dije mamá que cres vamos a celebrar san Valentin dijo mamá que vamos a ir a comprar ropa para la fiesta.

2. Por fin llego el día no pudia creelo mamá me había dicho deja las cartas mas alrato yo voy" Yo me fui mi maestra dijo que elegante pero no me importaba como me miraba. Mi estomago ya hacia ruidos tenia tanta hambre.

3. "Mmm mp que rico comimos HAPPY MEALS la maestra dijo que podiamos empezar a repartir las cartitas de San Valentin todos tenian dulces luego empezamos a jugar Bingo

fo 4 Todos fueron para afuera entonces le dije a mi mamá que si podemos ir a jugar en recreo mi mamá dijo que si pero primero que me cambie porque hiva a aruinar mi vestido luego me puse a jugar soccer

rrafo 5 Hoy disfrute tanto en mi escuela Ojala qu vuelvo a continuar este día tan bonito. Como paso hoy.

FIGURE 8.7 Lucinda's third grade Spanish writing sample. "My Best Day at School. I am excited. I want to tell you about what happened today. My teacher said 'We are going to celebrate Valentine's Day. You are all going to have to buy Valentine's Day cards.'

When I got home, I told my mom, 'Guess what? We are going to celebrate Valentine's Day.'

My mom said that we were going to buy clothes for the party.

The day finally came. I couldn't believe it. My mom had told me 'Leave the cards, I'll be there in a while,' so I left. My teacher said, 'How elegant,' but I didn't care about how I looked. My stomach was growling, I was so hungry.

Mmmm, how delicious, we ate HAPPY MEALS. The teacher said that we could pass out our Valentine's Day cards. They all had candies. Then we began to play Bingo.

Everyone went outside. Then I asked my mom if we could go to play at recess.

My mom said yes, but first I had to change so that I wouldn't ruin my dress. Then I went to play soccer.

I enjoyed my school so much today. I wish this great day that happened today would continue."

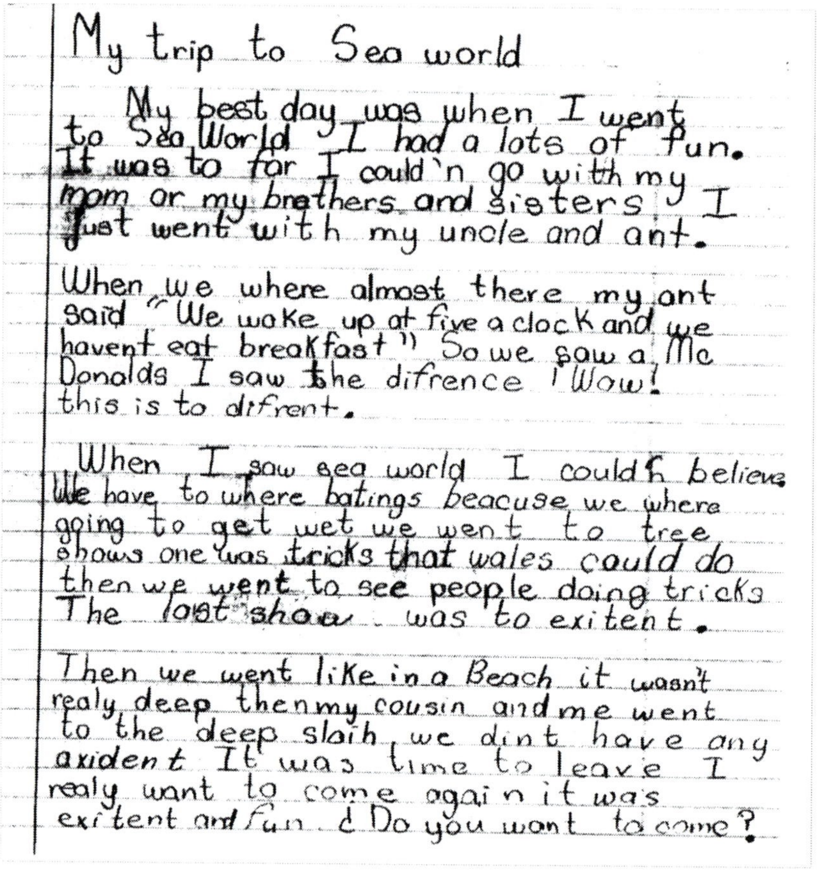

My trip to Sea world

My best day was when I went to Sea World I had a lots of fun. It was to far I could'n go with my mom or my brothers and sisters I just went with my uncle and ant.

When we where almost there my ant said "We wake up at five a clock and we havent eat breakfast" So we saw a Mc Donalds I saw the difrence I Wow! this is to difrent.

When I saw sea world I couldn believe We have to where batings beacuse we where going to get wet we went to tree shows one was tricks that wales could do then we went to see people doing tricks The last show was to exitent.

Then we went like in a Beach it wasn't realy deep thenmy cousin andme went to the deep sloih we dint have any axident It was time to leave I realy want to come again it was exitent and fun ¿Do you want to come?

FIGURE 8.8 Lucinda's third grade English writing sample.

Lucinda employed an effective structure, while at the same time varying her paragraph and sentence beginnings, thus demonstrating her understanding of how to keep her reader engaged. In contrast, many of the other third grade samples contained the highly structured sequencing vocabulary often taught in school such as *first, second, then, next*. Lucinda also wrote with rich description and voice, inviting her reader to join her as she retold her favorite experiences. She wrote, "Mi estomago ya hacía ruidos tenía tanta hambre." ("My stomach was growling I was so hungry.") Rather than merely telling her audience she was hungry, Lucinda drew in her reader with additional details, demonstrating her emerging knowledge of literary language. Similarly, Lucinda concluded her English narrative by saying what a great time she had and asking her reader, "¿Do you want to come?" Thus, although Lucinda scored below average in the number of words per T-unit, a third grade teacher with a bilingual perspective would likely consider her on a positive trajectory toward biliteracy.

The number of words per T-unit can also overestimate a child's writing capabilities. As Table 8.4 illustrates, although Raúl had a higher average number of words per T-unit in both languages, he did not demonstrate the same writing abilities that Lucinda demonstrated with fewer words per T-unit. While Raúl's Spanish and English samples (Figures 8.9–8.10) showed his ability to convey his ideas in a narrative, it was apparent that he was struggling to express them effectively. Although he framed his story within the formatted structure of *primero, segundo, tercero, luego* (first, second, third, later), he could only communicate specific events that happened or might happen, rather than describing his personal experiences during those events. For example, he wrote, "Tercero, La mamá de Ms. Levine se va a su casa para hacer comida para ella." ("Third, Ms. Levine's mom goes home to make herself food.") While Raúl was writing about the time his teacher's mom came to his classroom, rather than describing his actual experience throughout the event, he only wrote that Ms. Levine's mom showed the class how to make ice cream and then he began to describe what she did after leaving.

In his English sample, Raúl described a specific event and his experiences with that event, though he did not draw in his reader and explain his full experience. Though Raúl's third grade samples showed limitations in his writing, when examining his writing longitudinally from first through third grade, he demonstrated growth in linguistic complexity and quality. While the average number of words per T-unit has practical advantages in quantifying written linguistic complexity, such as its objectivity and ability to produce numerical values for comparison, the contrast between Lucinda and Raúl's writing demonstrates that such analysis does not necessarily provide a complete picture of the quality of a child's writing, and therefore other criteria should also be used when analyzing students' writing.

Because of the shortcomings of T-unit analysis, one must use caution when using such analysis so as not to overlook important developments in a child's writing. Our qualitative analysis provided insight into the quality of students' writing and students' resourcefulness in acquiring biliteracy, and it allowed us to examine some of the skills and strategies transferring in the students' work, none of which would have been evident through T-unit analysis alone. Thus, T-unit analysis should not be used in isolation, but instead should be used in conjunction with other methods of analysis such as the qualitative analysis we provided

TABLE 8.4 Third grade words per T-unit

Language	Average	Lucinda	Raúl
Spanish	9.60 (2.3)	7	11.6
English	10.74 (2.9)	6.8	11.7

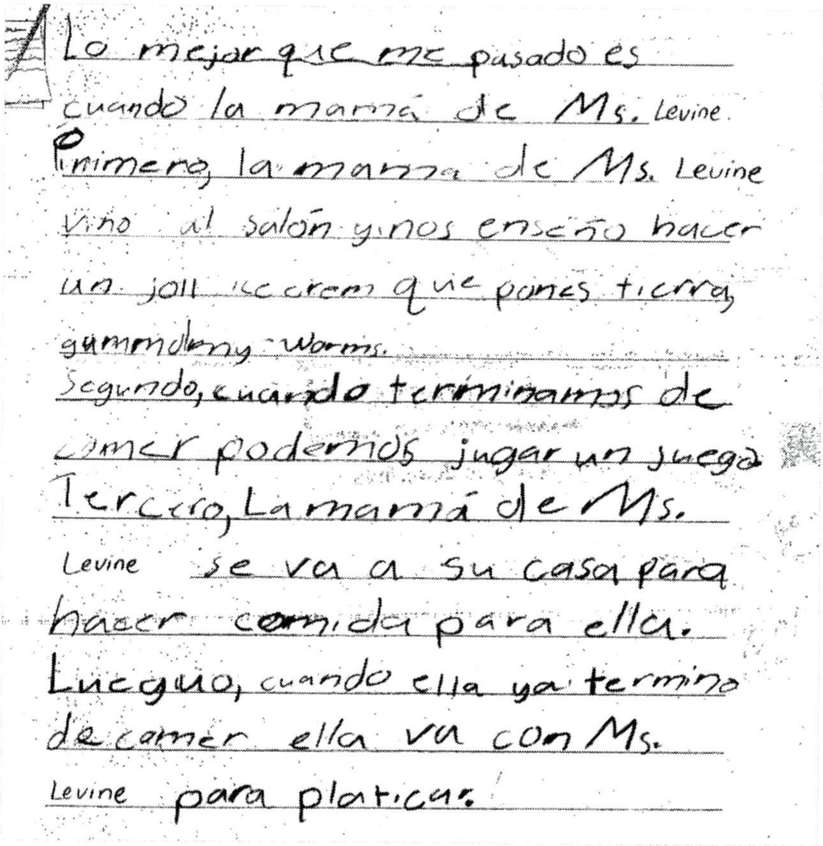

FIGURE 8.9 Raúl's third grade Spanish writing sample. "The best thing that happened to me is when Ms. Levine's mom. First, Ms. Levine's mom came to our classroom and taught us how to make ice cream in which you put dirt, gummy worms. Second, when we finish eating we can play a game. Third, Ms. Levine's mom goes home to make herself food. Then, when she already finishes eating she goes with Ms. Levine to talk."

in this chapter. Nevertheless, when performing any analysis, people must remember the importance of looking at emerging bilingual children's writing from a bilingual perspective, which, among other things, includes always taking each student's capabilities in both languages into consideration.

Discussion and Pedagogical Implications

Findings from this study suggest that emerging bilingual students receiving paired literacy instruction benefited from such instruction, and though writing development differed for each child, all continued on a positive trajectory

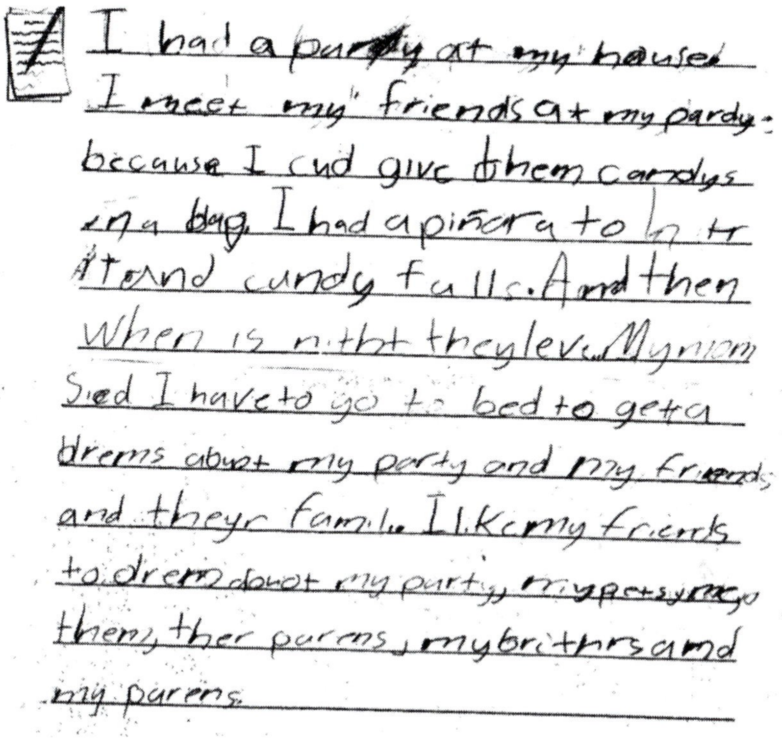

> I had a party at my house.
> I meet my friends at my pardy.
> because I cud give them cardys
> in a bag. I had a piñata to hit
> it and candy falls. And then
> When is nitht theyleve. My mam
> Sied I have to go to bed to get a
> drems abuot my party and my friends
> and theyr famil. I Lke my friends
> to drem abuot my party, my pets, me,
> them, ther parens, my brithrs and
> my parens

FIGURE 8.10 Raúl's third grade English writing sample. "I had a party at my house. I meet my friends at my party because I could give them candies in a bag. I had a piñata to hit it and candy falls. And then when it's night they leave. My mom said I have to go to bed to get a dreams about my party and my friends and their family. I like my friends to dream about my party, my pets, me, them, their parents, my brothers and my parents."

toward biliteracy. Our analyses of these writing samples has highlighted the importance of examining students in both languages in order to understand the student in a more holistic way (Grosjean, 1989). As illustrated briefly in the discussion about Diego's samples, it is difficult to determine a child's strengths and weaknesses without looking at a student's Spanish and English samples together. In fact, it can result in incorrect, and even detrimental, decisions regarding a student's needs. We therefore suggest that teachers regularly gather students' Spanish and English writing samples to help them understand students' writing development in both languages. While it may not be feasible to apply T-unit analysis to these samples each time they are collected, by collecting and reviewing them, the teacher can remain cognizant of the skills the child is developing in both languages.

While teaching emerging bilingual students in one language often assumes such instruction will foster development in the other language, teaching students literacy simultaneously in two languages allows them to gain proficiency concurrently in both languages (Davis et al., 1999). It is important to remember that developing biliteracy includes writing, thereby making it critical that writing instruction becomes an integral part of literacy and biliteracy instruction. Consistent and comprehensive writing instruction is as important as reading instruction for emerging bilingual children. The writing examined in this study illustrates the importance of teaching literacy in both languages beginning in first grade, as doing so does not have negative repercussions on literacy or language development. Furthermore, it allowed us to consider the totality of emerging bilingual children's experiences as a unique and unified whole rather than viewing them as two monolinguals in one person (Grosjean, 1989). In examining students as emerging bilinguals, Spanish and English writing samples need to be read and interpreted by bilingual individuals looking at students' work in both languages simultaneously.

When looking at students' longitudinal writing development in Spanish and English, it becomes evident that students have the capacity to develop biliteracy, without one language adversely affecting the other. Furthermore, learning in two languages allows students to use each language as a scaffold for the other, as the languages act symbiotically with one another. As students become bilingual and biliterate, each takes on a different trajectory toward this biliterate development, thus illustrating the importance of examining individual development from a bilingual perspective (Dworin, 2003; Edelsky, 1982; Grosjean, 1989). Grosjean explains, "The bilingual's communicative competence cannot be evaluated through only one language; it must be studied instead through the bilingual's total language repertoire as it is used in his or her everyday life" (p. 6). Because language and cross-language transfer are not linear, a set scope and sequence does not exist in biliterate development (Dworin, 2003). Our study adds further evidence to the theory that biliteracy develops in idiosyncratic ways, thus making it difficult to predict specific patterns of development. As teachers realize that emerging bilingual children do not follow a "normal" or predictable path toward biliteracy, it is imperative that they understand how emerging bilingual children use both languages as they develop biliteracy.

Through professional development and other experiences, it is critical that teachers learn to read and interpret emerging bilingual children's writing through biliterate perspectives to ensure that they are doing everything possible to support each student's biliteracy development. Findings from our study suggest that because emerging bilingual students' first grade writing is more complex in Spanish, they may transfer their knowledge of Spanish to their English writing, while in third grade, as their writing begins to show more complexity in English, they may use their English abilities to assist them in their Spanish writing. This finding may be specific to students receiving the Literacy

Squared intervention, which places strong importance on writing; but it also supports other researchers (Dworin, 2003; Hernández, 2001; Reyes, 2006; Reyes & Costanzo, 2001) who acknowledge the cross-linguistic transfer of skills and abilities between and across languages. Teachers and researchers must emphasize cross-language transfer because it acknowledges the emerging bilingual child's resourcefulness in applying knowledge across languages, rather than viewing such resourcefulness as interference or confusion.

Ideally, in bilingual programs, the same teacher would teach students in both languages, thus facilitating an understanding of each child's full linguistic repertoire. However, in recognizing that many emerging bilingual children are in monolingual contexts, we recommend that teachers provide opportunities for students to write in their native language even if they themselves do not speak the language. Such opportunities allow children to demonstrate their knowledge of writing, and teachers to discover their students' writing capabilities. Furthermore, teachers can gain an even deeper understanding of their students' writing by having someone else translate and discuss it, not only acknowledging and valuing the knowledge that their students bring to school, but also gaining a better understanding of their students' writing capabilities and helping to inform their instruction.

In terms of classroom practices, examining students' Spanish and English writing simultaneously showed that children strategically transfer knowledge from one language to the other. Therefore, teaching children explicit cross-language connections is of vital importance. Not only does it allow them to build on what they already know, but it also makes teaching and learning more efficient, as instead of reteaching the same strategies in both languages, time can be spent explicitly teaching the ways in which the written systems of the two languages are similar and how they differ (Escamilla et al., 2009). For example, after reading Lucinda's Spanish and English samples together, a teacher would notice her use of quotation marks in both languages. Knowing that she has mastery of quotation use in English, a teacher could easily compare and contrast such use with that of the *guiones*, the Spanish equivalent of quotation marks. Cognates are an example of demonstrating the similarities between the languages. In Diego's case, a teacher would see that he wrote "*tornadr*" for tornado in his English sample. All the teacher would need to do is explicitly teach him that the English word *tornado* is the same as the Spanish word *tornado* except in the way that it is pronounced.

In addition to making explicit cross-language connections, teachers can use oracy as a way to foster language and literacy development. Historically, literacy instruction has primarily focused on the receptive skill of reading, and the purpose of ESL instruction has been to develop oral language skills before introducing literacy. However, we posit that literacy instruction, and, more specifically, paired literacy instruction, should include both the receptive and productive aspects of language, which include reading, listening, writing, and oracy (Wilkinson, 1970).

Thus, while teachers continue to provide opportunities for students to use receptive literacy skills, they must also promote and develop productive literacy skills by providing explicit writing and oral language instruction. Diego's third grade English writing shows that he has been taught about similes, and he is beginning to experiment with them in his writing. Thus, he would benefit from oracy instruction in which the teacher provides alternative language structures that allow for ideas to be expressed more effectively.

Findings from our analyses illustrated that children who receive instruction in two languages have the potential to become biliterate. "Providing opportunities to write in both languages and promoting the use of both ... may enhance the repertoire of skills these children use in academic writing tasks" (Davis et al., 1999, p. 246). Literacy Squared provides such opportunities for students, and students therefore began to develop such academic writing skills. Our analyses of emerging bilingual children's writing also showed that the ability to express complex and sophisticated ideas preceded grammatical and mechanical competence (Geisler et al., 2007), again illustrating the importance of teaching students to express their ideas in both languages while recognizing that both languages may be in different stages of development. We believe that it is not only the opportunity to write in both languages that develops biliteracy, but that it is this opportunity combined with direct and interactive quality writing instruction. Using a bilingual perspective to understand emerging bilingual children's biliterate writing development over time provides insight into how emerging bilingual children utilize both languages as they progress on their trajectory toward biliteracy.

References

Carlisle, J. F., & Beeman, F. F. (2000). The effects of language of instruction on the reading and writing achievement of first-grade Hispanic children. *Scientific Studies of Reading, 4*, 331–353.

Carlisle, R. (1989). The writing of Anglo and Hispanic elementary school students in bilingual, submersion, and regular programs. *Studies in Second Language Acquisition, 11*, 257–281.

Carlo, M. S., & Royer, J. M. (1999). A cognitive components perspective of language transfer. In D. A. Wagner, R. L. Venezky, & B. V. Street, (Eds.), *Literacy: An international handbook* (pp. 148–154). Boulder, CO: Westview Press.

Clay, M. M. (2007). Child development. *Journal of Reading Recovery*, 69–76.

Collier, V. P. (1992). A synthesis of studies examining long-term language minority student data on academic achievement. *Bilingual Research Journal, 16*, 187–212.

Davis, L. H., Carlisle, J. F., & Beeman, M. M. (1999). Hispanic children's writing in English and Spanish when English is the language of instruction. *National Reading Conference, 48*, 238–248.

Dworin, J. (2003). Insights into biliteracy development: Toward a bidirectional theory of bilingual pedagogy. *Journal of Hispanic Higher Education, 2*, 171–186.

Edelsky, C. (1982). Writing in a bilingual program: The relation of L1 and L2 texts. *TESOL Quarterly, 16*, 211–228.

Escamilla, K., Geisler, D., Hopewell, S., Sparrow, W., & Butvilofsky, S. (2009). Using writing to make cross-language connections from Spanish to English. In C. Rodríguez-Eagle (Ed.), *Achieving literacy success with English language learners: Insights, assessment, instruction* (pp 143–159). Worthington, OH: Reading Recovery Council of North America.

Escamilla, K., Geisler, D., Ruiz, O., & Hopewell, S. (2005, January). Literacy squared: Transitions to biliteracy. Paper presented at the Annual Conference of the National Association for Bilingual Education, San Antonio, TX.

Gaies, S. J. (1980). T-unit analysis in second language research: Applications, problems, and limitations. *TESOL Quarterly, 14*, 53–60.

Geisler, D., Escamilla, K., Hopewell, S., & Ruiz, O. (2007, April). Transitions to biliteracy: Focus on writing of Spanish/English emerging bilinguals. Paper presented at the Annual Conference of the American Educational Research Association, Chicago, IL.

Gort, M. (2006). Strategic codeswitching, interliteracy, and other phenomena of emergent bilingual writing: Lessons from first grade dual language classrooms. *Journal of Early Childhood Literacy, 6*, 323–354.

Grosjean, F. (1989). Neurolinguists, beware! The bilingual is not two monolinguals in one person. *Brain and Language, 36*, 3–15.

Hernández, A. (2001). The expected and unexpected literacy outcomes of bilingual students. *Bilingual Research Journal, 25*, 301–326.

Hunt, K. W. (1965). *Grammatical structures written at three grade levels.* Research Report No. 3. Urbana, IL: National Council of Teachers of English.

Lanauze, M., & Snow, C. (1989). The relation between first- and second-language writing skills: Evidence from Puerto Rican elementary school children in bilingual programs. *Linguistics and Education, 1*, 323–339.

Miller, W. H. (1995). *Alternative assessment techniques for reading and writing.* San Francisco, CA: Jossey Bass.

Moll, L. C., & Dworin, J. E. (1996). Biliteracy development in classrooms: Social dynamics and cultural possibilities. In D. Hicks (Ed.), *Child discourse and social learning* (pp. 221–246). Cambridge: Cambridge University Press.

Moll, L. C., Sáez, R., & Dworin, J. (2001). Exploring biliteracy: Two student case examples of writing as social practice. *Elementary School Journal, 101*, 435–449.

Reyes, I. (2006). Exploring connections between emergent biliteracy and bilingualism. *Journal of Early Childhood Literacy, 6*, 267–292.

Reyes, M. L., & Costanzo, L. (2001). On the threshold of biliteracy: A first grader's personal journey. In L. Díaz Soto (Ed.), *Making a difference in the lives of bilingual/bicultural children* (pp. 145–156). New York: Peter Lang.

Rodríguez, A. (1988). Research in reading and writing in bilingual education and English as a second language. In A. Ambert (Ed.), *Bilingual education and English as a second language: A research handbook* (pp. 61–117). New York: Garland.

Slavin, R., & Cheung, A. (2003). *Effective reading programs for English language learners: A best-evidence synthesis.* Washington, DC: Center for Research on the Education of Students Place At Risk (CRESPAR).

Valdés, G. (1992). Bilingual minorities and language issues in writing: Toward professionwide responses to a new challenge. *Written Communication, 9*, 85–136.

Wilkinson, A. (1970). The concept of oracy. *English Journal, 59*, 71–77.

PART III

Reflections and Future Directions

9

REFLECTIONS AND DIRECTIONS FOR BILITERACY RESEARCH

Eurydice Bouchereau Bauer and Mileidis Gort

With rapidly growing numbers of emergent bilinguals in schools in the U.S., there is a critical need to explore the ways in which young children navigate multiple languages and cultures in the process of becoming literate. The complexities associated with these interrelated processes warrant a wider perspective and demand the consideration of political, social, educational, and cultural contexts affecting this development. This book represents a celebration of the diversity of skills that children across different language groups bring to being bilingual. Each chapter tells its own distinctive story; however, the stories intersect and interweave in ways that provide a tightly woven tapestry in which important and repeating patterns emerge. The young children across these chapters reveal that they are not confused by the use of their two languages, that they are able to use their knowledge of both of their languages to support their literacy development, and that the context of their learning shapes their literacy.

At the same time that we are given this opportunity to glance into young children's bilingualism, there is increased opposition to bilingual education for emergent bilingual children from language minority backgrounds in the United States. Paradoxically, two-way immersion programs are increasing and thriving (Crawford, 2004). As a country, we seem to be going in different directions at the same time. Although it is important to challenge prohibitive policies and practices that limit the potential of emergent bilingual children, it is equally imperative that we continue to investigate the ways in which young children become bilingual and biliterate as well as the contexts and practices that support that development. It is from this position that we came together to write this book.

The contributing literacy scholars, independently or in collaboration with their research team, know and understand the languages and cultures of the emergent bilingual populations with whom they work. With this knowledge and experience, they are able to conduct rigorous cross-linguistic and cross-cultural research in literacy and engage in alternative views and conceptualizations about language, literacy learning, teaching, and scholarship (Bernhardt, 2003). Such bilingual and bicultural approaches to literacy research challenges us to think differently about learning and teaching and provide unique insights into emergent bilinguals' complex and multiple paths to literacy.

The Early Years

Emergent biliterate children are actively involved in constructing their knowledge and skills about reading and writing in both of their languages. Bauer and Mkhize adopt a sociocultural approach to show how the literacy rich home environment of a German–English preschooler enhanced the child's emergent reading in German and English. Similarly, Soltero-González and Reyes underscore what a supportive school context in Spanish–English can do for children. In addition, these authors highlight the role of adults (parents, caregivers, teachers) and peers in scaffolding emergent bilingual children's reading and writing, and show how children and other participants can draw from children's linguistic and cultural resources to enhance emergent biliteracy. Importantly, these studies illustrate how the transfer of skills, within and across children's languages, impacts children's early language and literacy skills.

Addressing similar issues, Yaden and Tsai present a different perspective. They show how preschool emergent bilingual children's conceptual understanding of writing in the very early stages of development is similar to their monolingual counterparts. However, there is a stark difference in children's later development, as their conceptual understanding of writing reflects a bilingual stance. Similar to other authors in Part I of this text, Yaden and Tsai maintain that linguistic development is marked by variation within and across the two languages. This suggests that children are constantly restructuring their conceptual knowledge, which is influenced by the very nature of their two languages.

Collectively, the early years chapters reveal that across very diverse settings and language groups (Chinese, English, German, Spanish) emergent bilingual children were able to navigate two languages and used their developing knowledge of these languages to engage themselves and others in thinking about how their languages work. The studies suggest there is an interaction between the children's two languages and the interplay between the languages is evident even when the language pairs come from different language families. Moreover, emergent bilingual children seem to be aware of this connection between the languages and make use of that information as needed. Therefore, the concern that young simultaneous bilinguals are confused by their two languages in oral and written form is not supported.

An interesting finding across the three chapters is that the children were influenced by their linguistic environments, but the extent of that influence must be better understood. Different contextual factors impacted the children's language development. As a result, each setting afforded an opportunity to better understand the impact of the adults and the environment on the children. In Bauer and Mkhize, we got a glimpse into how caregivers used input from the child to continually move her learning within her zone of proximal development. The parents and caregiver positioned themselves to be responsive to the child's remarks across both of her languages.

In Soltero-González and Reyes' chapter, we saw children who resolved to use their L1 even when their learning context did not explicitly reinforce their usage of that language. Although the children's L1 was not forbidden, the teacher seemed unaware of the ways in which students drew upon their developing languages as they engaged with and processed print in both languages. Therefore, the teacher could not provide students with explicit support for cross-linguistic transfer. This is in direct contrast to the deliberate support provided by Elena's caregivers, who intentionally helped her navigate both languages and encouraged her to use both languages as resources (Bauer & Mkhize). The contextual contrast of the two studies supports the argument that the interplay between the children's use of their two languages is a normal part of simultaneous language acquisition. In both contexts, the children used both their language codes when thinking aloud or responding to text. If students have a tendency to use all their linguistic resources at a given time to accomplish a given task, researchers must continue to explore how children use their cultural and linguistic capital in sanctioned and unsanctioned spaces.

In Yaden and Tsai, the students were given very similar input across both languages; nevertheless, the children varied in their development. This finding indicates that language input and opportunities for interaction are important, but development is still individualistic. In the first two chapters, we noted how students were keenly aware of their languages and used them accordingly. In Yaden and Tsai, we see the emergence of that skill at the later stages of the language developmental scheme. It appears that once children in this study reached a developmental threshold in both languages, they were able to use their knowledge of the two languages to further advance their understanding of each of the different writing systems.

In sum, these studies suggest that it is important to adopt different lenses and apply different theories to understand how young simultaneous bilingual children's language knowledge shapes their emerging literacy development. Furthermore, the studies show that teachers should understand that for emergent biliterate preschoolers' language and literacy development are flexible and fluid processes. The two languages of these children represent different sides of the same coin that cannot be separated from each other. To help us better understand the biliteracy development and instruction of young bilingual children and to build on these findings, future research might investigate and document whether or not young children's awareness of the potential use of their two languages develop similarly across language pairs. In addition, it is important to document the degree of sophistication that students bring to their use of their two languages and how educators can capitalize on that knowledge to better support students. Finally, it is imperative we understand the role of context in shaping these young children's lives in and out of school. Finding answers to the above questions will help educators and parents support the reading and writing needs of these young bilinguals.

Biliteracy Development in School

Similar to the first three chapters, the chapters in Part II focus on understanding bilingual and biliteracy development from a bilingual perspective. Using different theoretical frameworks that underscore learning as a social process, the authors highlighted the importance of understanding how the languages of bilingual students interact with one another in shaping the development of biliteracy in the early grades. Furthermore, the authors contend that the interplay between the languages of bilingual students does not necessarily mean that these students are not proficient in each of their individual languages.

Sparrow, Butvilofsky, and Escamilla explore linguistic complexity in the development of writing in Spanish–English bilingual early elementary students and show how the strengths and weaknesses in the students' writing in both English and Spanish contributed to the students' biliteracy development. They argue that teachers' awareness and understanding of these complexities, particularly with regard to cross-linguistic transfer and other bilingual-based literacy behaviors, are crucial in supporting students' continued development. Following the same argument, Gort illustrates that when young bilingual–biliterate students use both languages to revise and evaluate their writing during story composition they not only come to appreciate writing as a meaning-making process, but also benefit from drawing from multiple strategies and resources. She maintains that, in addition to enhancing students' biliterate and bilingual development, this hybridization fosters students' bicultural and bilingual identities. Fránquiz contends that in order for students to benefit maximally from hybridized practices, teachers should promote instruction that helps students to unpack the dynamics and complexities of diversity. These chapters illuminate the kaleidoscopic ways culture and language shape and inform the human experience and challenge us to continue to conduct "research that concerns itself with culture and its relationship to literacy learning" (Gutierrez et al., 2002, p. 341).

Across all the early elementary grades studies, students reveal that they are able to use their languages strategically for different purposes. In Sparrow et al.'s chapter this was measured through the use of T-units. Although T-units can be problematic for evaluating writing, the researchers were able to document students' writing progression bilingually, developmentally, and longitudinally. What is worth noting in this context is that as students advanced through the grades, their English writing skills improved enough to reveal a slight advantage over their Spanish writing. This finding suggests it may be more difficult to maintain a good balance across the two languages as students progress to the upper grades.

An important lesson learned from Sparrow et al. is that classrooms can be spaces where teachers can support and engage students across their languages in meaningful ways. In addition, it is important for teachers to document students' development across both languages in order to better understand their language needs in reading and writing. Without this, it is difficult to know if students are trying to use their understanding of one language to assist them in another language or how the two languages interact with each other. In many ways, this study points to the need for bilingual professionals in our schools who can understand students' language development trajectories and promote the attainment of bilingual and biliteracy educational goals. The fact that biliteracy skills do not develop in unison makes it even more imperative that teachers have a greater understanding of typical progression in biliteracy. There is a tendency in education to try to create artificial boxes for students to be placed. In the case of young bilinguals, it is even more problematic to do this. To date, evidence suggests that students' languages interact with one another, but the trajectory of those language interactions is less clear.

These studies further support the position that school age emerging bilinguals use their L1 to support their L2 literacy development. For example, Çamlibel and Garcia documented the importance of Zehra's L1 literacy development on her continued interest in L1 and L2 literacy as well as its shaping effect on her view of herself as a learner. Often schools are in a hurry to help students reach a particular threshold in English reading without taking into account the emotional toll on the student. Zehra was fortunate to be in a school where she could receive both English-as-a-Second-Language and native language instruction. This combination helped her to emerge as a more confident student who viewed school as a positive learning space. We see from her case how quickly students can differentiate between their two languages when schools and teachers are responsive to students' needs. Early in the school year Zehra used her knowledge of the English alphabet, to which she was exposed first, to aide her in reading in Turkish. Soon thereafter, and with exposure to and formal instruction in literacy in her native language, Zehra was able to identify what distinguishes both languages. We contend that the parallel approach to her literacy development might have supported her ability to keep the languages relatively separate. What appears to have been essential to Zehra's development is the opportunity to explore and discuss the relationships between her languages. Working with a native speaker of Turkish who is fluent in English provided Zehra with a supportive context to analyze and thoughtfully contrast the two languages. There was a sort of playfulness in Zehra's interactions with the two languages, which may have accounted for her fast development as a Turkish reader.

Students demonstrated their abilities to transfer information bidirectionally as they emerged as writers. For example, in Gort's chapter we saw how, when given the opportunity to fully engage with their two languages on a regular basis, emergent bilinguals are able to explore their languages in multifaceted ways. This glimpse into these children's thinking shows us their ability to use all of their resources to further their understanding of written language. This is a departure from the view that these children's linguistic status puts them at risk. In contrast, this study shows that these children can use both of their languages as tools for learning to advance their understanding of new tasks and ideas.

Taken together, these studies reveal that teachers can create supportive contexts and opportunities that promote the development of literacy in more than one language. Across the early elementary grades chapters teachers were able to support biliteracy development by creating the space where students grappled with questions about the functions and forms of languages and discussed their possible (re)presentation in writing in collaboration with friends or through their independent self-talk. Ideally the students benefited from classrooms where the teacher and students shared both languages.

Questions remain, however, with regard to how teachers might effectively and thoughtfully recognize the different mediators of language and literacy in emergent bilingual children's lives in order to support their individual journeys toward bilingualism and biliteracy. Future research agendas can be developed to purposefully help us better understand how teachers can learn about, and build upon, the knowledge and experiences of emergent bilingual children. For example, it is important for researchers to explore in what ways emergent bilingual children's out of school knowledge differs from what counts as learning/knowledge in school. How can continuities in home and school language and literacy practices be strengthened? How can discontinuities/differences be a springboard for learning? How can teachers create classrooms where children's languages are promoted, modeled, valued, nurtured, legitimized, and utilized authentically and purposefully?

As researchers, it is imperative that we continue to document what students are able to do across their languages using a bilingual lens. We have a great deal to learn about language and literacy developmental patterns in bilingual–biliterate students from different language backgrounds, and much progress to make in our efforts to create quality educational programs and powerful learning contexts for these students. We hope that this book begins to fill some of these gaps, and, most importantly, that the emergent bilingual learners represented in these pages showcase the possibility and potential for bilingualism, biliteracy, and academic success in our children.

References

Bernhardt, E. (2003). Challenges to reading research from a multilingual world. *Reading Research Quarterly, 38*, 104–141.

Gutierrez, K. D., Asato, J., Pacheco, M., Moll, L. C., Olson, K., Horng, E. L., Ruiz, R., Garcia, E., & McCarty, T. L. (2002). "Sounding American": The consequences of new reforms on English language learners. *Reading Research Quarterly, 37*, 328–347.

GLOSSARY

Alphabetic hypothesis: A principle by which each sound or phoneme in a word has its own distinctive graphic representation; applying this principle, children analyze writing and speech beyond the syllable and assign one phoneme to each grapheme though the correspondence will not be complete nor conventional.

Bilingualism: The ability to speak and understand two languages, to varying degrees; bilingualism can be developed simultaneously or successively.

Biliteracy: The development of literate competencies in two languages, to varying degrees, either simultaneously or successively.

Case study methodology: An empirical inquiry that investigates a contemporary phenomenon within its real-life context and in which multiple sources of evidence are used (e.g., ethnographic field notes, video and audio recordings of interactions among participants, student writing/work samples).

Code-switching: The alternate use of two languages in oral or written language.

Communicative competency: The ability to communicate effectively in real situations.

Constant comparison method: A qualitative research method for finding commonalities and differences in the data by comparing new evidence to prior evidence which leads first to a description and then to an explanation of the ir/regularity.

Cross-linguistic transfer: The ability to use knowledge and skills acquired in one language in another language.

Decoding: The putting together, or blending, of sounds represented by letters.

Directed Listening-Thinking Activity (DL-TA): An instructional method that incorporates multiple symbol systems as integrated processes.

Discourse: Meaningful language units larger than a sentence; a component of communication relating ideas to a particular subject for a specified purpose.

Dominant language: The language of greater proficiency and/or use.

Dual language program: An academic program where two languages are purposefully used for teaching and learning.

Emergent bilinguals: Children who potentially could develop two languages and biliteracy if supported in their immediate environments, including home, school, and community.

Emergent biliteracy: The process through which children progress as they learn how to think, speak, read, and write in two languages.

Emergent literacy: The process of constructing knowledge about the uses of language and literacy from observation, interactions, and conversations about print at home and in the community before entering school; a child's early unconventional attempts at reading, writing, and listening.

English–language learners: Students who speak a non–English native/home language and are in the process of acquiring English as an additional language.

Environmental print: Familiar print found in the surroundings, such as logos, labels, road signs.

Ethnographic field notes: A qualitative research tool used to document the sociology of meaning through close observation of sociocultural phenomena.

Explicit instruction: A direct and intentional method of teaching.

Grapheme: A letter, or letter combination that represents a phoneme.

Graphophonemic knowledge: The recognition of letters of the alphabet and the understanding of sound–symbol relationships.

Grounded theory: A systematic methodology in the social sciences involving the generation of theory from data.

Head Start: A national program that promotes school readiness by enhancing the social and cognitive development of children through the provision of educational, health, nutritional, social, and other services to enrolled children and families.

Hybrid language practice: The practice of drawing from a variety of linguistic and cultural resources as well as using them competently in specific contexts.

Hybrid literacy practices: A systematic, strategic, affiliative, and sense-making process in which bilinguals draw upon multiple linguistic codes, semiotic modalities, or participation structures during literacy events.

Implicit knowledge: That which is learned naturally and not as a result of having been taught directly.

Instance of Conceptual Evidence (ICE): Evidence of a conceptual understanding of the writing system through a child's interpretation of his/her own writing with a further manipulation of the child's text by the interviewer.

Interlocutor: A participant in a conversation.

Intersentential code-switch: A switch from one language to another that occurs between sentences.

Intrasentential code-switch: A switch from one language to another that occurs within sentences.

L1: Native language.

L2: Second language.

Language Assessment Scales (Duncan & De Avila, 1990): A commonly used, standardized language proficiency test.

Language dominance: The language of greater proficiency.

Language experience approach: A language and literacy activity that builds on stories dictated by individual students, small groups, or the whole class. In language experience, the student provides the text, through dictation, that serves as the basis for reading instruction.

Literacy events: Children's construction and interpretation of texts that could be oral, written, drawn, dramatized, or multimodal productions.

Logographic: A writing system in which the smallest written unit of the language represents words (e.g., Chinese).

Longitudinal study: A research study involving recurring observations of the same phenomenon over a long period of time.

Metalinguistic awareness: A general ability to manipulate written and oral language as a formal system.

Microgenetic approach/study: A method of investigation that yields data about particular changes in an effort to understand cognitive developmental change mechanisms.

Minimum quantity principle: The belief that children conceptualize writing as having a minimum quantity of characters, usually three or more.

Miscue: An observed response in the reading process that does not match the expected response; a departure from the text in the act of reading.

Multimodality: The integration of different kinds of symbolic systems (e.g., drawing, drama, music, mathematics, movement, and talk).

Nepantla: A theoretical perspective referring to being positioned or positioning oneself somewhere "in the middle" ground between available positions (points of view about a subject); in-betweenness.

One-person-one-language: See *"une-personne une-langue."*

Oracy: An instructional technique intended to help children develop the productive language necessary for success in reading and writing.

Oral encoding: The sounding out of syllables and words as they are being written.

Orthography: A standardized way of using a specific writing system (script) to write the language; orthography describes or defines the set of symbols (graphemes and diacritics) used in a written language, and the rules about how to write these symbols.

Phoneme: The smallest unit of sound; sounds made by individual letters and combinations of letters that make a single sound.

Phonemic awareness: The ability to recognize that words are composed of a sequence of spoken sounds and being able to hear and identify these individual speech sounds. Phonemic awareness includes the ability to segment and blend individual sounds in speech. Phonemic awareness is strictly an oral activity without association to written symbols.

Phonetic: Of or related to the study of sounds.

Process writing: An approach to writing instruction that promotes writing as a craft in which the writer engages in a number of individual and interactive stages as he/she develops an idea and expresses it in writing.

Psychogenetic: An approach to studying bi/literacy development which focuses on the developing conceptual understandings children form about writing systems (i.e., the origin and development of literacy-related psychological processes or behavior).

Scaffolding: A type of assistance offered by a teacher or peer to support learning.

Semantic–phonetic compound: The most common type of Chinese character (symbol), usually composed of two /$zì$/, in which one part of the character relates to the pronunciation of the whole character and the other to its meaning.

Semiotic resources: Methods of understanding semantics, syntactics, and pragmatics.

Simultaneous bilingual: A person who learns two languages from birth (or from an early age).

Snapshot analysis: A research study that involves only one observation.

Sociocultural theory: A theoretical perspective in which language and literacy are not only viewed as socially, culturally, and historically situated tools, but are also used by participants in social settings such as homes and classrooms in order to mediate thoughts and experiences.

Sociolinguistic awareness: Awareness of the social uses of languages in particular contexts, including knowledge of culturally appropriate ways of using language.

Sound–symbol correspondence: The ability to relate speech sounds to the letters that represent those sounds.

Spanglish: A hybrid language and literacy form, characterized by the interaction and blending of Spanish and English, that is common in bilingual contexts and communities. Spanglish represents a positive way of identifying the normal borrowing and code-switching events of stable bilingual communities that reflect the bicultural experiences of Latino bilinguals living in the U.S.

Spontaneous biliteracy: The development of literacy skills in two languages without formal instruction in both languages.

Surface level emergent literacy awareness: Script specific knowledge.

Syllabic hypothesis: One of the early hypotheses developed by children as they begin to make sense of the written system of language. Children hypothesize that each syllable is made up of one letter or symbol. That is, at this stage of emergent literacy a child understands that each letter, written character/grapheme, or other part represents a single syllable.

T–unit: Any independent clause with all of its subordinate clauses and modifiers.

Tex–Mex: See Spanglish.

Two Way Bilingual Education (TWBE): A dual language educational model in which students develop bilingual proficiency by receiving instruction in English and another language in a classroom that usually comprises half native speakers of English and half native speakers of the other target language. The goals of two-way bilingual programs are academic achievement, bilingualism/biliteracy, and sociocultural integration for all participants.

Two Way Immersion (TWI): See TWBE.

Une-personne une-langue (one-person one-language): An approach to raising a bilingual child in which one parent/caregiver speaks only language A to the child and the other parent/caregiver only speaks language B.

Writing Workshop (WW): A process-based approach to writing instruction that stresses the notion of writing as a craft and engages writers in a number of individual and interactive stages to develop an idea and express it in writing.

/zì/ (字): The fundamental contrastive unit of writing in Chinese. Each /zì/ represents a syllable in the spoken Chinese language.

Zone of proximal development: The distance between a child's actual developmental level as determined by independent problem solving and the level of potential development as determined through problem solving under adult guidance, or in collaboration with more capable peers.

Reference

Duncan, S. E., & De Avila, E. A. (1990). *Language assessment scales-oral.* Monterey, CA: CTB McGraw-Hill.

CONTRIBUTORS

Editors and Authors

Eurydice Bouchereau Bauer is Associate Professor at the University of Illinois, Urbana-Champaign. Her research focuses on the area of second-language literacy and young children's biliteracy development. Dr. Bauer has served as PI and co-PI on several research grants, which focus on bilingual and ESL students. In 2007, she was an invited member of the National Research Agenda Planning Panel for ELL Students in Washington, DC. From 2008 to 2011 Dr. Bauer served as co-editor for the second-language column in *The Reading Teacher*. Some of Dr. Bauer's research has been published in the top literacy journals including *Journal of Literacy Research, Research in the Teaching of English, International Journal of Bilingualism, Reading Research Quarterly*, and the *Reading Teacher*.

Mileidis Gort is Assistant Professor of Language and Literacy at the University of Miami's School of Education where she teaches courses on language and literacy development and bilingual education. Her current research examines the early bilingual and biliteracy development of English and Spanish speakers in dual language programs and the effects of curricular reform efforts toward culturally and linguistically responsive teacher education. From 2007 to 2009, Dr. Gort was co-editor for the *Journal of Literacy Research*. Her research appears in the *Journal of Early Childhood Literacy, Research in the Teaching of English, Multicultural Perspectives*, the *Bilingual Research Journal*, and *Educational Policy*. Dr. Gort earned her doctorate in Developmental Studies with a focus on Literacy, Language, and Culture from Boston University.

Contributing Authors

Sandra Butvilofsky is a Professional Research Associate at the University of Colorado, Boulder. Her research interests include classroom-based research with a focus on the biliterate writing development of emerging bilingual Latino elementary children. Her elementary teaching experience includes five years as a bilingual classroom teacher and five years as a trained Descubriendo la Lectura®/Reading Recovery® teacher.

Zeynep Çamlibel earned a PhD at the University of Illinois, Urbana-Champaign in Language and Literacy Education. She currently works in Istanbul at Marmara University as an instructor in the department of English Language Teacher Training. Her current research areas are bilingual and biliteracy development, skills in language learning, teacher motivation, and culture in language education.

Kathy Escamilla is Professor of Education at the University of Colorado, Boulder. She does research on biliteracy development and assessment of Spanish speaking Latino children. She has over 35 years of experience in the field of Bilingual/ESL Education as a teacher, teacher educator, researcher, and school administrator. She served two terms as the president of the *National Association for Bilingual Education* and currently serves as co-editor for the *Bilingual Research Journal*.

María Fránquiz is Associate Professor at the University of Texas, Austin. She teaches undergraduate and graduate courses on the theoretical foundations of bilingual education, biliteracy and culture, Latino children's literature, and writing in bilingual contexts. She is a teaching consultant for the National Writing Project. Her research on ethnographic examination of language and literacy practices in K-12 classrooms has been published widely. She currently serves as co-editor for the *Bilingual Research Journal*.

Georgia Garcia is Professor of Education in the Department of Curriculum and Instruction at the University of Illinois, Urbana-Champaign. Her widely published research has focused on the literacy instruction, assessment, and development of students (preschool-8) from diverse linguistic and cultural backgrounds and has been influential in changing current practices in bilingual education. Her current research interests include investigating cross-linguistic transfer in bilingual students' reading and writing, the literacy engagement and motivation of bilingual students, and the use of new forms of literacy assessments with students from diverse backgrounds.

Dumisile Mkhize is a PhD candidate in the Department of Curriculum and Instruction at the University of Illinois at Urbana-Champaign. Her areas of interest include bilingualism, biliteracy, and teacher education. She has taught English as a second language to high school and undergraduate students in South Africa. In addition, she has taught African literature and linguistics to undergraduate and graduate students at the University of South Africa. At The University of Illinois, she has worked as a research assistant on language and literacy projects, taught undergraduate courses, and worked as a writing consultant.

Iliana Reyes obtained her PhD in psychology with an emphasis on early childhood development from the University of California, Berkeley. She is currently an Associate Professor in Language, Reading and Culture, and faculty of the Early Childhood Education program at the University of Arizona. Her areas of expertise include early bilingualism and biliteracy, language socialization, and child development. Her research has been published in the top journals of literacy education including *Reading Research Quarterly*, the *Journal of Early Childhood Literacy*, and the *Bilingual Research Journal*.

Lucinda Soltero-González is Assistant Professor of Education in the Division of Educational Equity and Cultural Diversity at the University of Colorado, Boulder. Lucinda has taught in Mexico and the United States. Her research includes the development of bilingualism and early biliteracy in young Spanish speaking children and children's biliteracy practices in U.S. classrooms. She uses qualitative research methodologies to explore the links between language, culture, and learning within the everyday interactions and the wider socio-cultural and political context of classroom life. Her research has been published in the *Bilingual Research Journal* and *Theory into Practice*.

Wendy Sparrow is a Professional Research Associate at the University of Colorado, Boulder. Her research interests include the bilingual literacy development of Latino elementary school children and the fidelity of program implementation in bilingual and dual language programs and interventions. Before earning her doctorate and becoming involved in research, she spent seven years as a bilingual classroom teacher and a Title I literacy instructor at the elementary level.

Tina Tsai, PhD, is the founder and director of the Literacy Guild, a literacy development center that provides high-quality K-12 instructional services in small group learning environments. Her research on biliteracy began with first-hand experiences, being immersed as a child in multiple language and writing system environments and later teaching a variety of immigrant students. Her research interests include literacy and biliteracy development, developmental learning theory, and reading and writing pedagogy.

David Yaden, Jr. (PhD, University of Oklahoma) is Professor of Language, Reading, and Culture in the School of Education at the University of Arizona. His research specializations include developmental issues in early childhood education, the acquisition of literacy and biliteracy in alphabetic and non-alphabetic scripts, family literacy, theories of reading disability, and the application developmental science methodologies to growth in reading and writing. His recent research has been published in the *Elementary School Journal*, *Reading and Writing Quarterly*, and the *Handbook of Research on the Education of Young Children*.

INDEX

Page numbers in *italics* denote tables.